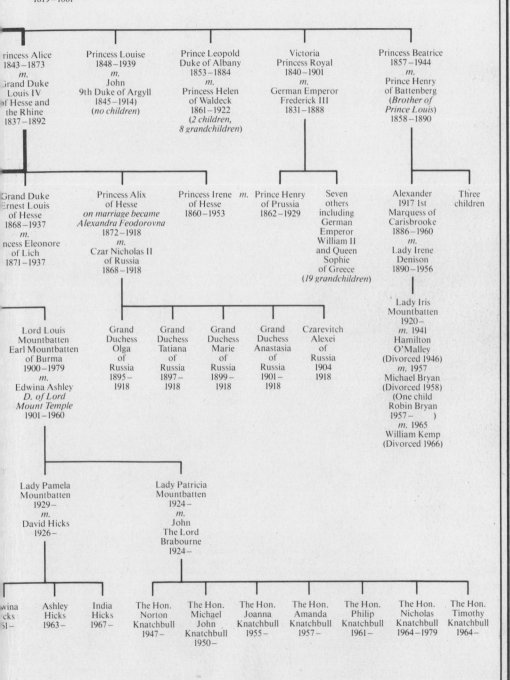

Prince Albert
of Saxe-Coburg
and Gotha
1819−1861

rincess Alice
1843−1873
m.
Grand Duke
Louis IV
of Hesse and
the Rhine
1837−1892

Princess Louise
1848−1939
m.
John
9th Duke of Argyll
1845−1914)
(no children)

Prince Leopold
Duke of Albany
1853−1884
m.
Princess Helen
of Waldeck
1861−1922
(2 children,
8 grandchildren)

Victoria
Princess Royal
1840−1901
m.
German Emperor
Frederick III
1831−1888

Princess Beatrice
1857−1944
m.
Prince Henry
of Battenberg
(Brother of
Prince Louis)
1858−1890

Grand Duke
Ernest Louis
of Hesse
1868−1937
m.
ncess Eleonore
of Lich
1871−1937

Princess Alix
of Hesse
on marriage became
Alexandra Feodorovna
1872−1918
m.
Czar Nicholas II
of Russia
1868−1918

Princess Irene m.
of Hesse
1860−1953

Prince Henry
of Prussia
1862−1929

Seven
others
including
German
Emperor
William II
and Queen
Sophie
of Greece
(19 grandchildren)

Alexander
1917 1st
Marquess of
Carisbrooke
1886−1960
m.
Lady Irene
Denison
1890−1956

Three
children

Lord Louis
Mountbatten
Earl Mountbatten
of Burma
1900−1979
m.
Edwina Ashley
D. of Lord
Mount Temple
1901−1960

Grand
Duchess
Olga
of
Russia
1895−
1918

Grand
Duchess
Tatiana
of
Russia
1897−
1918

Grand
Duchess
Marie
of
Russia
1899−
1918

Grand
Duchess
Anastasia
of
Russia
1901−
1918

Czarevitch
Alexei
of
Russia
1904
1918

Lady Iris
Mountbatten
1920−
m. 1941
Hamilton
O'Malley
(Divorced 1946)
m. 1957
Michael Bryan
(Divorced 1958)
(One child
Robin Bryan
1957−   )
m. 1965
William Kemp
(Divorced 1966)

Lady Pamela
Mountbatten
1929−
m.
David Hicks
1926−

Lady Patricia
Mountbatten
1924−
m.
John
The Lord
Brabourne
1924−

wina
cks
61−

Ashley
Hicks
1963−

India
Hicks
1967−

The Hon.
Norton
Knatchbull
1947−

The Hon.
Michael
John
Knatchbull
1950−

The Hon.
Joanna
Knatchbull
1955−

The Hon.
Amanda
Knatchbull
1957−

The Hon.
Philip
Knatchbull
1961−

The Hon.
Nicholas
Knatchbull
1964−1979

The Hon.
Timothy
Knatchbull
1964−

PRINCE PHILIP

BOOKS BY DENIS JUDD

NON-FICTION

Prince Philip, Duke of Edinburgh   1981
Eclipse of Kings   1976
The House of Windsor   1973
Livingstone in Africa   1973
The British Raj   1972
Posters of World War II   1972
The Victorian Empire   1970
Balfour and the British Empire   1968

FICTION

Return to Treasure Island   1978
The Adventures of Long John Silver   1977

PRINCE PHILIP

A BIOGRAPHY

DENIS JUDD

NEW YORK   1981

ATHENEUM

To JAKE
who has never had a book
dedicated to him before

Library of Congress Cataloging in Publication Data

Judd, Denis, ———
    Prince Philip.

    Bibliography: p.
    Includes index.
    1. Philip, Duke of Edinburgh, 1921-
2. Great Britain—Princes and princesses—Biography.
DA591.A2J82   1981   941.085'092'4   80-22691
ISBN 0-689-11131-2

CONTENTS

ILLUSTRATIONS

Between pages 96 and 97

1 Prince Philip's great-grandmother, Princess Alice, Queen Victoria's second daughter *Popperfoto*
2 Prince Andrew of Greece, Prince Philip's father *Popperfoto*
3 Princess Alice, Prince Philip's mother *Popperfoto*
4 Prince Philip of Greece, photographed in England, aged one year *Camera Press*
5 Seafaring Battenbergs *Popperfoto*
6 Alexandra of Greece, Prince Philip's cousin and biographer, with her husband ex-King Peter of Yugoslavia *Popperfoto*
7 Prince Philip in 1947, with his three surviving sisters, Margarita, Sophie and Theodora *Popperfoto*
8 Prince Philip and his mother in 1957, at his niece's wedding in Baden *Keystone Press*
9 Gordonstoun batsman walking from the pitch, towards the end of his time at the school *Camera Press*
10 Prince Philip adjusts his garters before a Gordonstoun production of *Macbeth* *Fox Photos*
11 Gordonstoun school athlete with spike trouble *Camera Press*. *Inset*, Dr Kurt Hahn, founder of the school *Popperfoto*
12 The thirteen-year-old Princess Elizabeth at a swimming gala in 1939 *Popperfoto*
13 Princess Elizabeth, watched by her father and Princess Margaret, plants a tree at Dartmouth Naval College in July 1939 *Popperfoto*
14 The bearded wartime naval officer, whose photograph adorned Princess Elizabeth's dressing-table *Camera Press*
15 Princess Elizabeth and Prince Philip of Greece photographed as they enter Romsey Abbey for the marriage of Lady Patricia Mountbatten and Lord Brabourne, 26 October 1946 *Popperfoto*
16 Courting couple: a newsreel sequence of October 1946 shows Prince Philip helping Princess Elizabeth (and Margaret) disrobe before the wedding *Popperfoto*
17 The first waltz – in public, anyway, at a Ball in Edinburgh in July 1947 shortly after the announcement of their engagement *Keystone Press*

8

Illustrations

54 Prince Philip flanked by Colombian stalwarts, with Michael Parker behind him, during his South American tour of 1962 *Camera Press*

55 Prince Philip meeting the 1955 cup finalists Newcastle United at Wembley *Fox Photos*

56 Delegate at the controversial meeting of the Olympic International Sports Federation *Popperfoto*

57 Prince Philip making contact with shocked villagers at Aberfan in October 1966 *Keystone Press*

58 Police fending off Canadians rapturous at the sight of Prince Philip in Toronto *Camera Press*

59 Prince Philip with Bing Crosby at Buckingham Palace in 1976 *Syndication International*

60 1962 *Express* cartoon featuring Prince Philip's somewhat antagonistic relationship with Lord Beaverbrook *Daily Express*

61 A member of the Iounhanan tribe in the New Hebrides which worships the Duke of Edinburgh *Camera Press*

62 Lord Mountbatten welcomes Prince Philip as he arrives in Malta in 1949 to take up his naval command *Keystone Press*

63 Prince Philip surveying the scene in a street in Rabat, Morocco, in 1964 *Keystone Press*

64 Prince Philip talking to Quintin Hogg (and nursing a polo-injured arm) in 1964 *Syndication International*

65 Prince Philip with a bare-backed Diane Cilento at a 1965 film première *Keystone Press*

66 Prince Philip with Margaret Trudeau aboard the Royal Yacht *Britannia Popperfoto*

67 Prince Philip's childhood friend, Hélène Foufounis (later Cordet), with her children Max and Louise *Popperfoto*

68 Prince Philip with Mrs Julius Nyerere during Tanganyika's independence celebrations in 1961 *Keystone Press*

69 Three pillars of the Mountbatten–Windsor connection: Prince Charles, his "Honorary Grandfather", Earl Mountbatten, and Prince Philip *Syndication International*

70 Nephew and "Honorary Great Nephew" follow Earl Mountbatten's coffin to the ceremonial funeral service at Westminster Abbey, 5 September 1979 *Keystone Press*

PREFACE

DURING THE WRITING of this book I asked Basil Boothroyd, whose earlier biography of Prince Philip I greatly admire, if he could help me solve some of the remaining problems of interpretation that I had defined. He replied, "I deeply sympathise, remembering how I used to wake up in the small hours ten years ago thinking I was out of my skull to have taken it on." Only the small band of authors who have attempted a serious assessment of a leading member of the royal family can know exactly how he felt. When I was first invited to write a biography of Prince Philip I was immediately aware of the problems facing anyone who undertakes such a task. The main problem is how to get at the truth. Only when principal members of the royal family are dead is access given to their private papers – and even then it is only the official biographer who is granted such access. Nor is it possible to interview the biographical subject, and in that sense he or she is as good as dead, though they continue to give almost daily proof of being very much alive. The author can, however, closely observe his subject as he or she goes about their official functions, he can read all he can lay his hands on, and he can talk to people who are close to, or who have a good working knowledge of, the royal person in question.

I have done all of this. In addition, I have been able to put particular questions to Prince Philip through his staff, and in this respect I am grateful for the cooperation of John Dauth, Assistant Press Secretary to the Queen. I was given some research facilities at Buckingham Palace where, seated in a room that could have been set in any modest country house in England, I consulted the official details of Prince Philip's career and overheard the porters talk in a proprietorial way of the royal family – one remarking "Oh yes, she's watching the 3.45 race on the television" – in between battling with someone higher in authority for a new electric kettle (they won in the end).

All the quotations in the book are drawn from works cited in the bibliography, from press or eye-witness accounts, or from records of interviews in the press or elsewhere. Where there have been areas of doubt I have checked with as many different authorities as

11

possible. Any biographer of the Duke of Edinburgh must owe a special debt to Basil Boothroyd's *Philip*, published ten years ago, which is crammed with original material, and which is wise and witty as well. I freely acknowledge that debt.

I have been sustained while working on the book by the friendship and professional skills of Alan Brooke and Jennie Davies at Michael Joseph, by my mother, who typed the text, by my father who scrutinised the manuscript for her, and by my wife Dorothy, who guaranteed me sufficient peace to complete the project – even after the birth of our fourth child.

Denis Judd
London, 1980

ACKNOWLEDGEMENTS

The author and publishers would like to thank the following for permission to reproduce extracts from the publications mentioned: Opera Mundi, *Prince Philip: A Family Portrait*, by Princess Alexandra; Hurst and Blackett, *Memoirs* by Prince Christopher of Greece; *Burke's Peerage*; Longman, *Philip: An Informal Biography* by Basil Boothroyd; the Trustees of the Broadlands Archives, *The Mountbatten Lineage*; Peter Davies, *Born Bewildered* by Hélène Cordet; Cassell, *The Little Princess* by Maria Crawford.

Thanks are also due to The Society of Authors as the literary representative of the Estate of John Masefield for an extract from a poem *For The Times*, to Campbell Thomson and McLaughlin for the poem *Heard of Him, Never Met him* by Nicholas Monsarrat and to Macdonald and Jane's for the diagram of The Royal Circle from *The House of Windsor* by Denis Judd.

INTRODUCTION

Britain's Most
Misunderstood Man?

"I doubt whether I've achieved anything likely to be remembered."
Prince Philip

THE OPENING IS EASY – and conventional: His Royal Highness, the
Prince Philip, Duke of Edinburgh, consort of Her Majesty Queen
Elizabeth II, was born on the island of Corfu on 10 June 1921.
Thereafter convention becomes less useful and the story contains a
good deal that is unorthodox, painful and uncertain, which is
perhaps odd for a man who occupies so prominent a position in one
of Europe's most stable, and orthodox, monarchies.

Above all, there is paradox. It starts with appearance: a Greek
prince with the fair hair and blue eyes of a Scandinavian? And how
Greek can he be, anyway, when he speaks perfect English and is
the epitome of an English gentleman, almost a chocolate box
English gentleman? Educated largely in Scotland, an officer in the
Royal Navy, a member of the Church of England, father of the heir
to the throne, Duke of Edinburgh, and yet signing himself "Philip of
Greece" only a few years before his marriage?

The paradox continues beyond background and circumstance.
The Prince is President of the British branch of the World Wildlife
Fund, but *The Sunday Times* reported on 11 February 1980 that:
"Prince Philip and his friends shot 6500 pheasants at Sandringham
during the past season. In the biggest shoot, at the season's end, 12
parties shot 900 cock birds in a day." Surely they were not able to
eat them all? Many will also remember the slaughtered tiger in 1961
– now, though not solely in consequence, a protected species. Prince
Philip is sometimes challenged over the apparent paradox and can be

13

brusquely defensive. In 1979 he was asked, by a reporter at the Perth Agricultural Show in Western Australia, whether he saw any conflict between his position as President of the Royal Agricultural Society and the royal family's involvement in blood sports. Gesturing towards the animal pens he said: "All the animals you see out there get killed. So what? I can't see any conflict."

He is the President of the Society of Arts, and a trustee of the Royal Maritime Museum, yet he once remarked, when the ex-Shah of Iran was showing the Queen some local exhibits, "Oh, let's get away from this bloody lot!" Though he has bought a good many modern pictures, (a hedge against inflation, or exile?) there is no doubt as to his own tastes, as illustrated by his comment when he first saw Victor Pasmore's *Relief Construction* in the San Francisco Museum of Art: "That looks to me like something to hang a towel on." He is, however, somewhat resentful of accusations of philistinism, and once remarked ruefully. "The art world thinks of me as an uncultured, polo-playing clot." At least painting pictures is one of his pastimes.

He has a delicate constitutional position as consort of the monarch in whose name the Mother of Parliaments functions, yet in September 1969 a *Daily Telegraph Magazine* showed him as first choice for a national dictator. He once antagonised British public opinion, moreover, by remarking to the dictator General Alfredo Stroessner of Paraguay, a protector of surviving Nazis, that it "was a pleasant change to be in a country that isn't ruled by its people" and where "the government decides what's to be done, and it's done". A somewhat limp official explanation of this gaffe was that he was thinking of meddlers back home like the Lord's Day Observance Society.

Although those associated with the monarchy are not expected to parade, or, in a sense, to have political views, it is conventionally assumed that Prince Philip has a broad sympathy with the right, and not simply because of a rash pronouncement long ago in a Latin American dictatorship. Perhaps his paternal Greek family background is partly responsible. His brother-in-law, Prince Christopher of Hesse, was certainly an active and influential Nazi, though Philip's brief stay at Salem school in Baden, shortly after Hitler came to power, was characterised by his unbridled mirth at the Nazi salute and similar pomposity; he was not invited to join, and did not join, the Hitler Youth, as did some of his contemporaries at Salem. His current political views tend instead to find

14

indirect expression when he sometimes appears to be, for example, a mouthpiece for the Confederation of British Industry rather than for the Trades Union Congress – a role which has sometimes seemed more acceptable to Prince Charles. Not that Prince Philip is above berating British management, as on the celebrated occasion in 1961 when he told one hundred and twenty leading British industrialists at a London lunch of the Industrial Co-Partnership Association: "I think it is about time we pulled our fingers out" – at least it was "our" fingers, not "your" fingers. This piece of advice has not only assumed its proper place in national folklore (and indeed might serve as an informal epitaph), but also lends some support to the view that Prince Philip is neutral, or centrist, rather than right wing in his opinions. A number of those close to him deny that he is particularly right wing and say instead that he is "neutral", "pragmatic", "objective", "above that sort of thing", "moderate" or not really interested in political infighting. Although it is possible to claim, at least within the British political context, that "moderate" is a code word for "centrist leaning markedly to the right", these views cannot be dismissed as merely being discreet and protective.

Indeed, Prince Philip's involvement in the spring of 1980 in the furore over the Olympic International Sports Federation's statements criticising the use of political pressure to bring about an Olympic boycott, provides a neat illustration of the "above politics" school of thought. Had Prince Philip, at the OISFs meeting, opposed the boycott, and hence the British government's collective view, or not? The *Guardian* correspondent, John Rodda, believed that he had. The next day the Palace denied that "the Duke was in any way a motivator of the statement by the committee [opposing the boycott]. . . . The Duke of Edinburgh has never personally criticized the position taken by Her Majesty's government." Clearly Prince Philip had got into a muddle both as a member of the OISF and as the consort of a constitutional monarch. On 27 May *The Sunday Times* discussed the matter on its centre page, asking "Did Prince Philip blunder?" On 9 May *Private Eye* quoted the Duke as telling Olga Maitland, "Now politicians are trying to control us. If only they would just accept that sport and politics do not mix. In any case, they have no right to tell us what to do." An interesting statement, if true, from a man who normally expresses his own views so plainly.

Hence a further paradox. A constitutional monarchy strives to steer clear of controversy and to inhabit a safe middle ground.

15

Whatever their personal views, British monarchs in the twentieth century have apparently accepted great political and social upheavals with equanimity, if not with enthusiasm; they have certainly not foisted whatever private views they may have upon the public. There are sound constitutional reasons for this, as well as a finely-developed instinct for self-preservation; British monarchs, after all, are not affected by the swing of the political pendulum, and, as they hold office for life, why rock the boat?

The Duke of Edinburgh, however, feels comparatively free of such restraint. Perhaps his status as consort, rather than monarch, has had a liberating effect. At any rate, he speaks his mind, and the popular press often reacts with the full "Shock! Horror!" treatment: "Duke Angers Drainage Men", "Philip in Tinned Fruit Uproar", "A Right Royal Rumpus", and so on. Whether or not this combative approach to matters in the public eye is part of a calculated strategy to keep people on their toes is unclear, but very likely. The Queen is by now resigned to it; she once said, "I gave up trying to stop him years ago." Prince Philip sees it as making "a sensible contribution" to the contemporary scene. A majority of British subjects would probably rather have the occasional provocative outburst than see him reduced to a silent, smiling dummy, or a compliant purveyor of cosy platitudes.

Are there any further explanations for Prince Philip's capacity to stir things up? It would be easy to pin it all on his disjointed early years when, in his own self-deprecating words, he was "a discredited Balkan prince of no particular merit or distinction". In boyhood he called himself "Philip of Greece", but not without some initial hesitation. While he was still a baby his father, Prince Andrew, like so many members of the Greek royal family, became a permanent exile. His parents' marriage then foundered on intractable political and personal pressures. As a boy, he was shuttled from one set of royal and aristocratic relatives to another, finding a more permanent roof over his head only in Mountbatten homes; firstly with the second Marquess of Milford Haven, after whose death the younger brother, Lord Louis Mountbatten, Philip's well loved "Uncle Dickie", took over. As with homes, so with schools – within ten years there were four, in France, England, Germany and Scotland. Next the Royal Navy provided him with a base that was no more permanent for him than for other officers and ratings. It was not until his marriage that he had what might properly be called a home.

Prince Philip has denied that his childhood and adolescence were spent in "unsettled and unhappy circumstances", and it is difficult at first sight to see symptoms of any early insecurities in his adult deportment. Yet his impatience, not only with fools, and his wit, often biting, even wounding, may stem from an unhappiness that is too deep and painful to acknowledge. Despite his extrovert personality, some who know him well talk of his having a "locked-in emotional middle". Certainly, apart from Michael Parker and perhaps David Milford Haven, he has not enjoyed any really close friendships with other men.

Despite, or perhaps because of, the "good copy" he provides, the Duke of Edinburgh's relationship with the press has been unsatisfactory, even deplorable. This is, at first sight, odd, especially in the light of the overwhelmingly uncritical attitude of the British press towards the Queen. It is likely, however, that the Duke, sometimes aided by his daughter, expresses a family dislike of press prying, which they see as persistent and unjustified attempts to disrupt their privacy. Moreover, unlike the Queen, he is "fair game".

With Prince Philip, though, it may be something more. In part, it may spring from the distrust once expressed by the Beaverbrook group of newspapers for his uncle Louis Mountbatten's allegedly "overweening ambition", for his wartime handling of the Dieppe raid and later, when Viceroy, for his "surrender" of India. In part, it may result from the press's insatiable hunger for gossip and from its endless capacity for muck-raking. Unlike his wife, Prince Philip has not led a sheltered, apparently blameless life. There are those "pro-German" Greek uncles, there is the Nazi brother-in-law, his two closest male friends, David Milford Haven and Michael Parker, have been resoundingly "dropped", there are varied and scurrilous accounts of liaisons with "other women", there is even talk of illegitimate children – though it is left to the foreign press to retail these more wounding stories and innuendoes.

Far from turning the other cheek, the Duke of Edinburgh has hit back in a most untraditional way; newspaper men, he once said, had "no obvious qualifications" for their work. In 1962 he called the *Daily Express* (then part of the Beaverbrook group) "a bloody awful newspaper. It is full of lies, scandal and imagination. It is a vicious newspaper"; he has been accused of dowsing reporters with a sprinkler at the Chelsea Flower Show; once, on the Rock of Gibraltar, confronted with both newspapermen and the famous apes, he asked ingenuously, "Which are the monkeys?" There is much more to say on this subject, but the quality and depth of the conflict has long been apparent.

Perhaps his prickly relationship with the press springs from a feeling of being "Britain's most misunderstood man" (a description attributed to Prince Philip in an article which appeared in *Look* in 1964) — a title to which Queen Victoria's Albert also aspired a century before. Superficially he could be regarded as a foreign parasite, feasting, amid national hardship and decline, on the fat of the land. This is a particularly galling image for a man who attends, mostly with zest, over three hundred functions a year, who writes his own speeches, and who generally asks the right, if awkward, questions. His index-linked allowance and his opulent surroundings are not unearned — though whether he gets an inflated rate for the job is another matter.

A quieter and less abrasive spirit would naturally provoke less criticism. Though he is notably unpompous, he is direct and challenging (some would say taunting) in his approach, which can look like taking unfair advantage of his position. There is good evidence, however, that he would behave in exactly the same way even if his victims were able to reply in as brusque and hard-edged a manner.

His "no nonsense", though often affable, approach is partly the tactic of the straightforward naval officer who expects his words to be taken at face value. But it also reflects the firmly held views of an able man who has thought through his approach to many things and expects others to have done the same. He can be powerful and ruthless in discussion, though occasionally allowing a smile to take the harshness from his words. He has sometimes cultivated an anti-intellectualism, mocking himself as "one of those ignorant bums who never went to a university", and this may account for his dislike of airy-fairy theorists and of *avant-garde* ideas. On the other hand he has addressed the British Association for the Advancement of Science and other learned bodies with flair and sufficient authority. Like Prince Albert he has been a consistent patron of science and technology, as well as of design.

His religious beliefs have not been particularly consistent. Despite his Greek Orthodox background he prudently and necessarily became a member of the Church of England before his marriage. For some time, buffeted perhaps by his years of insecurity and his parents' estrangement, he held no particular religious views and might even have considered himself an atheist. His capacity to

18

pry into corners (not only when inspecting factories and the like), and the rigour of his approach to his own, and other's, problems, are part of an intellectual honesty which has baulked at the obscurantism of formal religion. He was not even sure that Prince Charles should be confirmed at the age of sixteen. This uncertainty led him in turn (and not for the first time) to an act of provocation when he openly read a book (the Bible, as it happened) during the Archbishop of Canterbury's address at the confirmation service at Windsor in 1965. Archbishop Ramsey, normally a mild and scholarly primate, was moved afterwards to say to the Dean of Windsor, "Bloody rude, that's what I call it." Since then the Duke of Edinburgh has become reconciled with the Anglican faith, which is, after all, broad enough to accommodate most points of view, and especially changing ones.

Prince Philip's position is further complicated through being head of a family in which his wife has official precedence over him and the future belongs to his eldest son. Given his dominating, forceful, essentially masculine public image, how does this work out in practice? Fortunately there is no fundamental conflict. He presides over a family in which the big decisions, at least nowadays, are taken democratically (one vote each), and where discussion is preferred to dictation. He can, of course, be extremely influential, as is shown by the decisions about the choice of schools for his children. But, in sharp and happy contrast to Prince Albert, or even to George V – whose martinet-like qualities terrified his children – the Duke of Edinburgh's philosophy is that, "It's no use saying do this, do that, don't do this, don't do that. . . . It's very easy when children want something to say no immediately. I think it's quite important not to give an unequivocal answer at once. Much better to think it over. Then if you eventually say no, I think they really accept it."

Believing that his children's behaviour, overall, has been average to good, would he feel the same about his marriage? Certainly there was no lack of genuine and heartfelt love in the early days, and if their relationship is no longer a perpetual whirlwind of passion and romance, it is still a solid and loving relationship ballasted by thirty-three years of child-rearing, friendship, affection and mutual respect. They talk to each other a lot, and laugh together enough to smooth over differences and lighten the load of official duties. He is, above all, concerned for her welfare and is actively protective – keeping the press at bay is undoubtedly seen as one means of protection. Their silver wedding was eight years ago and was an occasion for realistic self-congratulation.

Not that Prince Philip is narrowly and obsessively a family man, rarely seeking the company of other males and reluctant to venture far from his wife's side. For one thing, he does not share a good many of her interests: racing bores him, for example, and she, in turn, does not share his passion for gadgetry and technology. He sometimes undertakes quite lengthy overseas trips without her – which sets the tongues wagging. He is at ease in the all-male company of a mess-room or a club, and for years was a member of the Thursday Club – an informal weekly get-together of artists, writers, sportsmen and others at Wheeler's restaurant in Old Compton Street in Soho. His patronage of sport, notably sailing, cricket and polo, has enabled him to flex his muscles in male company.

For a man who is so apparently straightforward, he is consistently (perhaps wilfully?) misunderstood, and his early life remains shrouded in an obscurity which is close to mystery. Very few of his wife's subjects would be able to name his father or his mother, though some would be convinced (wrongly) that Lord Louis Mountbatten was the former. He, too, is not altogether clear about incidents of his babyhood and childhood. Was his father present at his birth? He does not know. Was he bottle-fed or breast-fed? He can provide no information on that point. Perhaps it does not matter, yet the absence of such facts makes a curiously uncertain background to one of the most public and outspoken men in contemporary society.

It is easy to mock him as "Phil the Greek", or as "Keith", which is *Private Eye*'s pet name for him and is presumably meant to suggest an obdurate boorishness. Despite many attempts, however, he is difficult to caricature and quite impossible to stereotype. His life has been a compound of high drama, private tragedy, a convoluted family history, financial insecurity, rootlessness and a heritage richer, and poorer, than most people realise. But there has also been a solid marriage, a distinguished professional career, supervision of a successfully developing family, international regard, popular adulation, and the satisfaction of having helped to up-date the image of the British monarchy, and hence, presumably, to ensure its survival.

Though time has smoothed some of his rough edges, he is still a man whose infuriating qualities are as openly on display as his constructive and positive ones. If there is a harmony to be found in all this, it is the harmony of a restless spirit harnessed to the solemn and stately apparatus of the British monarchy and striving, despite occasional provocative outbursts, to promote its best interests as practically and firmly as possible.

Thus Prince Philip has invited time-and-motion experts to survey and improve the use made of Buckingham Palace; he has encouraged conscious acts of royal self-revelation such as the well-received television film *Royal Family*; he has brought the education of his children into line with the educational experiences of other, admittedly financially privileged, children; he has spent thousands of hours visiting factories, waving at onlookers in top-storey windows, asking intelligent questions of managers and workers, noticing the cut knees of children he meets, extending hospitality to visiting heads of state, and (mostly) smiling at the cameras. In short, the monarchy is the richer for his dynamic impact upon it, though he would probably be the last to admit it. Whether this impact would have been as dynamic if his background and upbringing had been cosy, conventional, and less traumatic is open to doubt.

THE ROYAL CIRCLE

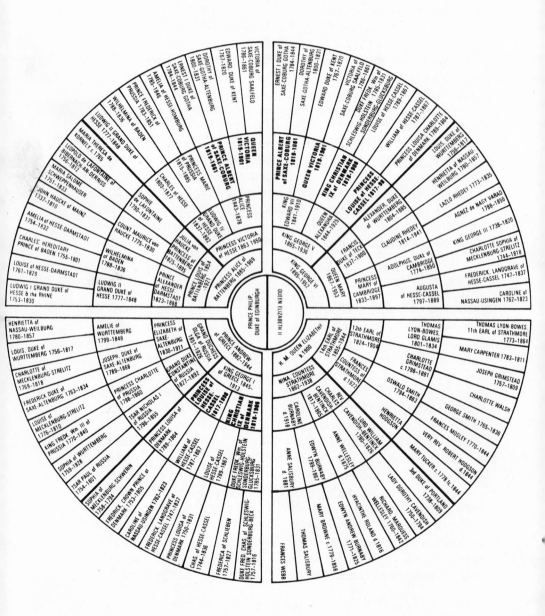

1

Family Trees

AN ATTEMPT TO SEE
THE WOOD AS WELL

"The trouble about any pedigree that goes back one thousand six hundred years is that it gradually shades off from the impossible through the possible to the probable and finally the certain."

Earl Mountbatten of Burma,
The Mountbatten Lineage

THE DUKE OF EDINBURGH'S GENEALOGICAL BACKGROUND is woven into such a wide and complex tapestry as to obscure clarity and defy all but the most persistent of researchers. Strands come together from such feudal residences as Frederiksborg Castle in Copenhagen, the Greek royal estate of Tatoi, and a Grand Duke's castle in Germany. They can be traced back to the Imperial Russian court at St Petersburg and to the less exotic though more durable palaces of the kings and queens of England. Even a cursory glance at Prince Philip's family tree, rooted in a lush and ancient royal jungle, is enough to show that the "unknown Greek prince" who, it seemed to many, came from nowhere to claim the hand of the heiress to the world's proudest and most stable throne had impeccable and impressive royal antecedents which rivalled those of Princess Elizabeth herself.

Like Elizabeth, Philip is a great-great-grandchild of Queen Victoria; like her, he is a descendant of German ruling houses. On his father's side he comes from a Danish royal line that goes back to 1448 and, by 1947, boasted sixteen kings of the House of Oldenburg and three of the House of Glücksburg or, more properly, Schleswig-Holstein-Sonderburg-Glücksburg – and Beck, according to the Duke of Edinburgh's cousin Alexandra of Yugoslavia in her book *Prince Philip: a Family Portrait*. Since 1947 there have been two more monarchs, one of them Queen Margrethe II who has reigned in Denmark since 1972. Six kings of Sweden and seven tsars of Russia grew on the branches of the same tree, not to speak of the

23

Glücksburg women who married into the British royal family, most notably Edward VII's Queen, Alexandra, who lived from 1844–1925. It was, in fact, the first of the Oldenburgs, Frederik VII, who transplanted his grandson (his heir's second son, William) to Greece, where he founded the troubled royal house that in 1921 produced Prince Philip.

Equally formidable was the heritage of Philip's mother, Alice of Battenberg and Greece, whose brother, Earl Mountbatten, began his work on the family's genealogy to coincide conveniently with the royal wedding of 1947. Published in a limited private edition in 1958, a somewhat battered copy of this rare work is available in the British Museum and, more exclusively, in the Tatoi library in Greece and on royal coffee tables up and down Europe. It is, in part, an essay in self-aggrandisement and the justification of family. For this reason, and others, it is a fascinating document which owes a great deal to the author's other specialist publication – a manual on naval signals – for it is dotted with cross-references in capital letters and figures – E4, F6 and on to E4F6-G8.

As an illuminating and unique piece of source material, Lord Mountbatten's genealogical survey is worth some attention. It opens thus:

The Mountbatten Lineage

The Direct Descent of the Family of
Mountbatten
From the House of Brabant
And the Rulers of Hesse

Prepared for private circulation
by
Admiral of the Fleet
The Earl Mountbatten of Burma
K.G., P.C., G.C.B., G.C.S.I., G.C.I.E.,
G.C.V.O., D.S.O., LL.D., D.C.L., D.Sc.

President of the Society of Genealogists
Patron of the Cambridge University Heraldic
and Genealogical Society
1958

In the Preface Earl Mountbatten reveals the complexity of his quest for a family that, according to Sir Iain Moncreiffe, Unicorn

Pursuivant of Arms, "was unique because it was the oldest traceable Protestant ruling house in the world". *Burke's Peerage* also raises up the ghosts of clanking, armoured, martial ancestors:

> The Mountbattens are a branch of one of the oldest traceable families in Christendom, the House of Brabant. Other branches of this great family made their mark in England long ago under other surnames, including the Lovaines (1186–1347), Lords Lovaine, and the historic Percies (1204–1607), Earls of Northumberland, among them the gallant and popular Harry Hotspur, hero of "Chevy Chase". As the mist of the Dark Ages clears away, their ancestors in the direct male line are already found in the soldier-statesmen maintaining order in parts of what is now Belgium and Luxembourg.

But where is the starting point of the lineage among these soldier-princes of the Dark Ages? Earl Mountbatten identifies three possible candidates.

First, there is "GISELBERT, Count of the Darnan, who abducted the Emperor Lothair's daughter in 846 AD . . . because from him onwards there is ample documentary evidence of the descent". Second, there is Duke MAINIER, Count of Sens, who died in 800 AD. Finally, there is Duke YDULF, "who flourished at the turn of the sixth to seventh century".

Beyond these three, there are figures even more shadowy. As Earl Mountbatten remarks, with a mixture of pride and vexation: "The legendary earliest ancestors of the Brabant/Hessian/Mountbatten family go back to the middle of the fourth century AD. The trouble about any pedigree that goes back one thousand six hundred years is that it gradually shades off from the impossible through the possible to the probable and finally the certain."

But what about the "Probable" ancestors, Giselbert, Ydulf and Mainier? After consulting Dr A. R. Wagner of the *Richmond Herald*, "one of the greatest genealogists in the Kingdom who wrote to me" and Sir Iain Moncreiffe, Lord Mountbatten took the plunge and "finally decided to start numbering [the generations] with YDULF, while making it abundantly clear that the descent established by adequate documents only starts with GISELBERT." Something between a plunge and a compromise, really, but at least it enables us to place the Duke of Edinburgh in the 42nd/43rd generation.

For all its antiquity and nobility, the Mountbatten lineage

becomes particularly relevant for the purpose of this book when it reaches the Grand Duke Louis II of Hesse-Darmstadt by the Rhine and his wife Wilhelmine, daughter of a Margrave of Baden (a name that will reappear in Prince Philip's time).

The eldest of Louis II's sons succeeded him in 1848 as Louis III, while the second, Charles, married Elizabeth of Prussia. It was their son who succeeded his heirless uncle as Louis IV, and who became the husband of Princess Alice, the second of Queen Victoria's three daughters. But the name which commands our immediate attention – because it leads us to the late Earl Mountbatten and to Prince Philip – is that of Louis III's other brother, Prince Alexander of Hesse (1823–1888), who somehow lost the "Darmstadt" from his name and could not even hand down "Hesse" to his offspring. It is idle to speculate about the course that Alexander's life might have taken had his younger sister Marie not become the wife of the future tsar, Alexander II of Russia, a marriage that enhanced the prestige of the house of Hesse-Darmstadt throughout the royal and princely courts of Europe. It also took her brother Alexander of Hesse to the sumptuous imperial court of St Petersburg where we must follow him in pursuit of the Duke of Edinburgh's line.

This is also where the austere, geometric (and confusing) genealogical tables, like many dry statistics, disguise romance and high drama. The mid-nineteenth century was a period when princes of German ruling families – Hesse-Darmstadt, Saxe-Coburg-Gotha, Hanover, Brunswick, Wittelsbach, and so forth, were so thick on the ground that there was little scope for them at home if they were not in the direct line of succession. Their best hope was to find employment abroad as soldiers, the only trade they knew. Raised with military discipline, they were worth their keep as fighting men and, wherever they went, could count on high rank in the forces they joined.

When Alexander of Hesse offered his services to the Russian army, the future Tsarina's brother was received with enthusiasm. His duties permitting, the able young officer enjoyed life at court, particularly surveying the galaxy of attractive ladies who enlivened the imperial scene. Eventually, however, his eyes came to rest on the wrong girl – wrong, that is, in terms of antecedents and status. The girl, Julie Hauke, was certainly handsome, but she had the misfortune of being a commoner and a maid of honour in the entourage of Alexander's sister, the future Tsarina.

A liaison at court was unexceptionable and easily condoned, but when news reached Darmstadt that Alexander intended to marry the girl, Grand Duke Louis III, according to a contemporary German account, exclaimed "Blödsinnige Gefühlsduselei!" (Idiotic, sentimental nonsense! comes nearest to rendering this idiomatic outburst in English.) Enraged with the younger brother who was naïve and daring enough to propose marriage to a girl without a title, he enquired contemptuously, "Do you expect us to have a Fräulein Hauke in the family?"

Undaunted, Alexander and Julie eloped and were married. Although they pleaded that Julie's father, a Polish officer who had risen to become War Minister before his death at the hands of nihilists in Warsaw, and had been created a Polish count (which, with European titles descending on all children, made her a countess), they had to pay for their obstinacy. Their marriage was declared morganatic and Alexander was drummed out of the imperial Russian army and obliged to look for employment elsewhere. He found it in the Austrian army and went on to serve the Habsburgs in many parts of the Austro-Hungarian monarchy.

The Grand Duke of Hesse-Darmstadt, whilst still disapproving of his brother's *mésalliance*, relented sufficiently to confer a lower German aristocratic title on his unwelcome sister-in-law and her future descendants. Prince Alexander's wife thus became the Countess of Battenberg. There were five children of the union, each born in a different Austrian garrison; the one of real relevance to the Mountbatten lineage was born in Graz, in the province of Styria. The boy inherited the title from his father, the surname from his mother, and – a hint of defiance on his father's part – the Christian name associated with the ruling Grand Dukes. He was Prince Louis of Battenberg, the father of Earl Mountbatten of Burma and grandfather of the Duke of Edinburgh.

It takes a good deal of dexterity and daring to hop from one branch of the intricate Mountbatten family tree to the other without losing one's footing and crashing down amid a rubble of Alices, Louis', Alexanders and the rest. However, Queen Victoria's daughter Princess Alice and Grand Duke Louis IV had seven children: Ernst Louis who became the next Grand Duke; Alix who married Tsar Nicholas II; Irene, the wife of Prince Henry of Prussia; Elizabeth, whose husband was Grand Duke Serge of Russia, a brother of Tsar Alexander III; two others, and Victoria, the eldest and her grandmother's namesake, who brings us back to Prince Louis of Battenberg who took her as his wife in 1884.

Princess Alice, mother of this Victoria, the third child of Queen Victoria, the grandmother of Earl Mountbatten and great-grandmother of Prince Philip, was an exceptional woman and worth pausing over. In 1974 Gerard Noel published her biography, *Princess Alice: Queen Victoria's Forgotten Daughter*. Earl Mountbatten wrote a foreword to the book, in which he expressed a family debt to Princess Alice's originality, intellect and liberalism:

> I was brought up on tales about my grandmother, Alice . . . with one accord they accepted her as the most remarkable of Queen Victoria's remarkable children. Had she not died so very young her impact on liberal history would obviously have been far greater.
>
> To me she was a fascinating personality and I was often told my mother took after her in progressive thought and ceaselessly taking the lead in discussions and conversations.

To be "the most remarkable of Queen Victoria's remarkable children" who were, in fact, a very mixed lot in both intellect and character, is perhaps not the highest of praise. Nonetheless, Princess Alice lived a passionately unconventional life which at times seemed compounded of all the ingredients of Victorian melodrama.

Princess Alice was the first of Queen Victoria's children to die, but death and family tragedy were no strangers to her. She was one of the carriers of the haemophilia which affected three of Queen Victoria's children and which spread, by inter-marriage, throughout the royal families of Europe, striking with particular ferocity at the Romanovs and at the sons of Alfonso XIII, King of Spain. One of Queen Victoria's sons, Leopold, was a haemophiliac, and both Princess Alice and Princess Beatrice (the old Queen's youngest child) were carriers of the deadly malady which as late as 1945 claimed the life of Waldemar, son of Prince Henry of Prussia.

Princess Alice's own death came tragically early. Two of her children were suffering from diptheria, and she was forbidden to nurse them or have contact with them. But when her daughter May died of the infection, she spontaneously broke the news to her sick son Ernest and, in the words of Disraeli's overwrought epitaph upon her, received "the kiss of death . . . My Lords, I hardly know an incident more pathetic. It is one by which poets might be inspired and in which the artist of every class, whether in picture, in statue or in gem, might find a fitting subject of commemoration."

Whether Disraeli would equally have approved of Alice's turbulent life is open to question. Certainly her marriage to Louis IV, Grand Duke of Hesse, was a stormy one. In the words of her biographer, "they quarrelled when together, even though they missed each other touchingly when separated." Alice gave clear expression to the ambivalence of their relationship when, urged by her mother in 1870 to visit her sister Vicky (wife of the Prussian Crown Prince Frederick) in Berlin, she wrote to Louis: "You know I prefer to stay here! And I believe it is what *you* prefer my darling – is it not?"

Alice, who was, it seems, basically tougher than her husband, tended to express her feelings in nervous, sensitive and more intellectual fashion: she "tended to be temperamental where Louis was taciturn; demanding where he was docile; critical where he was phlegmatic; demonstrative where he was reserved". Though all this might have added up to a perfect intermarriage of complementary qualities, Alice sought solace elsewhere in her "intellectual love affair" with David Friedrich Strauss, the philosopher, and in her passionate devotion to good causes. She campaigned vigorously for homes for the mentally handicapped, for the effective reclaiming of "fallen women", and so forth. Under her influence there sprang up the various "Alice Societies" in Germany – for example, the *Alice Frauenverein* to promote nursing and the training of nurses, and the *Alice Verein für Frauenbildung und Erwerb* – which were aimed at enabling women to achieve a proper education and to earn their own living.

Few princes or princesses could claim, or want to claim, so revolutionary an ancestor – an exponent of women's liberation almost a century before it became a fashionable and acceptable movement. But Princess Alice's blood flows through the veins of the Duke of Edinburgh and his children, a fact which ought to afford them more stimulation and pride than remorse.

Of course there are important intermediaries before the family tree forms its more recent branches. Prince Louis of Battenberg, father of Earl Mountbatten of Burma and grandfather of Prince Philip, is one of these. He made his first appearance in this history a short while ago, and will soon play a major role in the unfolding of the Mountbatten story. For the moment, however, a brief introduction will be sufficient.

Louis of Battenberg (1854–1921), whose life and accomplishments have stimulated several detailed accounts, followed the example of his father, Alexander, Prince of Hesse, and set his sights beyond the narrow confines of the Hesse-Darmstadt realm. As the husband of Queen Victoria's granddaughter, he joined the finest service open to him, the Royal Navy. A talented and ambitious naval officer, Prince Louis was clearly destined for an outstanding career. He and Victoria had four children – Alice, born in 1885, Louise in 1889, George in 1892, and Louis, the future Earl Mountbatten, who arrived in 1900 together with the new century.

Of these children, two must claim immediate and detailed consideration in any assessment of Prince Philip's life, and it is natural enough to start with his mother, Princess Alice of Battenberg who, in 1903, married Prince Andrew of Greece.

2

Alice of Battenberg
and Andrew of Greece

"There was a brief, fervent wooing and then a somewhat slower
but undoubtedly not less passionate courtship by correspondence."

Ex-Queen Alexandra of Yugoslavia

ALICE, APPROPRIATELY ENOUGH for a great-granddaughter of Queen
Victoria, was born at Windsor Castle in 1885, sixteen years before
the old Queen's death. She died in 1969 at Buckingham Palace, at
the age of eighty-four. A solid English beginning and a dignified
English ending for a life that was for the most part spent elsewhere
and amid a good many vicissitudes and tribulations.

She suffered from a congenital deafness which eventually became
so serious a handicap as to cripple her contact with others. She
endured exile and the break-up of her marriage. During the turbulent relationship between the Greek people and their imported
monarchy her life and the lives of her husband and children were
sometimes at risk. In later years, she withdrew more and more into
her religious shell, rarely appearing in public and then nearly always
dressed in a grey, nun-like, full-flowing robe and coif – the uniform
of the Christian Sisterhood of Martha and Mary which she founded
in 1949. Even before then, her devotional tastes were much in
evidence and her great-niece, Ex-Queen Alexandra of Yugoslavia
wrote: "Try as I will to separate present and past, I cannot build a
picture of Philip's mother . . . without often seeing her in one of her
severe grey gowns, a nun-like coif at her brow. Her brown eyes
would be fixed unwaveringly on my lips as she lip-read my gossip
and girlish talk."

Yet Alice of Battenberg was sufficiently resilient to survive her
disabilities and traumas (including, in 1966, an illness in Munich

31

which sent Prince Philip dashing to her rescue in a plane he piloted himself) and to see her youngest Windsor grandchild, Prince Edward, reach his fifth year. Described in 1908 as "the prettiest princess in Europe", she had been an eight-year-old bridesmaid at the wedding of the future King George V and Princess Mary of Teck in 1893 looking, according to Queen Victoria, "very sweet in white satin, with a little pink and red rose on the shoulder and some small bows of the same on the shoes". Towards the end of her life she was just a background figure, mysterious and remote, living obscurely at Buckingham Palace. To the casual observer, she was merely "an old Greek lady, some sort of religious crank. Hard to tie her in at all with the dashing, dominating and gratifying English Duke."

The Times obituary on her death in December 1969, said: "Of the many tragedies that afflicted members of European Royalty in this century, hers were perhaps among the most poignant and harrowing. She was a lonely figure in her late age." But even in the last two years of her life at Buckingham Palace, according to Basil Boothroyd's book, *Philip*: "If she didn't give the Queen any mother-in-law trouble in the music-hall sense, she was a force to be reckoned with, and domestic or family decisions that she had her own ideas about could get badly hung up."

Her great-niece, Princess Alexandra of Greece, the future Queen of King Peter of Yugoslavia, has left a warm account of her in her sometimes melodramatic but useful book *Prince Philip: a Family Portrait*. Alexandra's affection is apparent from the start: the book is dedicated to "My Dearest Aunt Alice". Ex-Queen Alexandra remembers her for "the warm sympathy and understanding she always displayed for my absurd little problems":

Though she was my great-aunt, tall, greying, elderly, she seemed to me to be one of the few adults willing to give a mere child her full and undivided attention. She would memorise the names of my friends so that she could enquire about them years afterwards. She could remember trivial incidents and recall them with laughter. She sat watchfully intent as I talked and then she would give her counsel and advice, throwing out her words as if they were pellets, forming her phrases with a staccato emphasis that seemed to enrich them with special significance.

Despite this affectionate picture of an attentive and caring Princess Alice, there are curiosities, eccentricities even, revealed in

Alexandra's account. Knowing that her great-aunt was "profoundly religious" she nonetheless accepted, without much thought, that "she never talked to me of religion". Alexandra was also aware that Alice "had been married for more than twenty or thirty years and had her four daughters, all far older than I, and a son [Philip], yet she *never* [author's italics] spoke of her husband, my Uncle Andrea". Alexandra's explanation of these odd silences is naïve, if not positively disingenuous: "Looking back, I can see that I must have always enjoyed more than my own full share in the conversation, for I cannot remember that Aunt Alice has ever talked of herself."

There are other vignettes which reveal more of Princess Alice's somewhat enigmatic personality: of her driving home furiously through the "pitched battle in the streets" of Athens during the Allied bombardment of 1916, and finding that "bullets had shattered the nursery window, scattering broken glass around her two youngest children, Cecile and Sophie, as they played on the floor"; of Alice being the first to come "into the room to put her arms round" Alexandra's mother to comfort her when the latter's husband, Alexander I, had been "called to the Throne . . . and my young mother and he were in tears at the awful responsibility that had so suddenly been placed upon them." Tears, incidentally, were quite in order. Alexander was to have a short, inglorious reign from 1917–1920 as the puppet of the pro-British Greek statesman Venizelos, during which time he lost contact with most of his family, had few friends, and eventually perished – as ignominiously as he had reigned – from blood poisoning after being bitten by a monkey. In view of the bitter antagonisms and recriminations within the Greek royal family at the time of Alexander I's accession, therefore, Alice's display of compassion was charitable, almost saintly.

There are more clues to Princess Alice's personality. Her greatniece Alexandra remembers in 1938:

when I was eighteen, visiting Aunt Alice in her little house near the Kolonaki Square. And I can see her now continually glancing at the clock at the hour when Philip was expected, while her old lady-in-waiting, Madame Socopol, came constantly running in with warning gestures whenever a car turned into the street. To welcome young Philip on these comparatively infrequent occasions a large meal was always prepared. One day, it included a compote of stewed oranges, oranges unpeeled and entire which

33

had first been boiled for hours. I must have pulled a face at the bitter-sweet taste, but Philip liked it, so I too politely tried to show appreciation. Thereafter, Aunt Alice often greeted me with the cry, "Sandra, we are having your favourite dessert – orange compote!" and I dutifully had to eat it almost to the point of feeling sick. On the other hand, Aunt Alice knew that I disliked sauces and attentively made her cook prepare plain food, usually something grilled.

Prior to the outbreak of the Second World War, Alice lived in Athens, in overcrowded rooms, "crammed with signed photographs of innumerable Battenbergs". When the German invasion of Greece was imminent in 1941, Alexandra recalls that Alice:

> opened a cupboard door and gave me all her crested notepaper, stamped with an "A" and a crown, because my initial was the same as hers. In its huge Asprey box nearly a yard long, this most impracticable parting gift had to be stowed aboard a destroyer for evacuation. All of our worldly goods were jettisoned overboard when the destroyer was involved in battle action but the heavy box of notepaper remained, and I used it to the last scrap.

A little eccentric, perhaps, but interesting.

Yet Alice is not simply revealed as a religious zealot, engulfed in a feuding and beleaguered royal family, and beset by diverse anxieties and her enveloping deafness. She was able to do more than comfort others and involve herself in their problems. It is not, as Alexandra, perhaps defensively, remarks:

> that Aunt Alice lacked a sense of humour. At one time she loved to frequent a cinema that showed old classic silent films, chiefly for the joy of lip-reading what the characters really said. With her infallible memory she would then retail these conversations for the amusement of her friends.

A dinner-party once nearly choked with laughter when Aunt Alice described one of the big scenes in, I think, Von Stroheim's *Greed*. In the midst of a passionate love scene, the hero was really telling the heroine that he was being evicted for not paying his rent. These glimpses of real life from the movies were admittedly all the more comical for Aunt Alice's explosive method of blurting them out.

But all of this came later.

At sixteen, Alice, pretty enough to turn any head, visited her father's family in Darmstadt where she met Prince Andrea (or Andrew) of Greece, the nineteen-year-old son of Danish-born King George I of Greece and nephew of Alexandra, Princess of Wales. After six years at the Military Academy in Athens, Andrew had recently passed an exhaustive examination by a panel including his father, the King, his brothers (Crown Prince Constantine and Prince Nicholas), the Prime Minister, the Archbishop, the War Minister and half the Military Academy's teaching staff, and he was duly commissioned and posted to Darmstadt on attachment to an élite cavalry unit, the Hessian 23rd Dragoon Guards.

Andrew and Alice were clearly attracted to each other at their first meeting. They met again the following year, when he came to London for the Coronation of Edward VII, which Alice attended as a Maid of Honour to the new Queen. Andrew visited her once more after that, and, before her eighteenth birthday, 25 February 1903, she was clearly in love with him.

What sort of a courtship was it? Alice was shy, a little withdrawn because of her deafness. In order to understand her suitor fully she would have had to read his lips. Though his parents mostly conversed in German, Andrew spoke Greek by choice and conviction; however, he and his brothers also spoke Danish, Russian, German and English. Alice spoke English and had recently learned German, so it was chiefly in the former, and perhaps a little in the latter of these languages that they communicated.

Despite the unusual problems posed by Alice's deafness, the first meeting was apparently "a brief, fervent wooing" followed by a "somewhat slower but undoubtedly not less passionate" courtship by correspondence. One day a friend found Alice crying bitterly because no letters had arrived, although she wrote to Prince Andrew every day. The friend tried to console her by explaining that delays occurred in the post. The next day, to Alice's undisguised joy, five letters from Andrew arrived all at once.

Prince Andrew was undoubtedly a fine prospect for the young princess. He was good-looking, tall, straight-backed, and fairhaired – part of the Danish ("Viking") heritage that is also Prince Philip's. His only physical disadvantage was poor eyesight: since boyhood he had worn spectacles, although he later favoured a rather Teutonic monocle. Andrew's myopia, like his stature and colouring, was passed on to Philip, who mostly wears contact lenses – despite his earlier tendency to lose them during polo games.

Ex-Queen Alexandra remembers Prince Andrew as "a tall, genial, smiling gentleman . . . who turned everything into a joke". Certainly he enjoyed practical jokes, not all of them in good taste if Alexandra's account is anything to go by. He also became reticent about his personal life: "Like Aunt Alice, he never talked of his secrets, the darker hours of his life." Was this merely a Balkan version of the stiff upper lip? Certainly, from Alexandra's evidence, there is little to suggest an open and constantly communicative relationship between Prince Philip's parents.

But, at least, despite his rare, "sterner moods", Andrew was mostly humorous and relaxed with his only son, who so much resembles him in manner and appearance:

> He always treated Philip with the same indulgent raillery. I heard him joking with my cousin sometimes on his athletic prowess or youthful escapades but, as Philip's Papa, he would give him advice, whenever it was sought, with a gentle gravity. Philip adored his father and, looking back, I can see physical resemblances that went unnoticed when I was younger. Not long ago, leafing through a magazine, I discovered the Annigoni portrait of Philip. I was absently awaiting a telephone call, I suppose, and I very naughtily pencilled in a monocle and the suggestion of a moustache. I scarcely noticed that I was doodling. And the result suddenly shocked me; for there, in one of his sterner moods, was Uncle Andrea.

During his courtship of Alice, some twenty years before Philip was born, Andrew must have begun, for her benefit, to unravel the complexities of recent Greek politics and to describe the family that provided Greece with its royal house.

The 1862 revolution that abruptly rid the country of its first imported monarch since independence, Otto of Bavaria, would have been the best place to start. Otto was dethroned while on a sea voyage, and all that was left of his dynastic pretensions were the colours of the Greek flag – blue and white like Bavaria's own.

After Otto's overthrow the Greek nation offered the throne to Queen Victoria's second son, Prince Alfred, later Duke of Edinburgh. When the Queen and her government declined the invitation, fearing that Alfred might all too quickly suffer Otto's fate, the powers sponsoring the Greek kingdom (Britain, France and Russia) put forward another candidate. This was Prince Andrew's father, Prince William of Denmark, who was only eighteen when he was eased into the accession – as George I, King of the Hellenes – with a coronation gift of the Ionian Islands, which had been a British protectorate for half a century. Corfu, which is the finest of the islands and still cherishes the English cricketing tradition, became the Greek royal family's favourite resort. The powers also added £12,000 a year to the pitifully small Greek civil list, one of the lowest in Europe.

There was one more problem: William, now George I, was the brother of Alexandra, Princess of Wales, and the Russians were worried that he might turn out to be too pro-British for comfort. Fortunately, William had been to St Petersburg where, according to family history, he had seen the sixteen-year-old Grand Duchess Olga Constantinova serving tea from a samovar with such grace that he fell straightway in love with her. No matter what really happened, romance and diplomacy (as is so often the case with royalty) neatly dove-tailed, and most of Russia's worries dissolved when William proposed to Olga and took her off to Greece as his Queen.

By the time that Prince Andrew met Alice, forty years had passed since his father's enthronement and marriage. George I's close family ties with Britain and Russia had helped Greece to acquire Thessaly. Though the King was relieved to have added considerably to his new country's territory and population, there was also bitter disappointment that his family and diplomatic connections did not enable him to reclaim Crete from the Turks for a considerable time.

Prince Andrew's family history was anything but straightforward and tranquil, and it would have taken Princess Alice a good deal of time to understand the lineal ramifications and his family's links with other royal houses. For instance, his father's sister Dagmar had taken the opposite route from the one which had brought his mother from Russia, and she became Marie Feodorovna, the wife of Tsar Alexander III; another aunt was Thyra, Duchess of Cumberland, whose descendants became the Dukes of Hanover-Brunswick; and, of course, there was his aunt, Queen Alexandra, but Alice would have known as much about her as he did. Andrew's grandfather, Christian IX, was still on the throne of Denmark.

In 1903, the year of Andrew's marriage to Alice, Andrew's uncle Nicholas and his wife, Grand Duchess Helen of Russia, had their first daughter, Olga (who eventually married Prince Paul of Yugoslavia), followed in 1904 by a second daughter, Elizabeth, and in 1906 by a third, Marina, the future Duchess of Kent, to whom Philip was to become greatly attached. Before long, a new generation would produce three more Greek kings and their three sisters, one of them, another Helen, the none-too-happy wife of King Carol of Romania and mother of Philip's boyhood friend Michael. He replaced his father as King of Romania before being deposed himself – by his father, who made a brief come-back.

Then there were Andrew's brothers and sisters. Alice may at first have been as confused as future historians, one of whom, a specialist on the Greek royal family, overlooked one sister altogether, while a more recent chronicler left out another sister and paid scant attention to a brother who played a significant part in Prince Philip's youth. To put the record straight, Andrew was one of eight brothers and sisters. The eldest was Constantine ("Tino"), who was married – inconveniently, it turned out – to Sophie, Kaiser Wilhelm II's sister; next was George, who married Princess Marie Bonaparte, Napoleon's great-grand-niece – Philip's unexpected link with the French Imperial family; the next child was Alexandra, then came Nicholas and Marie, who both married into the Russian Imperial family (though Marie's second husband was a Greek admiral); then Olga, who died in infancy; and, after Andrew, Christopher, who was also married twice.

Andrew and his brothers had been strictly brought up by a father who believed in military virtues and had pushed his sons to the very limit of their physical endurance – cold baths in the mornings, hard drilling by German instructors at the Military Academy and the like.

Christopher, Andrew's junior by nearly seven years, has left some idea of what life in the Greek royal household was like in his *Memoirs* published in 1938. Christopher suggests that he was "so much an afterthought that the Spartan discipline of the nursery had relaxed from long disuse and I met with far more indulgence from my parents than any of my brothers or sisters".

Nonetheless, Christopher was anything but a spoiled child. He recalled that he was tutored in an enormous classroom which was like all the rooms in the royal palace in Greece. The classroom had "bare white walls, with maps hanging about, a china stove and two desks, one for my tutor and one for me". Predictably there was a blackboard and, less predictably, "a set of hideous furniture".

38

Christopher was "hiked out of bed every morning at six for the detested cold tub; baths did not exist in those days". And this, we have been assured, was a relaxation of spartan discipline! By comparison, the regime at Gordonstoun School, where both Prince Philip and Prince Charles received a major part of their education, seems positively decadent, an unashamed indulgence of the senses. Not that Philip is by nature an early riser; complicated echoes from his father's upbringing may account for this.

As if the rigours of the palace were insufficient, in 1899 Prince Andrew was turned over to a merciless Greek taskmaster, Major Panayotis Danglis. Noting that the seventeen-year-old prince was, not surprisingly, "in some awe of his father", Danglis also saw that he was tall, quick, handsome and intelligent – which might serve equally well as a description of Philip. In fact, Philip's father and his four brothers were all physically impressive, upright and good-looking. They were also great players of practical jokes, which somehow goes together with cold baths at six o'clock in the morning. According to Prince Philip, "Anything could happen when you got a few of them together. It was like the Marx brothers." An apt description, and one that is strengthened when one considers their nicknames – "Tino" leading one gang and "Groucho" the other.

Danglis instructed Andrew in a number of military subjects: artillery, fortifications, military technology, military history, military geography and military topography. Not exactly a liberal education, but practical in view of Greece's violent history and uncertain future. Danglis drummed his lessons into Andrew's head for a year and a half. When the royal family went to Corfu in the spring of 1900, Danglis accompanied them, and Andrew had to forego family picnics and communal pleasures for his lessons. Later in the year, Andrew stayed with his elder brother George, High Commissioner of Crete, during a fretful period in the island's history; but Danglis came too, and Andrew's instruction continued unabated.

This unrelenting instruction appears not to have marred Andrew's sense of fun, for though single-minded, he retained the capacity to laugh easily and to appreciate quickly the ridiculous in any situation (traits which mark both Prince Philip and Prince Charles). Nor should one suppose that he disliked his father, King George, despite being in "some awe" of him, for George could also be relaxed and jovial, and he was given to unescorted strolls through the streets of Athens, chatting amiably to passers-by.

Andrew, moreover, was able to see things clearly, and he turned, sometimes impatiently, from stupidity, inefficiency and deviousness – yet more characteristics that were inherited by his son.

At any rate, by the time he married Alice, Andrew was free of Danglis' presence, and the latter was decorated for his services with the Gold Cross of the Order of the Redeemer. He went on to turn against his royal employer during the Greek troubles of 1916.

The betrothal was not exactly a blissfully straightforward affair. It was common knowledge that Alice's family was less than enthusiastic about her choice. Although her father, Prince Louis, by now Director of Naval Intelligence at the Admiralty, was not inordinately rich by any means, the Battenbergs were wealthy compared with the Greek royal family. "Willy", as relatives continued to call Prince Andrew's father long after he had become King George I of Greece, or "Willy of Denmark" (in order not to confuse him with "Kaiser Willy"), often referred to himself as "a poor man with a large family". What income would the young couple have to live on? Prince Andrew haughtily brushed all objections aside. If needs be, he would support his wife on his pay as a Greek officer. Puritanical, stubborn and admirable.

It did not come to that. As prominently reported in the recently created *Daily Express* (an early pointer to the paper's dogged and often uncharitable preoccupation with the Battenbergs right down to Lord Louis Mountbatten and Prince Philip), several royal relatives offered help to make the marriage possible. The most generous contribution came from the Tsar Nicholas II but it was nowhere near the amount of £100,000 that was rumoured. However, while there were eventually sufficient funds to permit Andrew and Alice to enjoy a reasonable standard of living, they never enabled the couple to rise above a level of contemporary bourgeois comfort. Alice, modest and frugal by nature, was not perturbed, and it was many years before Andrew found some compensation for his spartan upbringing in the relaxed atmosphere of St Moritz, Paris and Monte Carlo.

It was announced in May 1903 that Prince Andrew of Greece and Princess Alice of Battenberg had become formally engaged. The Prince and Princess of Wales, later George V and Queen Mary, gave an engagement party at Marlborough House which was attended by King Edward VII (who ran his fingers through Alice's golden hair and declared that no throne in Europe was too good for her), Queen Alexandra, and a sprinkling of Battenbergs and

Glücksburgs. Prince Louis of Battenberg, on becoming more closely acquainted with his future son-in-law, recognised with relief a kindred spirit – an officer dedicated to service. Prince Louis was destined to attain even higher naval rank, and Prince Andrew's military career looked equally promising. Ironically, however, both men – one in Britain, the other in Greece – were ultimately to be rejected and humiliated by the country each had chosen to serve.

Andrew and Alice were married on 9 October 1903 in Darmstadt in the Grand Duchy of Hesse-Darmstadt, despite murmurings in some quarters that a London wedding would have been more befitting. It was a lavish, Edwardian set-piece: one of those ridiculously ornate, overdressed, self-assured and sky-larking occasions when Europe's royalty proved their essentially ordinary tastes amid extraordinary pomp and wealth.

Heading the royal congregation in Darmstadt were the exuberant Tsar Nicholas II and his Tsarina Alix (of Hesse-Darmstadt), untroubled by any premonition of their murder at the hands of Russian revolutionaries fifteen years hence; they were accompanied by a retinue of Grand Dukes and Grand Duchesses, half Romanov, half Hesse, including Grand Duke Paul, brother-in-law of the bridegroom. Another brother-in-law, Kaiser Wilhelm II, sent his brother Henry, Prince of Prussia, and his wife Irene, the Tsarina's older sister. Queen Alexandra of England brought Princesses Victoria and Beatrice, King George of Greece was with Andrew's brothers. There was a covey of Austrian archdukes, representatives of the Italian royal house (the Duke and Duchess of Aosta), Romanians, Serbs, and scores of German relations. The bride's father and mother had their other children with them: Louise, a future Queen of Sweden; George, heir to Prince Louis' title (which would eventually be that of the first Marquess of Milford Haven); and three-year-old Louis, the future Earl Mountbatten of Burma, marking his first ceremonial trip abroad by a noisy chatter which, in church, was only drowned by the anthems of the Russian Imperial Choir, specially brought from St Petersburg.

On the wedding day, the guests emerged appropriately accoutred from the Grand Duke of Hesse-Darmstadt's Wolfsgarten, where most of them had been lodged, or from their suites at Heiligenberg Castle, which Prince Louis of Battenberg had inherited from his father. An official holiday was declared so that the populace might dutifully line the streets; no anarchists threw bombs, nor, indeed, were any seriously expected to do so.

The guests attended three ceremonies – an exchange of vows at the town hall to comply with the law of the land, a Protestant wedding in deference to a Protestant bride, and a prolonged and beautiful ritual of the Greek Orthodox Church which finally sealed the union in the eyes of Prince Andrew's family. They listened to the prayers, the litanies, the hymns, the choir's "Kyrie Eleison" (Lord, have mercy), and the archimandrite's address to the bridegroom, "The servant of God, Andrea . . . ." and to the bride, "The servant of God, Alice . . . ." They saw the blessing of the symbolic golden crowns which Andrew's brothers, Nicholas and Christopher, held over the heads of the couple and switched from one to the other to signify their union, after which Andrew and Alice, as the ritual demanded, circled the altar three times.

The only serious hitch occurred when the bride could not properly hear, or understand, the officiating Greek priest's questions as to whether she had consented of her own free will to marry Andrew or whether she had promised her hand to someone else. Perhaps she failed to read the priest's lips amid the profusion of his beard. At any rate, she replied loudly, "No" to the first question and "Yes" to the second. Prince Christopher nudged her sharply, and the errors were amended.

The wedding banquet at the Old Palace was the scene of those predictable high jinks which, rather than cultured wit, seem part and parcel of such occasions. Royal and noble eye-witnesses have handed down lurid descriptions of the festivities. The venerable Grand Duchess of Württemberg, who had secured her tiara with elastic, nonetheless had her spectacles knocked off, and in a myopic fury she hit the wrong suspect with her handbag. Tiaras and headgear were exchanged, apparently to much amusement. Led by the Tsar, whose simple spirit throve on horse-play, the wedding guests showered the departing couple with rice, rose petals and slippers, and pursued their carriage down the road. There was one incident, full of bloody portent, when paper bags were popped among the crowd with a noise which sounded like explosions and sent detectives pouncing on suspected assassins. The Tsar, however, had not done yet. Having caught up with the carriage, he threw a full bag of rice straight into the bride's face! He followed this up by hurling a slipper which she caught and brought down unceremoniously on his head, shouting, with some justice, "You're a stupid old donkey!" Weak with laughter, the Tsar of all the Russias stood in the middle of the street unable to move, while in the carriage Alice resumed her seat and, unruffled and charming, acknowledged the waiting crowds.

Andrew and Alice's first marital home, in sharp contrast to the opulence of their surroundings at Darmstadt, was a sombre suite in the austere royal palace in Athens, the Old Palace. But the gloom was doubtless relieved by the family roller-skating and cycling down its corridors, sometimes led by King George himself. Then there were holidays, and the occasional weekend, in one of the modest houses which King George had built for his sons in the grounds of his Tatoi estate at the foot of Mount Parnassos. Later Andrew and Alice moved into one of these houses, and their first two children, Margarita and Theodora were born there.

As her capacity for easy social contact was hampered by her deafness, Princess Alice attended the School of Greek Embroidery, first as pupil then as teacher, and led the life of a soldier's wife. Prince Andrew was away on active duty for long periods. During this time, Crete was a constant thorn in the side of the monarchy and Prince Andrew shared closely his father's anxiety over reverses in the inglorious conflict with the rebellious islanders.

The marriage of Alice and Andrew seems to have been comfortable rather than brilliant, tempestuous or extraordinary. At the very least they did their marital duty. Two years after the wedding, Alice gave birth to their first daughter who was named Margarita, followed a year later by another baby girl, Theodora. Still no boy; no possible successor to the Greek throne. Next came two more daughters, Cecile and Sophie. Margarita and Theodora, and later Cecile, enjoyed several summer holidays at Broadlands, the Hampshire estate of the Battenbergs, where several decades later their brother and Princess Elizabeth spent their honeymoon.

Meanwhile Prince Andrew's military career was, to say the least, unsettled. This was not because of an innate incompetence – quite the opposite – but because of the tangle of intrigue and uncertainty that enmeshed the Greek monarchy and the Greek people before, and during, the First World War. With the development of the Greek republican movement and the subsequent rise to political power of the able Cretan lawyer Eleutherios Venizelos, destined to be four times Prime Minister, it was difficult for a royal officer to avoid conflict.

In 1909 republican and anti-German agitation (the latter directed chiefly at Crown Prince Constantine for his family ties with the Kaiser) caused Andrew to resign from the army. His brothers

Constantine, Nicholas and Christopher resigned with him, and Prince George from the navy. There ensued two frustrated years for Andrew, spent, according to Alice, "in idleness, to his great grief".

Yet, in Greek politics, the only thing that could be safely predicted was that the unpredictable would happen. In the years before the First World War, no part of Europe was in greater danger of violent conflict than the Balkans. In the short run, it proved a blessing for Andrew and his brothers. With her neighbours Serbia and Bulgaria preparing to go to war against Turkey, Greece could not stand aside. In 1911, after constitutional amendments, the royal princes were restored to their military posts. Later, when the King read his proclamation ordering total mobilisation from the balcony of the royal palace, it was Prince Andrew who held a candle over the parchment. On 17 October 1912, the first Balkan War broke out.

A colonel in the 3rd Cavalry Regiment, Andrew was with Crown Prince Constantine at Army HQ in the drive against the Turks. Poorly equipped and lacking in many essentials, the troops were enthusiastic to reconquer Greek territory. There are some interesting images of the campaign: of Andrew, damp and bedraggled after a day's fighting, seeking shelter in the local church where the villagers offered "some straw, but you could sleep in the choir stalls"; of Andrew and his men roasting a pig and eating it with their hands. The fighting went well. By early November 1912, they were advancing into southern Epirus and Macedonia. Entering Salonica, Andrew was reunited with Alice who was carrying medical supplies for the troops. King George rode into the city in triumph.

Four months later on 18 March 1913, while on his daily walkabout to meet his new subjects in the streets of Salonica, King George was assassinated. Shot, to quote *The Times*, "by a degenerate who was immediately arrested"; in fact by a Macedonian whose motive was never established. The *Times* obituary, headed "The career of a Danish prince", gave the family name of the Duke of Edinburgh's grandfather as "Schleswig-Holstein-Sonderburg-Glücksburg", and described him as a good, industrious man who (it brings the grandson to mind) encouraged technical progress and taught his people how to make the best of their productive capacity.

Prince Andrew swore allegiance to his brother Tino, the new King Constantine I, who was soon embroiled in conflict with the Bulgarians in the Second Balkan War of June–July 1913. With the approach of the First World War, King Constantine's position was precarious and became well-nigh intolerable when war broke out the following year. Greece was in the British and French sphere of influence, but Constantine was considered to be sympathetic to Germany. In London and Paris, the fact that he was the Kaiser's brother-in-law rendered him suspect, as well as his brothers. While Venizelos was siding with the Western Allies, Andrew and Nicholas were thought to be in league with pro-German Colonel Metaxas who worked to bring Greece into the war on Germany's side.

In Britain meanwhile, the German-born Prince Louis of Battenberg was in an extremely vulnerable position himself; a position that was unlikely to be helped by reports of his son-in-law's involvement with the pro-German faction in Greece. It was as Admiral Louis Battenberg, First Sea Lord, that the Prince signed the order sending the Royal Navy into action against Germany. But while Battenberg's exceptional service record had earned him the confidence of the Commander-in-Chief of the Grand Fleet, Admiral Sir John Jellicoe, and the First Lord of the Admiralty, Winston Churchill, anti-German fervour engulfed anything and anybody remotely connected with the enemy. Beethoven became an unacceptable composer, dachshunds were booed in the streets and Battenberg was vilified for his German name and connections. Three months after the outbreak of war, Admiral Battenberg tendered his resignation to Winston Churchill. The xenophobia which drove him from office was later to cause King George V to change his family name from Saxe-Coburg-Gotha to the safe, anglophone Windsor. In the wake of this change in the royal family name in 1917, Battenberg was anglicised to Mountbatten, and Louis, no longer a prince, was compensated in some measure with the rank and style of Marquess of Milford Haven, Earl of Medina and Viscount Alderney.

If Alice's father had a difficult time in Britain – enforced idleness on his estate in the Isle of Wight was an ordeal – her husband fared even worse. Political and diplomatic tempers ran high in London in the summer of 1916 when Prince Andrew and Prince Nicholas arrived on a mission – which also took them to Paris and St Petersburg – to assure the government that King Constantine, far from being pro-German, was strictly neutral. A full-throated press campaign against the Greek emissaries was reinforced with the publication of a photograph showing Andrew with the openly pro-German Colonel Metaxas who, it was said, had supplied Berlin with secret information about Allied troop movements. Angry headlines included: "Tino's new treachery" and "Allied plans betrayed to Germans". King Constantine was accused of hatching plots in Tatoi and allowing German U-boats to refuel in Corfu. Though certainly not pro-British, he was perhaps mainly concerned to keep his country out of the war, though at the same time leaning a little towards one side, much as Franco did in the Second World War.

In the circumstances, it was not surprising that the mission which had brought Andrew and Nicholas to London was a total failure. The Greek princes lunched with Queen Alexandra at Marlborough House, and with King George V and Queen Mary at Buckingham Palace, where the King urged them to make Constantine see the risks he was running. The official Allied reaction was simply to put severe pressure on the Greeks to get rid of their pro-German King.

In August 1916 Venizelos, with his party leaders, seceded to Salonica where he established a provisional government. At the beginning of December 1916, an Anglo-French force landed at Piraeus and advanced, not entirely smoothly, upon Athens.

This was only the beginning of Allied interference. In 1917 Panayotis Danglis, Andrew's old tutor, and now a full general, made common cause with them and opened up Salonica for an Allied landing. Constantine was forced to vacate the throne – he later claimed that he had not formally abdicated – and ordered to leave the country.

With other members of the royal family, Andrew and Alice were at the palace bidding him farewell when news came that angry demonstrators were approaching. The couple only just managed to extricate themselves and made for Tatoi. Convinced that Constantine's eldest son, Crown Prince George, shared his father's pro-German sympathies, the Allies installed George's younger, twenty-four-year-old brother Alexander on the throne as a puppet of Venizelos, thus compounding the problems of the young man who had fallen in love with a commoner, Aspasia Manos. His first decision as King was to enter into a morganatic marriage with her. His next was to join the Allies in the war.

Constantine went into exile in Switzerland – Zurich, Lucerne, St Moritz; his brothers and their families followed a few days later. Exile for Prince Andrew, his wife and daughters had little to commend it. They spent the next three years short of cash, dependent on loans, often – we know on the authority of Prince Christopher –

46

wondering where next month's rent would be coming from. Nor were the Swiss overjoyed to have such politically embarrassing exiles on their soil. They watched them closely, and Christopher complained later that their friends had only been able to visit them in the strictest secrecy; but he failed to mention that the visitors included agents of the German government. Abetted by the Swiss authorities, the British Consul strongly advised the English servants of the Greek princes to seek more suitable employment, and, as a result, the children of Prince and Princess Nicholas – Olga, Elizabeth and Marina – and the four daughters of Prince and Princess Andrew lost their British nannies.

The end of the war brought no peace to the Greeks. The Allies wanted Alexander to continue on the throne, but Prince Andrew and his other brothers tried both to wean the young King from his dependence on the Western powers and, better still, to persuade him to make way for his exiled father, Constantine. Alexander's wretched and ignominious reign might have tottered on for some time had not fate intervened in macabre and comic style. On an autumn day – 2 October 1920 – as the King was walking in the gardens of Tatoi, a pet monkey attacked one of his dogs. Coming to the dog's assistance, Alexander tried to drive the monkey off, only to be attacked himself and severely bitten. Blood poisoning set in, the King's heart was affected and he seemed likely to die.

In Lucerne, ex-King Constantine called his brothers together. If his son died, the way would be open for him and the family to return home. As Alexander deteriorated, there were busy political manoeuvres on all sides: a government crisis in Greece and various calculations in Western chancelleries. Who was to succeed him? It was an involved and delicate matter. King Alexander died at the end of October, before his daughter Alexandra was born. His mother, Queen Sophie, returned to Greece from Switzerland and took over as Regent. Rashly, Venizelos offered a general election, with the electorate to choose between himself and Constantine. Venizelos lost by a landslide. A later plebiscite amply confirmed the popular will for a restoration of the deposed monarch. There was some diplomatic to-ing and fro-ing, and Constantine was restored as King of Greece. His brothers were free to return to their country.

Arriving at Phaleron Bay, Andrew and Christopher, the first of the brothers to reach Greece, were carried shoulder high by the excited crowd all the way to Athens. Christopher recalled, "I shot a glance of anguish over at my brother Andrew, but he did not even see it; he was too busy defending his garters from admirers who wanted them as souvenirs."

Andrew and Alice returned to Corfu and to their archly-named villa "Mon Repos" – echoes of semis from Bromley to Bognor! But they were not merely taking up their old life with the pattern undisturbed. Alice was pregnant once more, and the child was due to be born in the middle of 1921.

3

Early Days

"I don't think anybody thinks I had a father."
Prince Philip

"THEY WERE AS POOR AS CHURCH MICE," according to Agnes Blower, when she first allowed a reporter to inspect her photograph album in 1962. Then aged ninety-one, and living in an old people's home in Peterborough, she treasured the memories the album contained of the time when she was a housekeeper at "Mon Repos", the home of Andrew and Alice in Corfu. Agnes Blower's knowledge of church mice was obviously limited, because Prince Andrew was, in fact, able to afford to employ her, her husband, as steward and handyman, plus a couple of locals who came in to cook and clean, and Miss Roose ("Roosie"), the English nanny who had previously cared for Prince Nicholas's children.

This was hardly a deprived life style. Nor was "Mon Repos" – an elegant neo-classical villa built in the 1820s by the British High Commissioner of the Ionians – a royal slum. Approached by a road coiling up a hill, there was a narrow entrance drive skirting a magnolia tree, and, once through the front door, a broad sunny hall and a wide stairway curving up to the top floor. Downstairs were the study, the dining-room, the kitchen and so forth, while the main bedrooms were on the first floor, with two more a floor higher.

Admittedly there had been few improvements since Andrew had inherited the house from his father in 1913, and it had stood empty during the three years he and Alice had been away from Greece. In June 1921 there was still no electricity, no gas, no running hot water (on bath night buckets had to be carted upstairs) and, as in many

49

homes on the island, no proper heating facilities. Nor did the interior decoration match the exceptional view across the gulf and the green-blue Ionian Sea, or the beauty of the grounds, running down to the water's edge and awash with flowers between the sweet-smelling orange and lemon trees. Still, it was a pleasant enough home where, seven years earlier, the youngest of Alice's four daughters had been safely delivered.

Preparations for the new birth were modest enough. The local doctor was summoned to attend the delivery. He soon decided that Alice's bedroom was unsuitable for the birth, bodily carried her downstairs, and put her on the large dining-room table. Apparently Alice's high state of anxiety, doubtless intensified by Andrew having recently left on active service, rendered the table more suitable than a bed – though the medical reasons for this decision are not entirely clear.

Assisted by nurse Roose, and with her two elder daughters (aged sixteen and fifteen) available to help, Alice gave birth to a healthy, well-formed boy with tiny wisps of very fair hair. This successful delivery was certainly the first, and very probably the last, time that a future consort to the British monarch has been born on a dining-room table. At the very least, it provides an interesting contrast with the more luxurious circumstances of the births of Philip's own children.

The birth of a boy doubtless came as a joy to Prince Andrew and as something of a relief to the Greek royal family in which female progeny had recently heavily outnumbered male offspring. Not only did Andrew now have a son and an heir, but Philip immediately became sixth in line of succession to the Greek throne.

Though scarcely noticed in the outside world, Philip's birth brought warm congratulations from Athens and from royal residences throughout Europe. Still, it was unlikely that even the most doting of the new baby's relations anticipated a future that was to make him one of the best known of international personalities.

Not much is known of Prince Philip's first few weeks of life. We do know, however, that Nanny Roose had prudently laid in a stock of English baby foods and had ordered infant woollens from London. But baby foods, even English ones, could have had little relevance in the diet of such a young baby, and woollen clothes were probably not needed in abundance during the blazing Corfu summer. What the baby played with apart, presumably, from his fingers and toes, is also not well documented, though Agnes Blower remembered that he had a few wooden bricks and his nanny's pin cushion – from which he was allowed to pull the pins and needles.

Philip was just over three months old and in his pram when he was first transported on to English soil. He was with his mother and sisters who had come to Britain for the funeral of his maternal grandfather, Prince Louis of Battenberg, by then known as the Marquess of Milford Haven. When the family returned to Corfu, Prince Andrew, home from active service, complied with local law and formally registered the birth of his son. More than four months had passed since the birth when Andrew summoned the responsible officials to what he ironically called his "royal château". A record of the brief ceremony appears as "Entry No. 449" in the Corfu Register of Births:

In Corfu on the twenty-fourth day of the month of October in the year nineteen twenty-one, according to the law in force, I the undersigned, Vicar of the Church of Christ the Saviour located in the royal château of Mon Repos hereby declare that His Excellency Prince Andrew of Greece, son of our ever-memorable King George the First, aged 39, born in Athens and residing in Corfu, came before me and presented to me an infant of male sex stating that he was born on the day of the twenty-eighth of the month of May in the year 1921 on the day of the week Friday at 10 o'clock in the morning at his residence by Her Excellency Princess Alice, daughter of Ludwig Prince Battenberg, aged 36, born in Windsor Castle, the name given in baptism to the baby being Philippos by the godparent Her Majesty the Queen Mother Olga, represented by Her Excellency Princess Olga, daughter of His Excellency Nicholas, son of the King of Greece, and Corfu City Council, represented in accordance with a unanimous decision by the City Council by Messrs. Alexander S. Kokotos, Mayor, and Stylianos I. Maniarizis, Chairman of the City Council.

For this purpose the present deed has been construed, witnessed by Messrs. Theodor Chrysovitsianos, son of Nicholas, and Constantine Alamanos, son of Pericles, the former being a doctor, aged 45, and a city councillor, born in Corfu, the latter being a lawyer, aged 39, and a city councillor, born in Corfu, being signed according to the law by the person (Prince Andrew) appearing before me and by the witnesses.

The vicar, Spyr. Ier. Tryfonas
The person appearing before me, Prince Andrew of Greece

51

The Witness, K. P. Alamanos
The Witness, Theod. Chrysovitsianos
The Mayor in his capacity as Registrar, Alexander S. Kokotos

Since the Julian calendar was still in force in Greece, the actual date of Prince Philip's birth was, as stated, 28 May 1921. Only when Greece adopted the Gregorian calendar two years later was the date amended – put back thirteen days – to 10 June, which has ever since been Prince Philip's official birthday.

But 28 May was still the operative date in July 1922 when the infant Philip paid his second visit to Britain. It was prompted by another, but infinitely happier, family occasion. This time it was to attend the wedding of his uncle, Lord Louis Mountbatten, then twenty-two years old, handsome and sophisticated, but hardly wealthy, and Edwina Ashley, the attractive and intelligent grand-daughter of Edward V II's banker and friend, Sir Ernest Cassel, who was said to have settled two million pounds on her. Lord Louis (an intimate of the Prince of Wales) and Edwina were to become the leaders of a typically "twenties" crowd of bright young things who, released from wartime restrictions, enjoyed life on a grand and hectic scale – races, theatres, night-clubs, country house parties and trips to fashionable resorts. All good copy for the gossip columnists, but as yet providing no indication of the weighty and worthy careers that both were to follow, careers that were to entwine them inextricably in the last days of the British Raj and which, in Lord Louis' case, was to come to a bloody and inglorious end at the hands of Irish Republican assassins in 1979.

Though his four sisters, dressed in blue and white, acted as bridesmaids at their uncle's wedding, Philip, now a white-blond, cheerful toddler with undeniably solid limbs, stayed behind in the Kensington Palace nursery. Doubtless he remembers little of it, but he also took the air in Kensington Gardens – a tranquil setting for his first major excursion into English public life.

Such tranquillity, however, was not to be found so easily at home. Once back in Corfu, Prince Andrew's family were soon to be faced with a crisis that not only threatened Andrew's life but was to have the most profound effects upon the baby Philip's future.

The crisis arose from the current conflict between Greece and Turkey, an ugly and chronic left-over from the Balkan Wars and from the First World War itself. The central problem of Greek foreign affairs at the time of King Constantine's (and Andrew's) return from exile in 1920 was the Turkish clamour for the return of Anatolia (Asia Minor) which the Western Allies had helped Greece to occupy in 1919, and where hundreds of thousands of Greeks lived under constant Turkish threat. While ambitious Greek politicians indulged in dreams of a new Byzantine empire and a triumphant march on Constantinople, the revitalised Turks under Mustapha Kemal's clique of vigorous young officers turned the tables on them and prepared to drive the Greek army, and the Greek population of Anatolia, into the sea. Despite the hostility felt towards him in certain sections of the army, Andrew applied for a military command, and a few weeks after the birth of his son, he resumed his army career with the rank of Major-General. He was soon promoted to Lieutenant-General and given command of the 2nd Army Corps in Asia Minor. The old feuds were, however, shortly to be revived in the most spectacular fashion.

In fact, Andrew's re-admission to the army and to high military command was a prelude to one of the most painful chapters in his life and to a time of unmitigated disaster for Greece. When the major Turkish attack was unleashed it destroyed, once and for all, Greek influence in Anatolia. Prince Andrew's role in this catastrophic campaign has been painted in all the colours of the rainbow. Accounts of his activities and of his personality are so contradictory that it is difficult to know where to begin. It is most likely, however, that his influence on events was wantonly exaggerated by the antimonarchical faction in Greek public life, which was anxious to provide a royal scapegoat for the army's débâcle.

Andrew gave his own version of the catastrophe in a book gloomily entitled *Towards Disaster*, which was translated into English by his wife and published in the United Kingdom in 1930. It does not make happy reading. On the other hand, it presents a perfectly coherent and intelligible account of treachery, intrigue and incompetence on a grand scale. It is an apologia, but one which convinces by its prosaic style and its almost total lack of special pleading. It is a dignified book written by a dignified but troubled man.

According to Andrew, he was at odds with the Greek Commander-in-Chief General Papulas and opposed to his unrealistic strategy in Asia Minor. Dissatisfied, while commanding the 2nd Army Corps, with his men's equipment, suspecting treachery and disloyalty – and desperately trying to improve matters – he made a thorough nuisance of himself. Nonetheless he led his men in a victorious advance on Eshki Shehr. When, despite this success, his criticism and suggestions were disregarded, he went on leave (absenting himself without permission, it was later claimed), but eventually returned and reported at Greek headquarters in Smyrna. Unable to change the prevailing military strategy, he asked to be relieved of all command. Instead he was given command of the 5th Army Corps based on Epirus and the Ionian Islands, and with its headquarters at Janina. He was thus on the fringes of the fighting when catastrophe overtook the Greek army in Asia Minor.

In August and September 1922 the Greek army reeled back under a ferocious and sustained Turkish assault and was almost literally destroyed. As the Turks took Smyrna, casualties were appallingly heavy and the local Greek population suffered with the troops. Civilians were massacred, and an estimated million and a half Greeks were driven from the Asian continent. The political repercussions in Athens were inevitably of seismic proportions. King Constantine was once more forced to abdicate and leave the country. His eldest son, who succeeded him as King George II, was merely a puppet of the revolutionary military junta which now ran the country. The monarchy was apparently weakened beyond recovery, and George II's reign was to last little more than a year. Andrew was once more forced to resign from the army, though it was understood that he could rejoin his family in Corfu and remain in residence there.

Once in Corfu, Andrew composed a long letter to General Papulas setting out the military command's shortcomings, which he held responsible for the disaster in Asia Minor. In the event, his sojourn in Corfu was short-lived. Early in October 1922 he was summoned to Athens, ostensibly to give evidence in the proceedings against several of ex-King Constantine's ministers who were being held on serious charges. He walked into a trap. On his arrival, Andrew was arrested on orders from the revolutionary junta led by Venizelos. General Pangalos, now Minister for War, and earlier one of his contemporaries at the Military Academy, interrogated him, once suddenly asking, "How many children do you have?" Surprised at the question's irrelevance, Andrew told him, at which Pangalos shook his head, remarking, "Poor things, what a pity they will soon be orphans."

Eventually, after seven weeks' confinement, Andrew was charged before a military court with "having abandoned a position without orders when in contact with the enemy", with being "undisciplined", and with being "without the necessary experience for a superior command". In effect, he was accused of treason.

Was Andrew really in danger of execution? After all, the revolutionary junta was a far cry from the Bolsheviks, and Andrew was no Tsar Nicholas II – a figurehead whose liquidation was considered necessary to preserve the newly established régime. Despite Pangalos' threatening and overbearing behaviour, Andrew's execution would have provoked an intense diplomatic reaction and would have gained the new government little in return.

Still, fellow generals and ex-ministers were being condemned by revolutionary courts, and six of them were eventually to face the firing squad. Princess Alice left her children at "Mon Repos" and travelled to Athens to be near her husband. She was not allowed to see him.

Christopher, Andrew's brother, went to see his nephew, the puppet King George II. He found him "practically a prisoner, as his father had been"; he was "powerless to intervene, his own fate hung by a thread. He had less liberty than his poorest subjects, spies surrounded him night and day, and reported all his movements."

As for Andrew, Christopher later wrote:

No one was allowed to go near Andrew except his valet; even the dentist was not given permission to visit him when he broke a tooth and suffered great pain. It was impossible to communicate with him for his guards kept the strictest watch and confiscated all letters and parcels that came to the house. Even food sent in by sympathisers was closely examined and a *foie gras* in aspic, with which a dear old lady intended to console him, was hacked to pieces before he was allowed to eat it.

Finally I hit on the happy expedient of writing a letter on cigarette paper, rolling it tightly and putting it with other cigarettes into his valet's case. In this way it reached him safely. He answered it with a short note full of courage, but reading between the lines I knew that he had no longer any hope of regaining his freedom.

Fearful and helpless, Alice and her relatives appealed for intervention to any who might be sympathetic: King George V in Britain, the Pope, King Alfonso XIII of Spain, the French Prime Minister Poincaré. Messages of sympathy were quick to arrive, but, with one exception, the foreign powers and the Vatican did nothing practical.

Help finally came from Britain, beginning even before it was announced that Andrew and five others would stand trial before the Chamber of Deputies on 2 December 1922. In England, Alice's and Andrew's royal relatives exerted pressure. Queen Alexandra, widow of Edward VII, took up her nephew's cause. Louis Mountbatten went to see King George V and members of the government, including Premier Bonar Law and the Foreign Secretary Lord Curzon. The King asked the Foreign Office to save Andrew. "The King is most anxious concerning Prince Andrew," said an official Foreign Office telegram to the British Embassy in Athens. Although the Greek royal house was hardly popular in Whitehall (shades of those "German Greeks"), the British government launched a double-pronged action to rescue George V's cousin. Commander Gerald Talbot, a former British naval attaché in Athens, was instructed to go to Greece to extricate Andrew from his predicament one way or another. One lively account of Talbot's mission has him entering Greece with false papers and in disguise, planning to snatch the Prince from his gaolers, but goes on to say that he managed to see General Pangalos and warn him of the British sovereign's and government's deep concern.

In a brief revival of Palmerstonian gunboat diplomacy, HMS *Calypso* was ordered to go to Phaleron Bay to reinforce Talbot's hand. Between them, Talbot and *Calypso* did the trick. Even before the start of Prince Andrew's trial – with Pangalos a member of the tribunal – Talbot could report to London that the Greeks, while insisting that the proceedings must take their course, would convict the Prince but would not sentence him to death if he agreed to leave the country. As far as Andrew was concerned – but not his co-defendants – the trial, in spite of the prosecutor's bluster, was something of an anti-climax. When it ended at midnight, Andrew was found guilty of disobeying orders and abandoning his post in the face of the enemy. Humiliatingly, his "lack of experience in commanding a large unit" was taken into consideration as a mitigating factor. Instead of the firing squad, Andrew faced official degradation and condemnation to perpetual banishment. Of his trial he subsequently wrote, rather stiffly, "It is sufficient for me to say that only three witnesses for the defence were called, from the many whom I suggested. It suffices to read the accusations of the revolutionary prosecutor to be convinced of the prejudice of those who tried me."

Dull, dignified stuff, rather like a sober dispatch from the front line – which in a way it was. A contrast to the almost passionate exhortation Andrew allowed himself near the end of his book *Towards Disaster* where he describes and justifies the Greek invasion of Asia Minor that was to lead to the military catastrophe:

> For the first time after many centuries, since the time of the Byzantine rulers, a Greek King and a Greek Army trod the immense plains of Asia Minor. Full of eagerness, faith, and self-sacrifice, the Greek soldier threw himself into the age-old struggle of his race– the struggle of civilisation against Asiatic barbarism. The glitter of Greek bayonets was seen once more on the fields of Kintahia and Eshki Shehr ... Gordium, Justianopolis once more heard the shouts of Greek victory, the echoes reaching as far as Angora.
>
> Is it in vain, this last sacrifice in Asia Minor? No! For the seed sown by the Greek soldier will one day burst forth into a great and flourishing tree.

Nearly six decades on, this stirring rhetoric has a pathetic and hollow sound. No great Greek Empire stretching far into Anatolia has been established. Indeed, at the time of writing, Cyprus remains partitioned, with Greece unable to dislodge the Turks from the northern part of the island. It is, in fact, Turkey that has built on the military events of 1922, not Greece.

Still, Andrew was free, though the verdict rankled perpetually. Indeed, as recently as 1970 Prince Philip, when asked his opinion on an editor's footnote describing the verdict in a volume of British foreign policy documents being prepared for publication, hoped that the entry need not appear since, "People might think it was true."

Andrew was released at dawn following his midnight trial and reunited with Alice. General Pangalos then escorted him to Phaleron Bay. An act of courtesy? Or just to ensure that Andrew was actually leaving? Probably the latter. Certainly it neatly rounded off the state trial. Soon the *Calypso* was on her way to Corfu where as many of the family's belongings as could be gathered up were hurriedly packed and taken aboard the cruiser. The girls joined their parents, and a colourful story describes how eighteen-month-old Philip was put into a wooden orange box and carried aboard. Another version suggests that Philip was carried aboard in Nanny Roose's arms and that the orange box was produced by the

Calypso's sailors and fitted out as a cot. Either way, it was a sad and humiliating exit.

HMS *Calypso*'s first port of call was Brindisi; after a brief visit to Rome where Andrew and Alice were received by the Pope, they sailed for England.

For the young Philip the voyage of the *Calypso* was the beginning of a wandering and effectively stateless period that was to last for twenty-five years. From 3 December 1922, when he left Corfu, until 1948, when he moved into Clarence House as Princess Elizabeth's husband, he had no permanent home.

How this affected him is difficult to say. Perhaps the belligerence which characterised him as a small boy (and sometimes as a grown man) originated in the insecurities of his early childhood. There is no doubt about the infant belligerence. According to his sisters, Margarita and Sophie, "he was very pugnacious and the other children were scared to death of him," and his first teacher, Donald McJannet, remembers him as "a rugged, boisterous boy". On the other hand, he had a good deal to put up with from his sisters who decided at one stage that Princess Alice was spoiling him "and we were all very anxious to prevent it and were all particularly strict and disagreeable to him; he must have suffered awfully, poor child, in those days." With controlling sibling rivals like that, it is surely possible to excuse some aggressive displays of infantile independence.

In any case, Philip was not exactly living in a children's home, bereft of family love. Overwhelmingly, family and friends doted upon him and he repaid them in kind. Though he was mischievous and daring he was apparently rarely malicious, and, for the most part, could be generous and considerate. Very like the average run of small boys, in fact, and evidently more alert and polite than a good many.

The early days of exile, however, could not have been easy. On arriving in London Prince Andrew's family were given temporary shelter by the Dowager Marchioness of Milford Haven in Kensington Palace, but there was no prospect of them settling down there. Soon Andrew and Alice, leaving Philip with Nurse Roose, set sail for the United States as guests of Andrew's brother Christopher and his wealthy American wife Nancy – formerly Mrs Nancy Leeds, the widow of a tin plate magnate.

In America, aboard Nancy's yacht and at her house in Palm Springs, Andrew discussed his future with his brother. It must have seemed ironical to be considering so uncertain and impecunious a future surrounded by the lavish trappings of New World wealth. Andrew's various sources of income were slight enough for a Prince of Greece. There were the proceeds from the sale of a small agricultural property in Greece and, later, a small legacy from ex-King Constantine who died in 1923. Alice received an allowance from her brother George, Marquess of Milford Haven, which, however, did not even cover the school fees for the girls. Nor, apparently, was Andrew happy to accept financial assistance from his wife's family. He was greatly relieved when Christopher offered some assistance which was later to include Philip's fees at the exclusive infant school "The Elms" at St Cloud in Paris. Another significant contribution was to come from Andrew's older brother, George, whose wife Marie, the great-granddaughter of Napoleon I's brother Lucien, had inherited a fortune from her mother's family, the Blancs, founders of the Casino at Monte Carlo. Alexandra of Yugoslavia, who provides this piece of information, goes on to say, somewhat mischievously, "It is odd to think that gold francs from the roulette table gradually filtered through to pave the way for Philip's education," though she adds, "where they surely achieved the most good".

If the family's finances were now, more or less, solvent, they still had no permanent place to live. Andrew felt little inclination to settle in Britain, despite the dramatic intervention of HMS *Calypso* in his fortunes; after all, many still considered him a "German Greek", and his war-time mission to London had been strikingly unsuccessful.

He therefore accepted with relief an invitation from his brother George to bring his family to Paris and to take up residence on two floors of one of George's properties in the Rue Adolphe Ivan, near the Bois de Boulogne. Later George moved them to a small but pleasant house in the Rue du Mont Valerian at St Cloud, which became their semi-permanent home. From there the children were to set out on regular visits to the summer residences of their scattered but hospitable family.

We have a wealth of reminiscences from Alexandra of Yugoslavia for some of these holidays. She recalls, much in the style of Marion Crawford, the chronicler of the early years of Princess Elizabeth and Princess Margaret, how Philip, with his round face and ash-blond hair, loved the sea so much that he had to be dragged out of the water when he stayed at Panka by the Baltic Sea with his

Aunt Sophie, King Constantine's Prussian widow, and her sister. It was, incidentally, at Panka that Philip's sister Sophie first met Prince Christopher of Hesse whom she eventually married. We also learn, unremarkably, that like many other small boys, Philip's love of salt water did not extend to his daily bath at home.

Philip spent other holidays with his Uncle George of Milford Haven in England, and with his Romanian relatives, King Carol and Queen Helen and their small son, Michael. Darmstadt was yet another holiday home. These peripatetic summers certainly cemented the deep sense of family which characterised nearly all of Queen Victoria's descendants and which sometimes gave the impression of a royal mafiosa operating across innumerable frontiers.

Some of the most memorable summers of Philip's childhood were spent at a villa at Berck-Plage, near Marseilles, belonging to Madame Anna Foufounis, the wealthy widow of a Greek royalist who had befriended the royal exiles. As a boy of four or five Philip became a regular guest at Madame Foufounis' palatial house and played with her son Jean, who was about his age, and Jean's sister Hélène. The friendship between Philip and the Foufounis family was to include a close attachment to Hélène, who was one day to become well known to British television audiences as Hélène Cordet, the singer and cabaret star who featured in *Café Continental*. The friendship between Philip and Hélène was triumphantly to weather a temporary reversal of fortunes when Hélène entered marriage with, as she rather dramatically insists in her memoirs, "no money". As to whether Hélène was the "mysterious blonde" in Philip's young manhood we shall return later.

Hélène Cordet's autobiography entitled, with some justice, *Born Bewildered* reveals a good deal of Philip's boyhood. Hélène confesses that, when Philip began to stay with her family, she was "very worried by the fuss my mother made of him. I was terrified she would switch her affections completely from me to him, especially as I had the incredible idea that I was the least loved in our family." Though Philip's family was at that time comparatively impoverished and her own wealthy, Hélène apparently believed that "the little blue-eyed boy with the most fascinating blond-white hair seemed to have everything I lacked. In my mind he became a great danger, and I became ridiculously jealous."

Apart from stirring up feelings of displaced sibling rivalry, how else did Philip affect Hélène's life? Certainly she did not share his "passion" for "going round the farm [on land owned by the Foufounis family] feeding the pigs and cleaning the pigsties". Early signs on his part, perhaps, of keeping things shipshape and Bristol-fashion? But then he was especially fond of pigs, and was always happy to play one in a regular game with Hélène.

Hélène also recalls a notable act of generosity on his part, when, aged four, Philip insisted on giving her sick sister Ria, not only "his own battered toys" but also "his new one", when the latter had been left out by a tactless visitor. Whether this gesture was so unusual that it automatically warrants special consideration by posterity is not, however, made clear by Miss Cordet. What is plain is that some of Philip's staff nowadays believe that, "No one has a bigger heart, or takes greater pains to conceal it." At least the generous impulse with the toys was undisguised, though possibly, at four years old, attention-seeking.

A physical fight with Philip is also recorded by Hélène. She admits that she was the aggressor, though perhaps provoked. At any rate, she "grabbed him by his very fine hair with both hands" and only let go after she had pulled out several tufts. Years later in Paris, shortly after the Second World War, Hélène suddenly noticed that the hair on the top of his head was thinning slightly. Giving herself more credit than the male hormone she later wrote: "Oh! . . . but it gave me a terrible guilt complex! It took me a long time to persuade myself that our fight . . . years before had nothing to do with it." Unable to broach the subject then, she brought it up at their next meeting when Philip "thought it very funny, and roared with laughter".

How impoverished was his early childhood? Perhaps too much has been made of patched clothes, small amounts of pocket money, "saving up for a raincoat" and the occasional franc notes from the King of Sweden that helped to buy his first bicycle. Philip himself has said, "We weren't well off."

But by what standards are these matters judged? His childhood was certainly passed in very different material circumstances from, say, the childhood of Princess Elizabeth in Britain, or even a contemporary prince of Romania or Italy. Compared to millions of European children during the Great Slump of the late 1920s, however, he was positively rolling in riches. It is not even true that his mother supplemented the meagre family income by running a small shop called "Hellas" in Paris, selling Greek embroidery and arty knick-knacks. The shop existed, of course, but whatever profits it realised went chiefly to support Greek refugees – an early example of Alice's growing devotional and self-sacrificing tendencies. Moreover, during his early childhood he was never without a nanny, nor, come to that, was his father without a valet.

One way of judging Philip's early advantages, or disadvantages, is to consider his schooling in Paris. When he was five he went to a private and exclusive co-educational infant school called "The Elms", which was run by an American couple, Donald and Charlotte McJannet. It was conveniently near his home at St Cloud. So far so good. But the fees were paid by his uncle Christopher and doubtless came, in truth, from the latter's rich American wife. Hardly a disadvantaged position for a small boy, though probably a little galling for his father.

Perhaps the new schoolboy's chief problem was one of identity. When he was first asked to give his name to his class teacher Miss Catherine Lewitzky he answered: "Philip". "Philip – what?" "Just Philip," he answered, discomfited. "But you must have another name," Miss Lewitzky insisted. "Philip of Greece," he said finally. This seems to be the first of several identical stories which are associated with other phases in his life. At "The Elms" he did not apparently know that his parents had been issued with Danish passports in their original Danish-German name of Schleswig-Holstein-Sonderburg-Glücksburg; indeed he was later still signing himself "Philip of Greece" as a young man. More remarkable than this episode was the fact that he was little different in status and background from many of his school-fellows at "The Elms", for though most were children of American, and other, diplomats, there was a smattering of Bourbon princes and princesses, including Prince Jacques de Bourbon and his sister Anne, who later married Michael of Romania. The notable characteristics often attributed to the boy Philip – the fierce ambition to excel in sport, determination and self-assurance – owe much to hindsight. He was good at sports, liked athletics and later, cricket, but his accomplishments at swimming, yachting and polo were to come later. There was nothing much unusual about him at "The Elms".

Relations with his teachers were cordial. A letter, dated 11 March 1929, written, rather oddly, to Pomfield, a dog belonging to one of his teachers, Mrs Dorothea Huckel, while both were on holiday in the south of France, catches a relaxed mood: "Dear Pomfield," Philip wrote, "How do you like Cannes? Are you having a nice time eating candy? . . . Do not eat too much or you will get sick. I am very glad to have a letter from you. This summer, I am going to Romania. I hope that you are coming back soon and will play with me at the Elms. With a pat for your head. Philip of Greece." A joke, or an avoidance of a more direct communication with Mrs Huckel?

At this time, Philip was perhaps only dimly aware of his mother's growing preoccupation with religion, a piety and self-searching introspection which was at least partly due to her enclosing deafness. An increasingly lonely woman, Alice's communion was as much with God as with people, though she still ran the shop, "Hellas", which gave her some contact with the outside world. Interestingly her sister-in-law Helen, wife of Andrew's brother Nicholas (who sold his own paintings to supplement his meagre resources) worked as diligently on behalf of refugees from her native Russia. Marina, Nicholas and Helen's youngest daughter, and fifteen years older than Philip, often took the boy on tours of Paris, thus cementing what was to become a lifelong friendship. Andrew's daughters, meanwhile, were gravitating towards Germany and the Hesse family; almost old enough to be Philip's aunts, they were away from St Cloud a good deal.

During these years Andrew and Alice gradually drew apart. Perhaps Alice's deeper and deeper involvement with religion was both a cause and a symptom of the estrangement. But Prince Andrew could not have been easy to live with either. Still brooding on the humiliating circumstances of his flight from Greece, and subjected to almost daily reminders of his reduced circumstances, he had little enough cause for optimism. Lacking any serious prospect of a satisfying career, or even of returning to Greece, he was prone to periods of self-pity and withdrawal. Some relief could be found, however, in Parisian society, and Andrew, still a handsome man in his mid-forties, made the most of his opportunities.

While his parents drifted apart, the question of Philip's future upbringing became the subject of a discreet and dignified family wrangle. Though neither party proclaimed their interest with vulgar passion, Andrew and his daughters favoured Germany, while Alice and her Mountbatten brothers believed England to be the more suitable environment for Philip. It was a struggle which the Battenberg/Mountbatten faction were eventually to win. It was a victory, moreover, that was to have great consequences for the House of Windsor.

The upshot of Andrew's estrangement from Alice was the gradual dispersal of Philip's family. Alice gravitated towards Greece, hoping to return there permanently sooner or later. Andrew ended up in Monte Carlo. Their four daughters, already of marriageable age, looked towards the small army of German counts, margraves, dukes and princes who had (legally but not effectively) lost their titles with the fall of their Kaiser, but had lost by no means all of their wealth, their land or their castles. Hitler and the Nazis were still some years away from office, and few German aristocrats foresaw that the proudest of their class, the East Prussian *Junkers*, would eventually help so vulgar a regime to power.

Philip's destination, at the age of eight, was a Britain which contained his grandmother, the Dowager Marchioness of Milford Haven, and his uncles George and Dickie – the 2nd Marquess of Milford Haven and Lord Louis Mountbatten. At Kensington Palace, the ageing Dowager welcomed her grandson but soon found that it was not easy to cope with so boisterous a youngster. It was sensibly decided that he should live with Uncle George of Milford Haven whose son David, Earl of Medina, two years older than Philip, would doubtless enjoy the company of a cousin. Philip, who had already spent holidays at Lynden Manor, the Milford Haven residence near Maidenhead, quickly settled down in his new home, his fourth to date.

The influence of the eldest Mountbatten brother, George of Milford Haven, has been greatly overlooked when considering Prince Philip's boyhood. Philip himself has gone on record as saying, "I grew up very much more with my father's family than I did with my mother's. And I think they're quite interesting people. They're the sort of people that haven't been heard of much." This is certainly true for the first eight years of his life, but beyond that there is the clear and indelible imprint of the Mountbattens on Philip's development.

Nor is the imprint solely, even chiefly, that of Lord Louis Mountbatten. Certainly Prince Philip does not consider that he was brought up by Lord Mountbatten. During several crucial years it was George of Milford Haven who stood *in loco parentis*; it was George who entered Philip for Cheam School and who attended sports days and prize-givings. Indeed, as a sailor who had fought under Jellicoe and Beatty, George can claim as much credit as anybody else for Philip's choice of the navy as a career. There is, in fact, at least one account, "Boyhood of Raleigh" style, of Philip never getting tired of hearing his uncle tell what it was like in the forward turret of HMS *New Zealand* on that dangerous afternoon at Jutland, when the two great twelve-inch guns under his command were firing so fast that they got red hot, and three sister battle cruisers blew up from direct hits on their turrets. With his brother Louis on active service, and having recently retired from the navy himself, George was simply there much more, and therefore presumably a more consistent influence.

As we have seen, it was George of Milford Haven who decided where in Britain Philip was to be educated. He had himself been at Cheam in Surrey, one of the country's oldest prep schools dating back to Charles I, and that was where Philip, with his own son David, was enrolled. Cheam's old boys included future viceroys, as well as viscounts, commanders-in-chief (not all of them victorious) and Lord Randolph Churchill, whose son, Winston, noted that he had been most kindly treated there. The school was regarded as "progressive", which in those days meant that the rod was used sparingly. Philip was not, however, destined to avoid the cane. Introducing his former headmaster, the Reverend Harold Taylor to the then Princess Elizabeth when they attended the school's three hundred year anniversary in 1947, Philip told her: "This is the headmaster who used to cane me."

Reassured by the company of his older cousin, Philip, now proving himself adaptable and congenial, grew easily into the new routine. It was a harder life than he might have expected, but in practice an upper-class English education was not so different from the military discipline to which German and Greek instructors had subjected his father so many years before – hard beds, austere food, cold baths. Philip was prominent in the school sports, cricket, athletics and soccer, but his academic progress was not impressive. He hardly excelled, except in French, which he spoke as well as English and German and better than Greek.

The final disintegration of his parents' household started when the youngest of his sisters, Sophie, feeling stranded by the separation of her parents, rushed into a marriage which was hardly commendable politically (and not only from the English point of view). Shortly after her sixteenth birthday she married Christopher of Hesse, who was closely connected to her family and whom she had come to know better at the Baltic home of her Aunt Sophie of Greece and Prussia. The Hesse family tree had so many branches that some were bound to bear rotten fruit. Christopher was a convinced Nazi, rare as yet among German aristocrats.

He was, admittedly, a cruder, less sophisticated supporter of Hitler than his brother, Philip of Hesse, *Obergruppenführer* in the brown-shirted Nazi storm-troops and the husband of the King of Italy's daughter Mafalda. Philip of Hesse was also an intimate of Hermann Goering, and he helped to make the Nazis respectable in his elevated circles; he also used his family connections to cement the Nazi-Fascist Axis. On Philip of Hesse's recommendation, Goering, when he became Prime Minister of Prussia, gave the younger Hesse a job. It was nothing to boast about and was tactfully overlooked when the future Duke of Edinburgh's antecedents were first publicly discussed in Britain.

It was not overlooked at Buckingham Palace, though, when the list of guests for the wedding was being drawn up: "When he married the then Princess Elizabeth in 1947," the Hamburg news magazine *Der Spiegel* recalled on the occasion of the Queen's and the Duke of Edinburgh's first post-war visit to Germany eighteen years later, "he [the Duke] had difficulty in securing invitations to the London wedding for his surviving sisters. The officials in charge of protocol reminded the bridegroom discreetly that it was not forgotten that his brother-in-law, Christopher, had been head of the *Abhöhrdienst* in Goering's *Luftwaffe* Research Office." This job was even more sinister than it sounded. The *Geheimer Abhöhrdienst* (secret telephone-tapping service) was charged with the "supervision" of the telephone calls and correspondence of foreign embassies and diplomats, but soon extended its activities to Germans in sensitive and prominent positions. It was, alas, the nucleus from which grew the *Geheime Staatspolizei*, or Gestapo. At the time of Hitler's rise to power, it ought to be stressed, Philip of Greece was twelve years old. Still, the connections were potentially embarrassing.

Following Sophie's example, Philip's other sisters soon found German husbands of their own. All three married in the same year, 1931: Margarita, at twenty-six, became the wife of Gottfried, Prince Hohenlohe-Langenburg, a grandson of Alfred, Duke of Edinburgh; Theodora, one year younger, married Berthold, Margrave of Baden; and Cecile, only twenty, married George Donatus, hereditary Grand Duke of Hesse. This latter marriage, incidentally, was to end in tragedy only six years later: Cecile and her children were killed when the aircraft bringing them to the wedding of her brother-in-law, Prince Louis of Hesse, crashed in fog near Ostend.

One concrete outcome of this flurry of marriages was that Philip moved from Cheam to a school at Salem in Germany. It was not a move he relished: Cheam was enjoyable and, moreover, he had been playing for the school's cricket eleven – there was not much chance of cricket at Salem.

Why was he moved? In a way it was the result of a counter-attack by the "German" side of his family. Theodora's recent marriage to Berthold of Baden started the manoeuvre off. At first sight there was much to be said for the transfer: the famous Salem school founded in 1918 by Prince Max of Baden, Imperial Germany's last Chancellor, was on one of the family's estates at Schloss Salem, near Lake Constance, in southern Germany; it was a school closely associated with the controversial and illustrious educationalist Kurt Hahn; Philip would both receive an excellent, liberal German education, and be close to a married sister. As it happened it was to lead to the most formative educational experience of his life.

4

Salem and Gordonstoun

"It cannot be given to many to have the opportunity and the
desire to heap honours upon their former headmasters."
Prince Philip, Chancellor of Edinburgh University,
on making Kurt Hahn an Honorary Doctor of Law

As THE GERMAN EMPIRE COLLAPSED in the autumn of 1918, the last
Imperial Chancellor, Max von Baden, was assisted in his final
official duties by his personal secretary and advisor Kurt Hahn. At the
Versailles peace negotiations the German case, presented by Foreign
Minister Brockdorff-Rantzau, owed a good deal of its substance to
Hahn, a brilliant scholar who had risen to a position of considerable
political influence. The son of a Berlin industrialist, Hahn had been
a Rhodes Scholar at Oxford when the First World War broke out, but
had managed to return to Germany, via Scotland and Norway, and
had been employed by the German Foreign Office as an Intelligence
expert on Britain and Liaison Officer with the *Reichswehr* (the
Imperial army). Close to Max von Baden at the end of the war,
Hahn was one of the many German Jews who, to prove their racist
enemies and detractors wrong, were almost more German than
their Gentile compatriots, more patriotic than the nationalists.

It was no secret at Versailles, or in Berlin, that Hahn was the
author of Brockdorff-Rantzau's impassioned speech repudiating
Germany's "war guilt": "To acknowledge the guilt of my people
for the outbreak of war," was the key sentence, "would be a lie in
my mouth!" Ironically, with this sentence, Hahn helped to coin the
explosive slogan under which Germans soon started to campaign
against the *Kriegsschuldlüge* (the War Guilt Lie) which was to lead
to the clamour for revenge, rearmament, the Nazi regime and,
finally, the Second World War. The von Baden government did not

last long. After an abortive attempt to secure a separate peace with Britain (which was one of the only ways of avoiding total defeat and unconditional surrender), widespread revolution in Germany forced the Kaiser to abdicate; the von Baden government resigned and a Council of People's Delegates took over.

Germany's last Imperial Chancellor returned to his ancestral seat – the spacious, though somewhat forbidding Schloss Salem, a former Cistercian monastery. Defeat, revolution and loss of office seem only to have strengthened his relationship with Kurt Hahn who, his political and diplomatic ambitions frustrated, decided to become a teacher. The thirty-two-year-old Hahn devised a system of education designed to instruct children of outstanding families in special schools so they should become responsible, dutiful, clear-thinking, and liberal Germans capable of restoring and leading the shattered fatherland.

Max von Baden, sharing Hahn's views, provided funds and established the proposed school in a wing of Schloss Salem. In a gesture of optimism and national self-renewal, Schule Schloss Salem with Kurt Hahn as headmaster was formally inaugurated by Max von Baden on 21 April 1920, with a total complement of eight boarders and twenty day boys and girls. The boarders, including Max von Baden's son Berthold, then aged thirteen, came from families "with a cultural tradition"; among the day pupils were several local children. As new pupils joined, however, the upper-class element became so prominent that Hahn had to start a recruiting drive to attract children from the lower orders in order to achieve a more representative social mix.

Another fourteen years were to elapse before Philip came under the influence of Hahn's educational ideas, by which time the theories had become established practice. As Hahn later claimed, the system was not original, but a compound of several strands. It owed something to Dr Thomas Arnold, the legendary headmaster of Rugby School and one of the architects of the English public school system. It was partly based on one of Hahn's principal inspirations, Plato, and his distinctly élitist philosophy, and partly on the principles of Sparta, the austere soldier state of Greek antiquity. All three influences were adapted to Hahn's ideas and stamped with his formidable personality. Since Hahn has been described as "the man who made Philip" (although Philip is clearly a man who has largely made himself), it is essential to examine some of the former's ideas.

Hahn's principal objective was to foster self-discipline and community spirit through the performance of common tasks. He believed in "forcing a boy into experience" . . . "the more unpleasant it is, the more he must face his own weaknesses." Rigorous training was designed to produce character and enable pupils to make the best of their abilities without becoming fanatics. A great deal of emphasis (too much, critics insisted) was placed on physical prowess and games, and on saving lives at sea, on mountains and in fires. Hahn forbade drinking and smoking, not for the sake of monastic self-denial, but because he felt it was not good for the boys. He talked about liberating what he called his pupils' "non-poisonous passions". Plato's élitism can be found in Hahn's ambition to create an "aristocracy of accomplishment".

Achievement through struggle, an aristocracy of accomplishment, it is not surprising that Hahn, who disliked socialism, believed in a form of leadership not unlike the Nazi *Führer* principle; indeed, he once called his system a kind of non-Jew-baiting Nazism. He denounced Hitler for "making good things look bad", and was horrified by Nazi violence, yet, predictably, Nazi influences permeated his school as they did most of German society. When, in the near civil war atmosphere of 1932, shortly before Hitler came to power, some Salem teachers and pupils applauded the Nazis after they had perpetrated a particularly vicious outrage, Hahn, as Sir Robert Birley, Headmaster of Eton, later recalled, asked boys "who were active in the S.A. . . . to terminate their allegiance either to Hitler or to Salem." Hahn, in fact, hoped that his pupils would be self-confident enough to follow their own beliefs, not Hitler's.

With its pronounced emphasis on physical fitness, Hahn's system was not likely to produce intellectuals, and, in a way, harboured a bias against universities. Compared with other schools, the number of his pupils who went on to higher education was comparatively small. At least one ex-pupil has made a virtue out of this defect: "I am one of those ignorant bums," the Duke of Edinburgh once said with, presumably, heavy irony, "who never went to a university, and a fat lot of harm it did me." True. But, then, he had other advantages.

Prince Philip was still at Cheam School when Hitler was appointed Chancellor of Germany in January 1933. The new regime could not appreciate that the children at Salem were being brought up in a fiercely patriotic spirit; nor could it understand how implicitly Hahn believed in the greatness of Germany, and even thought that "Hitler's cause could be good or made good". To the

Nazis the most significant fact about Hahn was that he was a Jew, and no Jew could be allowed to educate the youth of Germany. The new government did not forget his rebuke to staff and pupils for their pro-Nazi sentiments, nor his mockery of Hitler. His fate was sealed. By March 1933 he was in a Nazi prison. Fortunately, friends and educationalists all over Europe came to his aid. Hitler was bombarded with requests from influential people, including Britain's Prime Minister Ramsay MacDonald, to set Hahn free. Since Nazi policy towards the Jews at this time centred on driving them from Germany, rather than putting them in concentration camps or exterminating them, Hahn was released and allowed to emigrate to Britain. The new Margrave of Baden, Berthold, took over as headmaster of Salem.

By a curious twist of fate, as Hahn was bound for Britain, the young Philip of Greece was on his way to Salem. Anxious to soften foreign reaction against Hitler's regime which had led to the withdrawal of many foreign, and quite a number of German, boys from Salem, Berthold von Baden had asked his wife to bring her brother to the school. It would be, at the least, good publicity for Salem. The official family line was that after his French and English schools, Philip would benefit from a spell of liberal German education. We have already considered the argument that the boy would also be better off under a sister's protective eye than with his more remote English relatives. It was not an argument that Princess Alice and the Milford Havens found easy to accept. Nonetheless, at the age of twelve, Philip of Greece reluctantly left Cheam and was transported into the strange and threatening environment of Nazi Germany.

It was not the best moment for the boy to join the famous German school. By the time Philip arrived in September 1933, Berthold von Baden had already endured eight months of Nazi pressure on his school. It was an ugly battle. So many pupils had left that two of the school's four houses had to be closed down. The staff was split into pro-Nazi and anti-Nazi, the pros busily denouncing the antis to the Nazi authorities. Some of the finest teachers were suspended, but an official of the Nazi Ministry of Education sent to investigate proved surprisingly helpful and several of the old Salem stalwarts were reinstated. Perhaps this ambiguity reflected the regime's uncertainty as to whether to close the school down or to exploit its prestige for propaganda purposes.

Many of the remaining children and staff showed remarkable

resilience and strength of character, in the best Hahn tradition. But von Baden, depressed by the conflict, decided to close down the school rather than submit to official demands for total *Gleichschaltung* – Nazification of staff, pupils and curriculum. A Nazi commissar retaliated by threatening to send Berthold von Baden and his supporters to prison and take over the school.

Under this threat, the Margrave agreed to carry on, while hoping to keep Nazi influence within acceptable limits. He had little real chance of succeeding. Presently the Hitler Youth appeared on the scene to enrol the pupils into their ranks. It was made obligatory to join, and Hitler Youth *Führer* were invested with special powers – hardly the kind of leaders Hahn originally had in mind. Claiming authority independent of the teachers, these leaders ordered Hitler Youth groups to attend indoctrination and training classes, and also disrupted the curriculum. Younger teachers and older boys even joined the S.A. storm-troopers, thus creating an even more malevolent and threatening atmosphere. There was, in Philip's words, "a lot of ghastly foot-slogging".

"Prince Philip of Greece", as a foreigner, was exempt from the Hitler Youth activities and had no inclination to regret the fact. Indeed it seems that he found his closest friends among boys who regarded the Nazi drill as an unwelcome intrusion into their routine; moreover, he poked fun at Hitler, and mocked the Nazi salute. Of his contemporaries at Salem (except for Prince George William of Hanover, who later became his brother-in-law) only a boy called Breitling later crossed Philip's path. Other well-known contemporaries at Salem included Golo Mann, son of the author Thomas Mann, and two German post-war politicians, Eric Blumenfeld, the Hamburg MP, and Knut Kühlmann-Stumm, the Liberal leader; both Mann and Kühlmann-Stumm were, however, a good deal older than Philip. Another contemporary was Jocelyn Winthrop-Young, who became a distinguished teacher and later founded a Greek offshoot of the school, as well as tutoring the future King Constantine II of Greece. He was later to return to Salem.

The Duke of Edinburgh remembers the Nazis of Salem with distaste. In a preface to a symposium for his former headmaster, *Kurt Hahn*, published in London in 1970, he recalls the Nazi flags flying and senior boys joining the Hitler Youth: "Some stuck out against the Nazi take-over, and one senior boy . . . responsible for us juniors so displeased the thugs that they caught him . . . and shaved his head. I lent him my Cheam 2nd XI cricket cap and hope he has got it still." Prince Philip went on: "I realize now that it was probably the dreadful mass hysteria of the Germans of those days which made Hahn so aware of the need to encourage boys to develop as responsible individuals: strong enough in mind and character to reject the standards of the mob and to resist the temptation to run with the herd." A sensible conclusion, but these were, of course, ideas which Hahn had developed long before the Nazis came to power.

Ironically, while Philip's brother-in-law Berthold von Baden was battling against the Nazis at Salem, another brother-in-law, Prince Christopher of Hesse, was serving the Nazi regime as an S.A. officer in Berlin. Though von Baden remained nominal head of Salem, the Nazis eventually took control of the school's administration. Interestingly, they continued Hahn's schemes for sports competition with English public schools, thus enabling them to maintain international contacts at a time when Germany was anxious to avoid all forms of isolation. Was this school, torn between conflicting ideologies, suitable for Philip of Greece? Certainly he was not enjoying it – unusual in one who was normally able to enjoy most things. Abruptly, his sister Theodora and her husband decided that he should leave: "We thought it better for him, and also for us." An ideal alternative now existed, and, less than a year after entering Salem, Prince Philip returned to Britain.

His destination was Kurt Hahn's new school at Gordonstoun in Scotland, which opened in 1934. It is a tribute to Hahn's charismatic and persuasive powers that within so short a time of being ejected from Germany he founded a new school in a foreign land and assembled a board of governors of extraordinary distinction and authority. The board included William Temple, Archbishop of York, and later Archbishop of Canterbury, Claude Elliot, the Headmaster of Eton, John Buchan the novelist who, as Lord Tweedsmuir, was subsequently to become Governor-General of Canada, and the historian G. M. Trevelyan. A high-powered board, certainly, but hardly progressive; indeed, Trevelyan was the only one of recognisably radical views. But, then, Hahn's ideas were a strange amalgam of the revolutionary and the reactionary.

Overlooking the Moray Firth, near Elgin, Gordonstoun was soon successfully under way. Oddly, however, for one who had been accused of trying to anglicise German education, Hahn was soon to be reproached for germanising British education. Neither jibe is substantive; Hahn was too much his own man for that. What did emerge at Gordonstoun was a system of education which blended the expected with the unconventional, while containing a good deal that was downright quirky.

It was at Gordonstoun that Philip came fully under Hahn's influence; the confused and Hahn-less year at Salem was a quite separate experience. The curriculum at Gordonstoun was at least varied. Together with the first pupils, thirty in all, Philip underwent coastguard training and spent a good many nights on look-out duty. He was also required to join in rambling, mountaineering, and mountaineering exercises on which the school placed as much emphasis as on regular fire-drill practice. A heavy emphasis in fact on life-saving of all sorts which, though the pupils fortunately had little need to put theory into practice, was an intrinsic part of Hahn's philosophy.

In later life, Prince Philip was at pains to put the record straight regarding Gordonstoun's alleged "spartan, tough, rigorous, generally body-bending" qualities. (Perhaps his decision to send Prince Charles there had something to do with the apologia.) At any rate, he regretted the prevalent misunderstanding over Gordonstoun's physical regime: "I think it rationalises the whole of the physical activities. Instead of this obsession with games, which is the standard public school thing . . . we in fact had a great many more activities. This is why it got that reputation . . . But these are alternatives . . . not everybody does everything."

Conventional sports were, however, very much to his liking. One of Hahn's quirks was to attribute extraordinary healing powers to high-jumping, claiming, "I once cured two stuttering boys by forcing them into high-jumping." Even without stuttering, Philip was good at jumping and excelled at the Interscholastic Sports at Inverleith and other meetings. He was also good at hockey and cricket and eventually captained the school team in both sports, though he has subsequently displayed a disarming, almost bloody-minded, modesty over such matters, denying that he was much good at cricket and adding that, though he was in the first eleven, "There were so few of us, anyone who could hold a bat was in." Since there were nearly a hundred and fifty boys there when he left, the achievement was real enough, though admittedly falling short of captaining Eton.

Apart from the physical and sporting activities, pupils had to apply themselves to a wide range of personal and intellectual challenges. According to the Gordonstoun school reports to parents, pupils were expected to develop the ability "to state facts precisely", "to take the right course in the face of Discomforts, Hardships, Danger, Mockery, Boredom, Scepticism, Impulses of the Moment", and "to plan, organise, and deal with the unexpected". This was all good training for a young man who was eventually to make a career in the Royal Navy. Gordonstoun also demanded "Mental Concentration", "Conscientiousness" and "Manners" – qualities in which the Duke of Edinburgh has not so far proved notably deficient, though some might query the "Manners".

But, as Hahn's critics never tired of pointing out, studies in English, ancient languages, modern languages, history, natural science and mathematics, came rather low on the list of requirements, only just above practical work, art work (which included music and drawing and at which Philip did not shine), fighting spirit and endurance, of which he apparently had plenty. He came to share, perhaps too early, Hahn's concern over the modern decays – the alleged decay of physical fitness, self-discipline, enterprise, skill and care and, above all, compassion. Not that he strove to emulate Hahn's practice of clothing basic human decencies in abstruse philosophical language, nor of intellectualising the robust routine imposed on Gordonstoun boys. Nonetheless, the values he learnt from Hahn have re-emerged now and again in varied criticisms of modern British society – after all, no apostle of Hahn need be reminded to "pull his finger out" for the finger was unlikely to be in anyway. As to whether physical training provides a valid moral exercise for the young, there are a variety of answers. At least the Duke of Edinburgh later put the precept to the test in his Award Scheme, and it is clear that a large number of young people found the physical challenge worth taking up.

The subject he enjoyed most at Gordonstoun was sailing, under the guidance of Commander Lewty, a retired naval officer who led the boys on expeditions to the Shetlands and the coast of Norway. Life at sea suited him and he did not mind doing the cooking, if not exactly to gourmet standards; nor apparently, did he ever shirk hard and unpleasant work, though there are plenty of whom the same could be said.

Did the sailing at Gordonstoun help push Prince Philip towards a naval career? Obviously it was no hindrance, but he has subsequently claimed that it did not help the decision all that much. Rather, he had to do something for a living, and eventually accepted the logic of a career in the Royal Navy. Indeed, almost perversely, he has denied, according to Basil Boothroyd, that either his uncle George of Milford Haven or his uncle Louis Mountbatten were powerful, irresistible forces urging him towards the Navy. Of the latter, however, he has at least admitted, "He may have persuaded me. Or said that it would be easier to get in. I just sort of accepted it. I didn't feel very strongly about it. I really wanted to go into the Air Force. . . . Oh, yes. Left to my own devices I'd have gone into the Air Force without a doubt."

The necessity to choose a career, however, did not concern Prince Philip when he first went to Gordonstoun. More pressing, perhaps, was the need to establish an identity and satisfy his emotional needs. With his parents separated and far away, it was always likely that Philip would find emotional solace with his fellow pupils. Hahn (accused in Germany of corrupting youth) was certainly concerned to protect his boys from what he called "the poisonous passions of puberty". How much protection was needed is doubtful. Years later, Endymion Wilkinson, a former Gordonstoun headboy (or Guardian in Hahn's Platonic borrowing), argued that the headmaster was mistaken in railing against practices which were more common in conventional public schools than in Gordonstoun: "It is highly unlikely," Wilkinson wrote in the Cambridge University magazine *Granta*, "that more than a few boys ever slept together. The majority learned various habits of self-indulgence which from time to time, in greater or lesser degrees, they practised in common."

The hard work of the Gordonstoun timetable no doubt did something to stifle these gross passions. Philip worked as vigorously as anybody else, helping to convert an old stable into a dormitory and labouring on the construction of a pigsty (pigs and pigsties *again!*). The school system obliged boys to confess their sins daily and to accept appropriate punishment. It was a regime that was both unconventional, almost eccentric, yet ordered.

Philip made an immediate and favourable impression on Kurt Hahn. The latter quickly noted that, "his most marked trait was his undefeatable spirit" – high praise from a man who had carried his principles unscathed from the barbarisms of Nazi Germany. Hahn also noticed that Philip, "felt the emotions of both joy and sadness deeply, and the way he looked and the way he moved indicated what he felt. That even applied to the minor disappointments inevitable in a schoolboy's life."

Joy, though, seems to have been predominant – or at least

laughter, which is not quite the same thing. "His laughter", Hahn wrote, "was heard everywhere. He had inherited from his Danish family the capacity to derive great fun from small incidents." (Just like Tsar Nicholas at his mother's wedding all those years before.) He was, in addition, "often naughty, never nasty".

As for his school work, though no one was expecting, or even hoping for, an academic high-flyer, "He showed a lively intelligence. In community life, once he had made a task his own, he showed meticulous attention to detail and pride of workmanship which was never content with mediocre results."

Apart from ending up as school Guardian for the years 1938–9 Philip's schooling under Hahn confirmed and strengthened traits of character that were plainly evident before. He has remained solidly loyal to Hahn and his methods, once remarking, a trifle defensively, "For some reason it is perfectly respectable to teach history and mathematics, electronics and engineering. But any attempt to develop character, and the whole man, tends to be viewed with the utmost suspicion." The Duke of Edinburgh's Award Scheme was Hahn's idea, though not in all its details: "I would never have started but for Hahn, certainly not. He suggested I ought to do it, and I fought against it for quite a long time. Because you know what the British are like about that sort of thing."

About one thing there is no doubt; Prince Philip flourished at Gordonstoun. "I must confess I enjoyed my days at Gordonstoun. . . . I would like as many boys as possible to enjoy their schooldays as much as I did."

Of course, there were the holidays. Lacking a permanent home of his own, these might have been a trial and a disappointment to a less resilient boy. As it happened, he enjoyed his holidays as much as his schooldays – perhaps a testimony to the warm welcome he received at his relatives' homes.

Philip was still closer to his cousin David than to any Gordonstoun boy, and he spent a good deal of time at the Milford Haven homes in London and Maidenhead. The Marquess apparently often left the two boys to their own devices, and they would sometimes steal away at night and slip down the Thames in a canoe. Lord Louis Mountbatten's house in Upper Brook Street was another refuge, and an exotic one, with its dining-room that served as a cinema, its fast lift, and the bedroom decked out like the cabin of a cruiser. Then there were visits to the homes of his married sisters in Germany.

Reunions with Prince Andrew in Paris or Monte Carlo were mutually satisfying to both father and son; Prince Andrew must have cut a rather dashing figure, monocled, smartly-dressed and sophisticated. Philip clearly still admired his father, and there is ample evidence of the father's pride in the son – whether it arose from accounts of pigsty building at Gordonstoun or from pleasure at a good school report. Nearer home, his cousin Marina, daughter of Prince Nicholas, married George V's fourth son the Duke of Kent in 1934; Princess Elizabeth, then eight years old, was one of the bridesmaids.

Meanwhile, in the chaotic political history of Greece, the wearisome game of musical chairs in which kings and republicans alternately grabbed the seats of power saw, in 1935, the return to the throne of King George II after eleven years of exile in London. For Philip, the major significance of this change lay in his mother's decision to return to settle in Athens. Between London and Athens, in Florence, there were the remains of King Constantine I, Queen Sophie, and George I's widow, Queen Olga, who had all died in exile. George II undertook to bring them to Athens for reburial and to make the reinterment a great ceremony of state. He invited relations, exiled or otherwise, to come to Athens where, undeterred by the republican sympathies of the owner, they booked into the luxurious Hôtel Grande Bretagne.

This macabre ceremony of reburial at least provided Philip with the chance to visit Athens for the first time. For the purpose he was obliged to equip himself with formal clothes, including a top hat. For a boy of fifteen who mostly went around in shorts and shirts and never owned more than two suits, this must have been a mixed blessing – but it was, at the very least, a symbol of some sort of status.

Prince Philip's visit to Athens was not only charged with the emotions natural to a returning exile, it also offered him the potentially painful experience of seeing his mother and father together for the first time since he had left St Cloud. There is not, alas, much evidence of what this reunion meant for Philip. He spent some time with his mother in her house in Kolonaki Square where, amid the photographs of assorted Battenbergs, he rummaged among family heirlooms and studied albums illustrating his father's life. Princess Alice, who shared the house with a female companion, asked Philip to come and live with her. He gave an unspecific reply, though it meant "no" all the same. It would have involved turning his back on the challenge and excitement of Gordonstoun, and he had recently astounded other relatives with details of his life there: of being in charge of a cutter sailing the North Sea, or of making ironware in the local village smithy.

Philip also made use of his time in Athens to try to establish a greater degree of identity. According to his cousin Alexandra, "He asked one of our aunts so many questions that she had to ask him to stop. Zestfully, for the first time, he wanted to know precisely who he was. He sought to have relationships defined and dated." Legitimate curiosity, or a frenetic search for genealogical roots? Either way, far more significant than the fact that he was overcome with nausea during the ceremonial reinterment and, later, in a coach, had no other choice but to vomit into his new top hat. On the other hand, that episode could be seen as a symptom of an upset that went very deep indeed. Or it could, after all, have been the lobster he had eaten the night before. Perhaps, knowing the man, the lobster is the better bet.

It was not long before Philip was back in Greece again, this time for the wedding of the King's younger brother, Paul, to a German princess who was destined to become Queen of Greece and to provoke her share of political problems. She was the Duke of Brunswick's daughter, Frederika, whose brother, George William of Hanover, nine years on, would be the second husband of Philip's youngest sister.

While Philip attended these festivities Prince Andrew was pressed to enrol his son in the Greek Nautical College from where he would go on to join the Royal Hellenic Navy. Philip would have been a prestigious catch for a service that did not enjoy a great reputation, for, although Greece was an ancient seafaring nation, her naval vessels in those days hardly rivalled those of the Royal Navy. In any case, Prince Andrew's own military career had been brought to a sharp and ignominious end by the unpredictable shift of politics. This could easily happen to his son. Nor did Philip wish to leave Gordonstoun or Britain. The proposition was, therefore, never seriously put to him. Diplomatically, Prince Andrew replied that his son would return to Gordonstoun for a year and then enter the Royal Naval College at Dartmouth; after this he might well wish to join the Greek navy. But, in fact, this was an increasingly remote possibility.

The deepening world crisis had personal implications for Philip. Hitler's march into the Rhineland in 1936 was welcomed by most

79

of the German side of his family but disturbed his British relatives. Where did Philip's loyalties lie? One of his Gordonstoun schoolfellows recalls that he was careful and diplomatic in his comments – "intelligently non-committal" was the phrase used. In 1936 he did not attend the funeral of King George V, who had played host at his parents' engagement party, though there is probably little significance in this. But he did refuse to discuss the abdication crisis of 1936, which subjected the British monarchy to upheaval of the sort normally reserved for foreign royal families – such as that of Greece. It is said that Philip sympathised with Edward VIII's voluntary dethronement and exile, and these events must undoubtedly have reawoken painful echoes of his father's fall from grace fourteen years earlier. He attended the coronation of George VI in 1937, however, where his sister Cecile adorned the Coronation Ball in a dress of classical Greek design.

Within half a year Prince Philip was to suffer the first of two bereavements which affected him deeply. In November 1937 his sister Cecile, her husband George Donatus, who had recently succeeded as hereditary Grand Duke of Hesse, their two sons and the Dowager Grand Duchess were killed en route to the London wedding of George Donatus' brother, Prince Louis of Hesse, and an English girl Margaret Geddes. The three-engined Junkers of the Belgian airline carrying this branch of the Hesse family had flown into a thick fog over Ostend; trying to make an emergency landing it had hit the top of a chimney and crashed. The Hesse family, six other passengers, and the crew were killed. Philip had thus lost a sister to whom he was apparently greatly attached despite the ten years that separated them. The tragedy cast an inevitable shadow over the wedding which had promised to be a welcome family reunion. Postponed by three days, it became a sombre, solemn private affair. The Duchess of Kent, Princess Marina, attended, but Philip chose to stay away.

Six months later he had to endure an equally hurtful loss when his uncle George of Milford Haven died of cancer at the age of forty-six. The death of this man, who had been a generous and immensely understanding father figure, was a tremendous blow. Yet, oddly, there is little evidence of conventional expressions of grief; perhaps Philip chiefly showed his feelings, as Kurt Hahn had earlier observed, by his looks and by his movements. Perhaps, also, he was developing an emotional resilience, a strength in the face of adversity, that was to become a marked characteristic of his personality.

In any case he had always, and quite naturally, found it easier to express enjoyment and amusement than grief.

The death of the second Marquess of Milford Haven had one profound consequence for Philip: it meant that Lord Louis Mountbatten took over his late brother's role as chief adviser and friend. The results of this change will be dealt with later, but it is enough to say that, arguably, they include Philip's marriage to Princess Elizabeth.

In the summer of 1938 Philip holidayed in Venice, where his activities showed little sign of grief. Indeed he seems to have spent most of his time either eating hugely, or in amorous dalliance – though not of a particularly serious kind: "Blondes, brunettes and redheaded charmers, Philip gallantly and I think quite impartially squired them all." That is his cousin Alexandra's somewhat tart description, and may owe something to jealousy; after all, her descriptions of him at this time are either warmly admiring ("my blond handsome cousin", "very handsome and graceful", and so on), or censorious.

Alexandra's not altogether welcome presence in Venice was unavoidable. Philip was the guest of her mother, Aspasia, the widow of King Alexander of Greece, and thus Philip's aunt. Aspasia had her instructions from Prince Andrew as to Philip's welfare. "Philip still has to pass his exams," he wrote. "Whatever you do, keep him out of girl trouble."

This was easier said than done, especially since Philip was "immensely gregarious, so quickly ready for each new experience". He was much lionised by various Italian families, among them the Volpis (Count Volpi had been Mussolini's Foreign Minister) and the immensely rich Castelboros. Perhaps it went to his head, for when Lady Melchett threw a party at a taverna, Philip, overcome with wine, danced "about the terrace like a young faun" and "began swinging from the pergola", which eventually collapsed, bringing the vine down with it. Wealthy Americans were also in the swing of things including Mrs Cobina Wright, whose name was later to be linked with Philip's.

His aunt Aspasia, conscious of her responsibilities, did her best to ration and control his exploits, only allowing him twenty minutes to see home "some lovely young thing in tulle or organdie", according to the watchful Alexandra. There was one girl in particular to whom he paid attention, finally begging to be allowed to take her for a cruise in a motor launch. Aunt Aspasia reluctantly agreed but issued the firm instruction, "You are to cruise round and round the island and don't stop the engine! I shall be listening!" But the chugging of the launch across the lagoon and down the canal was punctuated by unaccountable silences. "We had trouble with the sparking plugs," was Philip's explanation the next morning. At least it was an excuse that was hard to disprove.

From Monte Carlo, Prince Andrew heard of these adventures and sent off a stern warning that Philip was not to dissipate his energies. Certainly, in Alexandra's version, he was exhausted most mornings: "He used to lie in bed until eleven or twelve o'clock. . . . Then he would come down demanding a full English-type breakfast of eggs and bacon from our Italian cook, which had to be done particularly as he wanted." Hardly the Gordonstoun ethic, but, then, it was a holiday.

If his cousin's account is to be relied upon, Philip appeared rootless, restless and hungry for food and affection. He "gave me the impression of a huge, hungry dog; perhaps a friendly collie who had never had a basket of his own and responded to every overture with eager tail-wagging." Despite his welcome to other people's homes, "there were undertones of complete heartlessness . . . to be fed and looked after meant such a lot to him."

Philip's feelings of deprivation, no matter how skilfully masked, would not have been obliterated by a holiday he later took in Monte Carlo with his father. On the contrary, Prince Andrew's life style, though comfortable, was melancholy and without distinction. He lived at the Villa Alexandra, one of the four houses belonging to the Hôtel Metropole. Philip accompanied him when he took his daily aperitif in the bar of the Hôtel de Paris under the sharp, but not unfriendly, scrutiny of Victor the head barman.

When Philip returned to Gordonstoun, his place by his father's side in the bar and at lunch at the Salle Empire (and when it was later closed during the war, at the Salon Louis XV) was taken by Madame Andrée de la Bigne, a tall, discreet and very attractive French woman with whom Andrew had formed a close relationship. Fair-haired, with light grey eyes, Madame de la Bigne, a wealthy widow, could look back on a brief career in films (as Mademoiselle Lafayette) and, more significantly, owned a small yacht, the *Davida*, in which Andrew lived for a time, and on which they occasionally went cruising. From 1940–1941 onwards, during the German occupation, the couple led a quiet and unostentatious life.

Until the outbreak of the Second World War, Prince Andrew

received regular reports from Gordonstoun monitoring Philip's progress. During his five years at the school he had developed into a rather self-possessed, mature youth. He had graduated in the quasi-military hierarchy of Gordonstoun from Room Leader to Captain to Colour Bearer to Helper (one of the ten boys in charge of particular activities – his was sailing) and now, in his last year, he was elected Guardian or head boy, a distinction conferred on the school's most responsible and authoritative young man. Impatience and intolerance were his chief faults, and, despite the mellowing effect of experience, and of personal fulfilment and international fame, they remain so.

Kurt Hahn's final report was, however, warmly complimentary: "Prince Philip is universally trusted, liked and respected. He has the greatest sense of service of all the boys in the school. Prince Philip is a born leader, but will need the exacting demands of a great service to do justice to himself. His best is outstanding; his second best is not good enough. Prince Philip will make his mark in any profession where he will have to prove himself in a full trial of strength."

Stirring stuff, and certainly a justification of Hahn's educational ideals. As for the "great service" in which to do justice to himself, Hahn was thinking of the Royal Navy, though with hindsight, Prince Philip's contribution as consort to the stability and improvement of the British monarchy has been the greater service.

So, Dr Hahn was pleased with his product. Whether Gordonstoun, with its unconventional, lopsided curriculum and its rigorous pursuit of physical excellence, fully developed Philip's potential in intellectual and academic areas is open to question. At the time, it probably seemed an irrelevance: naval officers could get by without participating in discourses on Proust or Descartes – come to that, so could members of the British royal family.

The impending entrance examination to the Royal Naval College at Dartmouth was not taken lightly. Indeed, on his uncle Louis Mountbatten's advice, he went for a time to stay with a retired naval officer and his wife in Cheltenham, where the coach, Mr Mercer, put him through a course of intensive study. A sign of academic insecurity? Or part of an "attempt to prove himself in a full trial of strength"?

At any rate, the Mercers found him co-operative, hard-working, eager to get on, and quite without "side". Mr Mercer also noted, clearly with surprise, that he had very little pocket money. Apart from Saturday night visits to the cinema and occasional radio or record sessions with the Mercers' daughter, he dedicated himself to the cramming that appeared so necessary for success.

He had a good many advantages: uncle Dickie as patron; the encouragement of his cousin David Milford Haven, with several years of naval service behind him; a martial family tradition on the paternal side; and, above all, the seafaring experiences of Gordonstoun, coastguard training, sailing expeditions and so forth.

The examination results were encouraging, though not outstanding. His marks put him sixteenth of the thirty-four entrants, most of them from naval schools. It could be considered a failure only in the eyes of those who took Hahn's claims for his system of education entirely at face value. Philip did best in the oral examination, in which he gained nearly maximum points for self-reliance, judgment and leadership. Gordonstoun had been least successful in teaching him correct English spelling, though this was to improve later.

Early in 1939, therefore, he entered the Royal Naval College at Dartmouth, the demanding, levelling, training ground which had played an important part in shaping the characters of the three most recent King-Emperors, George V, Edward VIII and George VI. That Dartmouth would play its part in the development of a future consort of a British Queen could not, of course, be predicted in 1939. What could safely be predicted was that the new cadet would not be content with his middle-order ranking. The "exacting demands of great service" would soon enable him, as Hahn had foreseen, "to do justice to himself".

5

War at Sea

"An enjoyable Greek cocktail party. Prince Philip of Greece was
there. . . . He is to be our Prince Consort, and that is why he is
serving in our Navy."

Sir Henry "Chips" Channon,
21 January 1941

THE ROYAL NAVAL COLLEGE AT DARTMOUTH was not overawed by
royalty. King George V had received what was probably the most
formative period of his education as a cadet in the Royal Navy, and
his two eldest sons had followed his example. There was no
feather-bedding for princes. George V, who affected naval dress,
beard, and manners all his life, recalled:

> It never did me any good to be a Prince, I can tell you, and many
> was the time I wished I hadn't been. It was a pretty tough place
> and, so far from making any allowances for our disadvantages,
> the other boys made a point of taking it out of us on the grounds
> that they'd never be able to do it later on . . . they used to make me
> go up and challenge the bigger boys – I was awfully small then –
> and I'd get a hiding time and again.

The future King Edward VIII had felt himself "nearly over-
powered" when he first joined the Royal Naval College at Osborne,
before going on to Dartmouth. He was a nervous, shy, diminutive
boy who earned the half-contemptuous, half-affectionate nickname
of "sardine". He was bullied by the older boys and suffered such
indignities as having red ink poured down his neck, and being
"beheaded" by a sash window to remind him of the fate suffered by
one of his ancestors, Charles I.

George VI had rounded off his education with a spell at

Dartmouth. He had enjoyed his time there, though not distinguishing himself in the final examinations in 1912 — coming sixty-first out of sixty-seven. George VI, however, had considered himself well-suited to a naval career. Indeed, when his elder brother abdicated in December 1936, the new King, close to tears, said to his cousin Louis Mountbatten, "Dickie, this is absolutely terrible. I'm only a naval officer, it's the only thing I know about." To which Mountbatten robustly replied, "George you're wrong. There is no more fitting preparation for a king than to have been trained in the Navy." (Presumably the same thing holds for those who marry kings' daughters?)

Prince Philip had hardly settled in at Dartmouth when George VI, Queen Elizabeth and Louis Mountbatten (then the King's personal aide-de-camp) paid a visit to the college at the end of July 1939. The two princesses accompanied them. The royal visit, however, faced complications. These complications were not of the heart, but, rather, connected with less romantic parts of the body. A double epidemic of chicken-pox and mumps had broken out, and it was decided to keep the princesses away from possible infection. The officer in charge of the college, Admiral Sir Frederick Dalrymple-Hamilton put his house at the disposal of the royal family. The two princesses, once they had alighted from the royal yacht *Victoria and Albert*, were taken to the house while their father and Dickie Mountbatten revelled in a nostalgic tour of the college. But how, in the meantime, were Elizabeth and Margaret Rose to be entertained?

Enter Prince Philip of Greece, "a fair-haired boy, rather like a Viking, with a sharp face and piercing blue eyes", according to Miss Crawford, the princesses' nanny and later a writer of memoirs that are both useful and trivial. Why Prince Philip? Because he was there, for one thing. Because he was a distant cousin, for another. Was there more to it?

Was it, in fact, a plot? Can we discern the machiavellian hand of Lord Mountbatten making the first move in a calculated strategy to marry off his nephew to the future Queen? The start of Mountbatten's retaliation for the fall of Louis of Battenberg and associated humiliations? Who can say? Certainly "Uncle Dickie" was later to campaign with skilful persistence on Philip's behalf.

There are numerous versions of this meeting of Prince Philip and Princess Elizabeth. One thing must be cleared up at the start; it was the third time they had met, not the first, though the previous occasions were hardly meetings of the face-to-face variety – both had attended Princess Marina's marriage to the Duke of Kent in 1934, and Philip had been a family guest at George VI's coronation in 1937.

What is clear, however, is that at Dartmouth they noticed each other for the first time. How far Philip noticed the thirteen-year-old Elizabeth, or what precisely she made of it all, is difficult to ascertain. Did they have a "glorious time", as one version insists, or was it rather a flop, as another account makes out? Probably somewhat between the two, mainly because it is hard to see Philip associated with a flop on such an occasion.

Miss Crawford remembers that, "He said, 'How do you do?' to Lilibet [Elizabeth], and for a while they knelt side by side playing with the trains." According to another authority, Philip found it easier to relate to Margaret, who was rather plump and far less shy than her sister. He teased her a lot and she asked, with royal disdain, "Who is that boy?"

One thing is certain: Philip displayed his athletic prowess. They went outside and he proceeded to jump over the net on the tennis court and to play croquet with the visitors – though not at the same time. Showing off, in a word; it was not the first, or the last occasion.

Was Princess Elizabeth amused? She seems, according to Miss Crawford, to have been impressed: "Lilibet said, 'How good he is Crawfie! How high he can jump!' He was quite polite to her." Another commentator has Elizabeth saying repeatedly, "When are we going home?" A bit of a dampener that, and rather unlikely, unless she considered the yacht *Victoria and Albert* to be home. Cousin Alexandra of Yugoslavia, who was not there (and who seems to have wished that she had been), insists that Elizabeth also said, "How good he is" after the croquet game.

"How good he is" seems to have been Elizabeth's main contribution to the conversation, and then only as an aside. Perhaps she was struck almost dumb with admiration. Alexandra has recounted hearing Philip say years later to his wife, "You were so shy. I couldn't get a word out of you." Perhaps Elizabeth felt she had nothing much to say to this tall, ebullient eighteen-year-old. When later that evening Philip and a group of cadets came aboard the royal yacht for dinner, she had already been put to bed.

The next day contact was renewed. "Uncle Dickie", we learn, had "steadfastly procured his nephew an invitation to lunch on the royal yacht. Philip contributed to the conversation mainly by teasing Margaret [again!] and laughing a good deal." Note the words "steadfastly procured", it is cousin Alexandra's sharp pen again. Miss Crawford has a more charitable description of the meeting:

> Lilibet asked him, "What would you like to eat? What would you like?" when it came to tea. The Queen said, "You must make a really good meal, for I suppose it is your last for the day."
> Philip had several platefuls of shrimps, and a banana split, among other trifles. To the little girls a boy of any kind was always a strange creature out of another world. Lilibet sat pink-faced, enjoying it all very much. To Margaret, anyone who could eat so many shrimps was a hero.

What did Philip make of it all? Some versions have him making heavy weather of it, suggesting that he was "entirely unamused at the prospect of attending . . . on two small girls." Cousin Alexandra, predictably, describes Philip being "hauled out of chapel to help squire the two young girls", and continues, apparently with relish, "Philip rather resented it, I believe, a youngster of eighteen called to help entertain a girl of thirteen and a child of nine."

Prince Philip now professes an imperfect recall of the details of this first, proper encounter between himself and Princess Elizabeth. He certainly does not remember it as a wearisome and time-wasting ordeal; after all, jumping over tennis nets (albeit to applause) and eating several platefuls of shrimps indicates something more than a bored aloofness of spirit.

Moreover there is a further piece of significant "Philip and Elizabeth" lore. As the royal yacht left, a flotilla of small craft, manned by cadets, followed in her wake: launches, sailing dinghies and rowing boats. Philip was among those who sailed so close to her that the King grew apprehensive: "This is ridiculous and quite unsafe," he told his captain, Sir Dudley North. "You must signal them to go back!" The cadets all obeyed except one. The wind probably did not carry the King's outburst far enough for the delinquent to hear the three angry words: "The young fool!" (Or, according to another version, "Damned young fool".) Louis Mountbatten added his "high-pitched but commanding voice" to the rumpus; megaphones were used; arms were waved. It was almost certainly the arms that did it. The solitary oarsman turned back. There are no prizes for guessing the identity of the rash young man who had provoked the wrath of a King-Emperor.

Why did Philip do it? More showing off? An aquatic version of jumping over tennis nets? Attention-seeking? Love? One version of the escapade assures us that, "He was extremely attracted to his pretty little cousin who looked at him through adoring blue eyes." Another is certain that, "Elizabeth watched him fondly through an enormous pair of binoculars." We are further assured that she "had caught a disease more dangerous than mumps; she had an advanced case of puppy love" – love at last sight presumably, or had it been first sight? At any rate, Philip had picked on an excellent way of getting himself noticed; a farewell with a flourish. He was not to be easily forgotten.

With the *Victoria and Albert* gone it was back to the grindstone. Philip's achievements at Dartmouth belied his average performance in the entrance examination. He was awarded the King's Dirk as the best all-round cadet of his term and went on to win the Eardley-Howard-Crockett prize for the best cadet. These were gratifying achievements, especially for one who had not been a notable prize-winner earlier in his education, and who had been obliged to enter Dartmouth as a Special Entrant at seventeen and a half years of age, when many of his fellow cadets had been there since prep school.

More than a decade later he was handing out prizes himself to naval cadets aboard HMS *Devonshire* with the comforting words: "I would like to congratulate heartily all the prize-winners and at the same time to offer my sympathy to all those who were unsuccessful – an experience with which I am quite familiar." In fact, his capacity to pass naval examinations with distinction was confirmed when in the summer of 1941 he came through his sub-lieutenant's examination with four first-class marks and one second-class mark.

While Philip was at Dartmouth, Europe was moving closer to war. Ever since Hitler had annexed Austria in 1938, wrested the Sudetenland from the Czechs, and exposed the folly of Neville Chamberlain's over-optimistic promise of "peace in our time" by occupying the whole of Czechoslovakia, war had become increasingly likely. There was no question as to where Philip's loyalties lay, despite the complication of having three sisters married to German husbands – one of them, Christopher of Hesse, joining the *Luftwaffe*, another, Gottfried Hohenlohe-Langenburg, the German army.

Nonetheless, a war between Britain and Germany could hardly be an event to strengthen family bonds that were already stretched thinly over frontiers and conflicting ideological and nationalist convictions. It is thus significant that Philip spent the book token of two pounds from the Eardley-Howard-Crockett award on a copy of Liddell-Hart's *The Defence of Britain*. It was an outward and visible sign of where his loyalties lay.

He was, of course, still a Greek subject. When Neville Chamberlain announced over the radio on 3 September 1939 that, "We are now at war with Germany," Philip could not technically identify with that comfortingly collective "we". Plans for him to apply for British nationality were frustrated when naturalisation procedures were suspended. At least, with his Greek passport, he was a citizen of a neutral country. Still, he was not officially a British combatant. It has since been argued that, by virtue of his descent from Queen Victoria and the Battenberg-Mountbatten family, he could have claimed British nationality as of right (British nationality was, in fact, later accorded to the hardly more deserving German Brunswick-Hanovers on these grounds), but from a constitutional point of view this is debatable. Moreover, being a prince complicated things further.

Lord Louis Mountbatten proceeded to pull a few of the strings that connected him and Philip to the British crown and establishment, and the Admiralty gave permission for Cadet Prince Philip of Greece to carry on in his career. It was a common sense decision: in spirit and outlook, in manner, and by inclination and education, he was unmistakably British.

Even though Philip was passed out as midshipman less than a year after entering Dartmouth, their Lordships of the Admiralty were still uncertain as how best to deal with their "neutral" Greek prince. In fact, the Foreign Office, the Home Office, and the Palace were all involved with the deliberations, with Lord Louis robustly taking up his nephew's cause.

The solution was to have him posted to HMS *Ramillies*, an elderly, lumbering ship that was escorting transports of Australian vessels and troops to European war zones. It seemed a fairly safe assignment. During a short leave in London prior to joining *Ramillies*, Louis Mountbatten invited Philip to join a party with the King and the Queen to see a revue, "Funny Side Up". An indication of the possible match going through Lord Mountbatten's and, maybe, the King's mind? There was, however, no opportunity for Philip to meet Princess Elizabeth again before the young midshipman, still four months away from his nineteenth birthday, left for Colombo in Ceylon to join his ship.

It was not a glamorous assignment. The quarters were so cramped that, as he said, "Nobody ever turns in. The most popular sleeping quarters are in the gun room where the midshipmen sleep in two armchairs, two sofas and on the table. It is very hot at night." He was "Captain's doggie" and one of his duties was to make the cocoa. But at least he was at sea and contributing to the war effort. Nor was the *Ramillies* uninteresting. Convoys were met, marshalled and escorted, mostly ships of the British Empire-Commonwealth, but, according to the midshipman, sometimes "Dutch passenger ships with completely unpronouncable [sic] names".

Shore leave in Australia saw him leaving fellow officers to sample the depravity of Sydney's night life while he went four hundred miles inland to inspect a sheep farm. Not an orthodox release for a young seaman, but rather an early example of the capacity to look and learn that has, with the passage of time, made the Duke of Edinburgh a uniquely well-informed man.

On 12 April 1940, he was transferred to HMS *Kent*, a flagship with heavy armament and infinitely better facilities in every respect, including cocoa brewing. "The ventilation is so much better," he noted, "that it is quite possible to stay below decks in comfort. There is no danger whatsoever of hitting one's head on the deckhead or beams." The ventilation was good but, at first, the atmosphere was decidedly cool. Philip was not received with open arms. Anxious to get home after a two and a half years' tour of duty, the crew had been caught by the outbreak of war and had remained as far away from home as ever. To be saddled with some foreign prince as well seemed, to many of the ratings, to be altogether too much.

The evident goodwill and eagerness of their unwelcome addition, however, soon won them over. One of the crew has said, "I can honestly say that when we first saw this gangling youth, running all over the ship trying to obey instructions from a host of gold braid, smiling and cheerful to everyone, no matter what their rank, he immediately became endeared to us." Nor was it so bad being on watch with royalty: "We had the pleasure of his company for long periods, and he often rolled and smoked our home-made cigarettes with us." An early sign of a happy knack of making contact at any level.

Soon afterwards the *Kent* put in at Durban and the crew was received with liberal hospitality. Durban's girls must have been more hospitable and generous than most because, when the *Kent* sailed, midshipman Mountbatten wrote, "The fact that many hearts were left behind in Durban is not surprising." And yet, "At 06.30 we were leaving the jetty, a grey, damp morning laden with hangovers. There was no one there to wave us goodbye, because nobody knew we were leaving." Still, there were other ports of call: Fremantle, Aden, Bombay, Mombasa, Port Said, Athens, Alexandria. There is no reason to suppose that Philip left more hearts (or hangovers) behind in these ports than any other young naval officer. Indeed, one who sailed with him is of the opinion that he avoided any serious emotional entanglement like the plague. Not ready for them? Or keeping himself free for an infinitely more spectacular match? Durban remained a favourite place for shore leave though, and is usually favoured with an exclamation mark in his midshipman's log.

Like all midshipmen, Philip was required to keep Admiralty Form S.519, Journal for Use of Junior Officers afloat. Basil Boothroyd has described it as "a ruggedly bound volume with marbled endpapers and a hundred and fifty foolscap pages, ruled feint". S.519 was to be periodically inspected by superior officers, and in it, "Midshipmen are to record in their own language all matters of interest or importance in the work that is carried out, on their stations, in their Fleet, or in their Ship. The objects of keeping the Journal are to train Midshipmen in (a) the power of observation, (b) the power of expression, (c) the habit of orderliness."

Admiralty Form S.519, as kept by "Philip, Prince of Greece", as he wrote on the title page (crossing out the printed "Mr"), provides a mass of information about the early wartime experiences of the Journal's keeper, coming to an end on 9 June 1941. It also tells the reader a good deal about the personality of the writer. There is a great relish for technical data, and the pages are littered with cringles, shackles, rams and thrust-blocks. There are diagrams, plans, maps, charts of courses steered and a sketch, in three colours, of the Suez Canal. The spelling, as at Gordonstoun, remains erratic: Hitler's Axis allies are consistently the "Italiens" – which probably serves them right; buoys pop up as "bouys"; there are "misstakes", and a "c" is missing from "exept".

Such quibbles aside, and, after all, there was a war on, the Journal reveals excellent powers of observation, and the entries are direct, sometimes humorous, colourful, and showing a good eye for detail. A particularly receptive mind was receiving a host of impressions and images.

Extracts from the Journal give a good impression of Midshipman Mountbatten's war. Sailing from Durban in *Kent* (presumably without their hearts), the crew was alerted to the menace of a German raider in the Indian Ocean. The raider did not appear, but on the route to Colombo the Trades hit the ship instead. The roll was often over twenty degrees: "Seas were breaking over the fos'cle [sic] almost continuously . . . a lot of innocent fun was had in the mess, watching the Genoese stewards diligently laying the table, and then the plates, knives, forks, spoons, butter dishes, toast rack and marmalade landing in a heap on the deck." We do not learn if the Genoese stewards shared the amusement.

Meanwhile, in Europe the shape of the war was changing. The *Wehrmacht* relentlessly drove across France, eventually accomplishing the expulsion of the British forces from the Continent which contemporary Allied propaganda promptly transformed into the "triumph" of Dunkirk. Britain and her Empire were facing the prospect of fighting on alone. On the day that Prince Philip celebrated his nineteenth birthday (10 June 1940) Mussolini, sensing victory for the Axis powers, took Italy into the war; four days later the triumphant Germans entered Paris; another three days and France asked for an armistice.

Philip spent a brief leave in London at 16 Chester Street, Lord Louis Mountbatten's new town house, modest by comparison with Brook House but neatly symbolic of the Mountbatten metamorphosis from "playboy" of the thirties to "war hero" of the forties. It can hardly have been the Mountbattens and their friends who left Philip with the impression recorded in his log that, after Dunkirk, "The situation in Europe seems rather bad. Knowing what the atmosphere was like in certain circles in London before the German offensive, I should hate to think what kind of panic they must be in now."

Who on earth did he mean? Effete aristocrats? Over-fed businessmen? Defeatist workers? And why expect panic when he and his shipmates were being assured that, while the situation was grave, "the home front was taking everything very calmly"? He follows this with the tart remark that, "Politicians are doing their utmost to beat all previous tongue-wagging records." Not a particularly shrewd observation considering the principal tonguewagger of the moment was Winston Churchill, who was inspiring the nation with some of the finest and most rousing speeches in modern British history.

Still far removed from the home waters, Philip was next posted to Lanka, a shore station in Colombo. There was not much for him to do there, though he did go "fishing", which in practice meant blowing fish out of the water with small explosive charges and then presenting fifty or sixty of them to the Captain's table. Much of the time he was bored, impatiently groping and searching for something useful to do, pleading with his superiors to let him participate in various projects. A survey at Trincomalee Harbour: "I asked whether I could be sent there to see how it was done." He plainly wanted to see and know as much as he could. He thus set off through the jungle in a ramshackle old car which only just made the one hundred and sixty miles to Trincomalee. Next, there was mine-sweeping and again he asked to be in the party.

Another lull and he borrowed the C.-in-C.'s barge and set out for the festival of the "Buddha's Tooth" in Kandy, the ancient capital of Ceylon. There he marvelled at the colourfully dressed elephants and the chiefs with their pointed red leather shoes and "four-cornered gold crowns on there [sic] heads", preceded by their dancers. Obviously a feast for the eye and the Journal, and also good for "the power of observation" – he counted 80 elephants, not 79 or 81, but 80, which takes some doing.

Far away from elephants and, indeed, "four-cornered gold crowns", London and other British cities were enduring the Blitz. We have no record as to whether the loyal midshipman thought at all of his brother-in-law Christopher as the *Luftwaffe* flew above burning buildings.

A little later he was posted to another ship, and wrote wryly, "A few minutes after one o'clock on Sunday, October 1st, 1940, I walked aboard His Majesty's Ship *Shropshire*, the third ship in eight months to receive this singular honour." Just over three months later on 2 January 1941 a fourth ship, HMS *Valiant* had the honour, and this time he was on his way to real action and, to his unconcealed pleasure, no more cocoa-making. This was a grim phase of the war: Rommel's Afrika Korps had pushed back Britain's Eighth Army and invested Tobruk; in Europe there had been a shift of strategy as the *Luftwaffe* spearheaded a *Wehrmacht* assault on the Balkans. Belgrade was taken while the Italians attacked Greece from Albania, thus bringing British aid to the area.

Greece had at long last entered the Allied camp in October 1940 and Philip could no longer be considered technically a neutral.

HMS *Valiant* was in the Mediterranean fleet, and was much more pukka than the old Country Class light cruisers on which Philip had served in the Indian Ocean and beyond. *Valiant* was a battleship of the Queen Elizabeth Class, with eight formidable fifteen-inch guns, fourteen six-inch guns, and a hefty amount of anti-aircraft armament. It was an enviable transfer for Philip, and no doubt Uncle Dickie had done something towards bringing his nephew into a more prominent theatre of the war and, incidentally, into close proximity to himself.

Philip had barely settled on to the *Valiant* when he saw action at the bombardment of Bardia on the Libyan coast: "We went to action stations at 07.30, and at 08.10 the bombardment commenced. . . . The whole operation was a very spectacular affair." He was put in charge of a section of the searchlight control – just the right, exposed, sort of place to see exactly what was going on.

A few days after Bardia there was an encounter with enemy vessels south of Sicily. Philip's Journal records that, "Gun flashes were recorded on the starboard bow. . . . *Bonaventure* signalled that *Southampton* and herself were engaging two enemy destroyers. We could just see one of these destroyers blowing up in a cloud of smoke and spray . . . sixteen German dive-bombers attacked the *Illustrious*. She was hit aft amidships and fires broke out. Then the bombers concentrated on us and five bombs dropped fairly close."

After this he took leave in Athens, where he spent two days with his royal relatives. The Greek royal family were soon to scatter as the Germans, brought in to boost the ineffective Italian invasion, pushed towards Athens. Their first temporary refuge was to be Crete, then Alexandria, and next several scattered destinations.

There was a desperate and frenetic pace to Athenian social life at this time. While Philip was there, parties and dances were punctuated by the thud of falling bombs, and revellers took time off to watch the air-raids. He was reunited with King George II, Crown Prince Paul and his wife Frederika, and with his watchful cousin Alexandra, now a young woman. His reunion with his mother was overshadowed by her declared intent of not leaving when the Germans arrived. To her credit she stuck stubbornly to her word and went on to risk her safety by sheltering orphans and various fugitives from the S.S., including a family named Cohen. Perhaps the fact that two of her sons-in-law were high ranking German officers gave her immunity.

What sort of impression did naval officer Philip of Greece make upon his relations and friends? According to Basil Boothroyd, some felt, while watching the air-raids, that he "showed off a bit by making knowledgeable comments on the action", while another version claims that he "never talked shop and never had a word to say on his personal naval duties" – which seems the more unlikely of the two versions.

Mainly he seems to have been ubiquitously charming, in a mature and restrained sort of way. He was a particular hit with one guest at a party, the Tory MP Sir Henry "Chips" Channon. Writing in his diary on 21 January 1941 Channon recorded his attendance at "an enjoyable Greek cocktail party", adding, somewhat wistfully, "Prince Philip of Greece was there. He is extraordinarily handsome, and I recalled my afternoon's conversation with Princess Nicholas." But then the bombshell: "He is to be our Prince Consort, and that is why he is serving in our Navy."

Had it really been decided by January 1941? On the strength of some skill at jumping and the intrepid but foolhardy pursuit of the *Albert and Victoria*? There is no doubt that Princess Elizabeth cherished warm memories of the Dartmouth meeting. But was it likely that George VI and Queen Elizabeth were already committed to marrying off their fourteen-year-old daughter to a young man they scarcely knew? Yet Channon apparently based his information on a conversation with Princess Nicholas, Philip's aunt by marriage, and mother of Marina, Duchess of Kent – a direct link between Athens and the British royal family. Prince Philip has given his own verdict on the Channon rumour:

Well. This is precisely the sort of language that they used. It had been mentioned, presumably, that "He is eligible, he's the sort of person she might marry." I mean, after all, if you spend ten minutes thinking about it – and a lot of these people spent a good deal more time thinking about it – how many obviously eligible young men, other than people living in this country, were available? Inevitably I must have been on the list, so to speak. But people only had to say that, for somebody like Chips Channon to go one step further and say it's already decided, you see what I mean?

2

3

1 Prince Philip's great-grandmother, Princess Alice, Queen Victoria's second daughter. Princess Alice, who was well-known for her progressive views, was the grandmother of Prince Philip's mother, Alice of Battenberg, and of Earl Mountbatten of Burma, who resembled her.
2 Prince Andrew of Greece, Prince Philip's father
3 Princess Alice, Prince Philip's mother
4 Prince Philip of Greece, photographed in England, aged one year

4

5

5 Seafaring Battenbergs. *From left to right*, Lord Louis Mountbatten, Prince Louis of Battenberg (his father), and George, later 2nd Marquess of Milford Haven (his elder brother)

6 Alexandra of Greece, Prince Philip's cousin and biographer, with her husband ex-King Peter of Yugoslavia

7 Prince Philip in 1947, with his three surviving sisters, *from left to right*, Margarita, Sophie and Theodora

8 Prince Philip and his mother in 1957, at his niece's wedding in Baden

9

10

11

9 Gordonstoun batsman walking from the pitch, towards the end of his time at the school

10 Prince Philip adjusts his garters before a Gordonstoun production of *Macbeth*, in which he played a minor part

11 Athlete with spike trouble. *Inset*, Dr Kurt Hahn, founder of Gordonstoun.

12 The thirteen-year-old Princess Elizabeth at a swimming gala in 1939, a month before she met Prince Philip at Dartmouth Naval College

13 Something to commemorate? Princess Elizabeth, watched by her father and Princess Margaret, plants a tree at Dartmouth Naval College in July 1939, shortly after she had just met Prince Philip

13

12

14

14 The bearded wartime naval officer, whose photograph adorned Princess Elizabeth's dressing-table

15 Princess Elizabeth and Prince Philip of Greece photographed as they enter Romsey Abbey for the marriage of Lady Patricia Mountbatten and Lord Brabourne, 26 October 1946

16 Courting couple: a newsreel sequence of October 1946 shows Prince Philip helping Princess Elizabeth (and Margaret) disrobe before the wedding

17 The first waltz – in public, anyway, at a Ball in Edinburgh in July 1947 shortly after the announcement of their engagement
18 Engagement! Official! A delighted Princess Elizabeth displaying her engagement ring as well as her feelings

17

18

A somewhat self-deprecating, studiously vague, disclaimer. Still, he did consider himself to have been "inevitably" on the list, which was no small matter for somebody able to describe himself as a "discredited Balkan Prince". His Greek relations had obviously already sniffed the scent of a propitious marriage alliance. Moreover, he and Princess Elizabeth were corresponding by the summer of 1941, though whether they did so as early as January is not clear. There seems little doubt that she had become infatuated with him, and Sir John Wheeler-Bennett's official biography of George VI, approved and closely scrutinised by Queen Elizabeth, says unambiguously of Philip of Greece: "This was the man with whom Princess Elizabeth had been in love from their first meeting."

Philip's preoccupations were soon to be deflected by more pressing matters. Shortly after he was back at sea Greece was conquered by the Germans. The King, Crown Prince Paul, old Prince George, and Alexandra and Frederika were forced to leave the mainland for Crete, some by flying boat and the King, eventually, in the destroyer HMS *Decoy*. When Crete fell *Decoy* took them on to Egypt. According to Alexandra, "history now records" that *Valiant*, with Philip aboard, escorted *Decoy* to Alexandria. History records no such thing because it was not true. *Valiant* was in the thick of the sea battle around Crete, Philip still directing the searchlights as *Valiant* escorted convoys of British troops to Crete, or tried to intercept seaborne Germans en route to the island, with the *Luftwaffe*, swooping and menacing, in attendance.

On 28 March 1941 Philip found himself in the thick of the Battle of Matapan, two months before the German assault on Crete that started on 20 May 1941. At Matapan, the Royal Navy intercepted part of the predictably elusive Italian navy. Philip and his searchlights played a vital part in HMS *Valiant*'s contribution to the battle. He logged a judicious, underplayed, and very "stiff upper lip" account, beginning, "My orders were that if any ship illuminated a target I was to switch on and illuminate it for the rest of the fleet." Promptly following instructions he illuminated a target while Admiral Cunningham's flagship, HMS *Warspite*, unleashed a broadside, followed within seconds by *Valiant*'s own guns. The Italian cruiser was soon blazing. The noise "was considerable". Orders came to switch the searchlights to another area to see whether there was a second enemy vessel. He hesitated; the thought of another target had "never entered my head". But when he moved the searchlights, another cruiser suddenly loomed up, so close that she could not be fully illuminated. Another salvo and, "Almost at once she was completely blotted out from stem to stern." *Valiant* only ceased firing when the enemy "had completely vanished in clouds of smoke and steam". This unvarnished, and notably honest, account did not, however, mention the names of the stricken Italian cruisers – the *Zara* and the *Fiume* – nor that the action all but put paid to the Italian fleet, which never again ventured out of safe harbour – except to surrender.

The German assault on Crete began in earnest on 20 May 1941. *Valiant* was one of the warships deployed to beat off the German convoys attempting the seaborne invasion of Crete. On the opening day of the battle the *Luftwaffe* dropped heavy bombs at British ships in the sea around Crete, and shortly afterwards German transport planes disgorged a division of airborne troops who, led by General Student, became the first parachutists to comprehensively conquer enemy territory from the air. The naval battle took a fearful toll. Though the German convoys were beaten back, terrible damage was done from the air. Two days later, as Philip recorded: "*Juno* was sunk. *Naiad* and *Carlisle* were hit. A signal came asking for assistance, so we turned and steamed at 20 knots. . . . As we came in sight of the straits [of Cythera] we saw *Naiad* and *Carlisle* being attacked by bombers. We went right in to within ten miles of Crete and then the bombing started in earnest." Coolly and correctly, the midshipman's Journal goes on to record the havoc caused by the German Stukas (dive-bombers): "*Greyhound* was hit right aft by a large bomb, her stern blew up and she sank about twenty minutes later. . . . *Gloucester* was badly hit and sank some hours later." The fleet then received some more attention from the *Luftwaffe*; "We were bombed from a high level by a number of small bombs dropped in sticks of 12 or more." Then came a near miss: "One Dornier came straight for us from the port beam and dropped 12 bombs when he was almost overhead. We turned to port and ceased firing, when suddenly the bombs came whistling down, landing very close all down the port side."

The description is a far cry from the "blood and thunder" school of military history writing, and is all the more impressive for that. Its prosaic, trim qualities are much more powerful than journalistic hyperbole. It makes the reader realise that the writer was actually *there*, with bombs showering from the skies. Nor can it have been very comfortable to see the stricken *Greyhound* sink in "about twenty minutes".

In another part of the Battle of Crete, Philip's uncle, Captain Louis Mountbatten, had brought the flotilla under his command into the conflict. On the morning of 23 May a formation of twenty four dive-bombers attacked Mountbatten's ship the *Kelly* and the *Kashmir*. Both ships were quickly sunk with a loss of 210 lives. Fortunately the destroyer *Kipling* was nearby and, despite being continually bombed, managed to pick up from the sea 279 officers and men including Louis Mountbatten. It is interesting to wonder whether or not Philip would have ended up by marrying Princess Elizabeth if his Uncle Dickie had perished when the *Kelly* sank. He would certainly have lacked the backing of a patron who, by the end of the war, had emerged as one of the greatest of Allied commanders.

There are various accounts of the aftermath of the loss of the *Kelly*. There is the patriotic image of the *Kipling* carrying Lord Louis and the *Kelly*'s ragged survivors slowly through the fleet while its massed crews gave them a "tremendous roaring ovation". Then there is the version of Philip greeting Lord Louis when he landed "oil-smeared, exhausted, haggard with grief" with an ill-considered joke about "looking like a nigger minstrel". Why did he do it? Gaucheness? Embarrassment? An attempt to hide his own pain at the sight of his bedraggled uncle? At any rate, according to this account, Uncle Dickie "promptly gave him hell for not writing more often, for Philip was a lazy correspondent" (except with Elizabeth?) and Lord Louis a prolific letter-writer. Alexandra of Yugoslavia saw a completely different Louis Mountbatten in Alexandria, "urbane and smiling in white, but furious because he had lost a dressing case of gold-backed brushes". Can it be true? At least this provides ammunition for those who see Lord Louis as a vain and ruthless careerist.

There is one other interesting spin-off from the sinking of the *Kelly*. When, a couple of years later, Noël Coward's film *In Which We Serve*, dramatising the *Kelly*'s fight and tragic end, was released, a copy of the *Daily Express* was shown in one scene, trailing in the gutter, with a close-up of the rash and over-optimistic pre-war tag-line, "There will be no war this year or next year." Lord Beaverbrook, it is said, took it as a calculated, inspired insult, and proof that Lord Mountbatten and his family, including Philip, were enemies of his press empire. The Beaverbrook counter-attack went on for years and will be examined later in the book, but it may well have been partly provoked by the film version of the *Kelly*'s wartime exploits.

HMS *Valiant* did not escape from the Battle of Crete unscathed. Amid the scream of the Stukas and the thud of the recoiling guns, Prince Philip did not notice until much later that she had been hit twice on the quarterdeck. "There were only four casualties," he noted. Not until the crippled ship arrived in Alexandria to be patched up did he discover another big hole. *Valiant* was in dock while the Navy snatched as many British, Australian, New Zealand, and Greek troops as it could from the *Wehrmacht*'s grasp – a Cretan re-run of Dunkirk. Even so, the conquest of Greece's biggest island from the air had been a costly business for the Royal Navy.

Alexandria provided something of a respite for Philip, despite an embarrassing incident when, in charge of the last picket-boat bringing shore-leavers back to the *Valiant*, he rammed the battleship's bows. "Now what the hell have you done?" was the question from the exasperated Duty Boat Shipwright, wearily hauling out his tool-bag once more, to which the midshipman cheerfully replied, "Very sorry, Chippy," and proceeded to lend a hand for two hours of clearing up and hoisting aboard.

And, lo and behold! Who should be in Alexandria but (appropriately enough) cousin Alexandra? And David Milford Haven, whom Alexandra had not apparently seen since that not altogether satisfactory holiday in Venice several years before, though she candidly admits that she had been mainly "worrying about Philip". Still, "for the first time" she found her two cousins "handsome and attractive beaux, most useful for taking me around".

Philip had every cause to feel pleased with himself. After Matapan he had been mentioned in Admiral Cunningham's despatches, and his commander, Admiral Sir Charles Morgan, had noted, "Thanks to his alertness and appreciation of the situation, we were able to sink in five minutes two eight-inch gun cruisers." No medal from the British, however, though King George of Greece was quick to award him the Greek War Cross of Valour. Did he feel slighted? Alexandra congratulated him on the War Cross but, "he simply shrugged". Modesty? Or a feeling of having been awarded a second-class decoration? Alexandra also states that, years later, Philip seems to have had some misgivings over his dexterity with the searchlights at Matapan: "It was as near murder as anything could be in wartime. The cruisers just burst into tremendous sheets of flame." At least his searchlights had been seen scouring the sea for survivors immediately afterwards.

With his cousin David Milford Haven, and sometimes with Alexandra, Philip went swimming and drinking and made the most of Alexandria's night life. It was not all fun. The city was bombed, the port's oil tanks went up in flames and the midshipman's Journal noted, rather impatiently, "All Egyptians with their famillies [sic] and those who can afford it, evacuated themselves to Cairo. The result is that there are no taxis to be had, and very few Gharry's." He did acquire, however, "an absurdly small car", though how he did it is not clear.

Soon, cousin Alexandra, "distressed at leaving them [Philip and David Milford Haven] behind", was sent off to the comparative safety of Cairo. Interestingly, "Philip soon tracked us to Shepheard's Hotel. In his little wasp of a car we went out to the Ghezira Club, swam or just talked through the long . . . afternoons when he was off duty. We explored the old bazaars and the magnificent botanical gardens, or in chatty mood went to Grappi's for tea."

A few fascinating pieces of information emerge from all that chatting. One is that "Philip used to talk even at this time of a home of his own, a country house in England." Surely not Sandringham? They talked of Princess Alice: "Philip did not think the Nazis would disturb her and indeed was philosophic on the score that his sisters had married Germans. There was no news of Uncle Andrew in Monte Carlo. But after all, the war could not last very long. . . ."

Even when Alexandra and some of her relations sailed from Port Said, bound for South Africa, they had not seen the last of Philip. He turned up, only a week or two later, at "Groote Schuur" General Smuts' official home near Cape Town. What was he doing? Pursuing Alexandra at last with the amorous intent that had been so clearly lacking in the past? Alas, (for her), no. He had left the *Valiant* in June 1941 to take his sub-lieutenant's examination in Britain. With four other midshipmen he had boarded a troopship at Port Said bound for the Cape run back to Britain.

At Cape Town he took a short shore leave and, typically and indefatigably, went off in a car belonging to Crown Princess Frederika to explore Cape Province. He saw something of Alexandra, though, and she recounts one particularly significant episode:

One evening in Cape Town, when I wanted to chat, Philip insisted on finishing a letter he was writing and I cousin-like [and jealous?], enquired, "Who's it to?"

"Lilibet," he answered.

"Who?" I asked, still rather mystified.

"Princess Elizabeth in England."

"But she's only a baby," I said, still rather puzzled as he sealed the letter. Aha, I thought with family candour, he knows he's going to England and he's angling for invitations.

Maybe there was something in it – the angling for invitations, that is. But there was obviously a great deal more than this in the letters to, and from, Elizabeth, even though, for his part, they were more likely to contain bluff descriptions of the life he was leading than passionate endearments. Still, something was plainly going on. Indeed, according to Alexandra, she eventually "learned that Philip had sent Lilibet a Christmas card from Athens in 1940 and the ever-polite Princess discovered with alarm that he was not on the Family's Christmas mailing list. Long into the New Year [1941] she was still bothering Uncle Bertie [George V I] to send a return card. 'As long as he gets it I don't mind,' she wrote. The following year she carefully chose a card for Philip herself."

Once back in Britain, Philip would have the opportunity to put his contact with Elizabeth on to a firmer, more direct, footing. First, though, he had to get there. He eventually left South Africa to take his sub-lieutenant's examinations in June 1941, aboard an old transport, bound first of all for Halifax, Nova Scotia, to pick up a detachment of Canadian troops. En route, the captain made the mistake of putting in at Puerto Rico where the Chinese stokers jumped ship and made off. The midshipmen aboard were ordered to "volunteer" to take their place. Instead of sitting back and enjoying the voyage, Philip and his fellow midshipmen found themselves shovelling coal in the boiler room. He was eventually rewarded with a certificate as a "trimmer" from the captain to thank him for his labour in the antiquated boiler room. New stokers came aboard at Newport, Virginia, where Philip, true to form, used the brief stop-over to hire a car and drive to Washington for a quick visit. Joining the Navy had certainly helped him to see the world, as well as the sea. The final stage of the voyage home, via Halifax, was uneventful.

He passed the sub-lieutenant's examinations with ease and distinction. He then went back to sea in HMS *Wallace*, an elderly destroyer, as a sub-lieutenant with nine months seniority out of a possible ten. Promotion to First Lieutenant and second-in-command came in October 1942 when, at twenty-one, he was one of the youngest seconds-in-command in the Royal Navy. A rapid rise: due to natural ability, or the Mountbatten connection, or maybe a mixture of the two?

There was no cause to doubt his ability to run a tight ship. *Wallace* was engaged on the unglamorous but hazardous work of escorting convoys down the east coast of Britain from Rosyth to Sheerness. Now in his third year in the Navy, he was popular among his fellow officers but had made few close friends – hence his reputation for being somewhat reserved. Despite his attraction for the opposite sex, he was no pin-up to his crews – few naval officers who run a tight ship ever are. Testimonials from shipmates interviewed years later provide little in the way of fulsome praise for Lieutenant Philip of Greece. Most said he was a perfectionist, a naval euphemism for a disciplinarian; he was intolerant of sloppy work, and bawled out offenders – which was at least good for discipline. He was strict but, as they usually add, fair; he did not cut corners and worked as hard as he expected others to do. His way of doing things in the Navy is still characteristic of him. That he was by no means insensitive about the men who served with him has emerged on several occasions when spontaneous reunions with past shipmates have occurred during various royal visits. He knew the names of all the ratings who served under him aboard *Wallace* and, doubtless, on other vessels as well.

Very much concerned to establish his ship's reputation as the finest in the squadron, Philip encountered some competition from HMS *Lauderdale*. He soon traced the threat to *Wallace*'s supremacy to his opposite number in *Lauderdale*, Lieutenant Michael Parker, an intelligent and direct Australian who had transferred to the Royal Navy a year before the war. The two men met, recognised fellow spirits, and became close friends. They spent some boisterous leaves together, and shared a love of the ridiculous. A rare, and ultimately inconvenient, relationship had been established.

While at Scapa Flow and Rosyth, Philip could at least enjoy shore leaves on British soil, except for a brief period in July 1943 when *Wallace* was dispatched to the Mediterranean to patrol the sea while American airborne troops and British paratroops descended on Sicily. Part of Philip's assignment was to protect the British Eighth Army divisions which invaded the beaches.

Apart from the Mediterranean excursion, First Lieutenant Mountbatten made the most of his leaves in Britain. In November 1943 *Wallace* was taken into dock for a refit which lasted four months. That Christmas Philip, who had, in his own words, "nowhere particular to go", was invited to spend the holiday with the royal family at Windsor Castle. He arrived on Christmas Eve, looking rather weather-beaten but as handsome as ever. There were nine to dinner that night: the King and Queen, Elizabeth and Margaret, Philip, and four others. Apparently the visiting naval officer entertained them at dinner by giving a humorous account of German dive-bombers attacking HMS *Wallace* off the coast of Sicily; it was doubtless meant to impress the father as well as the daughter, and apparently did.

The Christmas festivities at Windsor in 1943 have since generated a good deal of speculation as to whether this was the occasion when Philip and Elizabeth became identified as a "couple". The Duke of Edinburgh believes not: "I thought not all that much about it, I think. We used to correspond occasionally. You see it's difficult to visualise. I suppose if I'd just been a casual acquaintance it would all have been frightfully significant. But if you're related . . . it isn't so extraordinary to be on a kind of family relationship terms with somebody. You don't necessarily have to think about marriage." True, but it seems that Princess Elizabeth's thoughts at that time were not so far away from a possible marriage.

None of this was in the open, of course. There were ghost stories after dinner, with the lights out. Princess Margaret later wrote, "We settled ourselves to be frightened, and we were NOT. Most disappointing!" Alexandra of Yugoslavia allows herself a little speculation here: "But was it so disappointing to Lilibet and Philip, close together in the shadows for perhaps the first time?" Alas, who can say?

Then there were the amateur pantomimes, a Windsor tradition dear to the royal family. The costumes were, as usual, first-rate, though King George made sure that Elizabeth, as Principal Boy, was not wearing too short a costume. The jokes were not for the fastidious:

Widow Twankey: There are three acres and one rood.
Princess Margaret: We don't want anything improper.
Widow Twankey: There's a large copper in the kitchen.
Princess Elizabeth: We'll soon get rid of him.

It was clear who was getting all the best lines. In the audience Prince Philip "was nearly falling out of his seat with laughter" – which ought to tell us something significant, if only that the extended family shared a taste for dreadful "groan" jokes. According to Miss Crawford, Elizabeth acted better than she had ever done before: "I have never known Lilibet more animated. There was a sparkle about her none of us had ever seen before."

There was more sparkling to come. On the last night David Milford Haven arrived and a group of young army officers manning the Bofors guns around the castle joined them. They played charades and danced a good deal. Margaret later told "Crawfie" that "David Milford H . . . and Philip went mad."

As the younger sister, Margaret's attitude seems to have been tinged with jealousy. She was already infatuated with the King's good looking aide-de-camp, Group Captain Peter Townsend, and yet could hardly talk about it. Apparently she brought Philip's name up frequently in conversation, perhaps to use as a weapon against her more reserved and vulnerable sister. It was at about this time that the press got hold of the story that Philip's photograph adorned Elizabeth's dressing table. Elizabeth was deeply upset by the ensuing speculation.

Even at this point in his life Philip, if we are to believe his cousin Alexandra, was by no means committed to Elizabeth. While waiting for the *Whelp*, his next vessel, to be finally built, we learn that, "The fascination of Philip had spread rather like influenza, I knew, through a whole string of girls. I always recognised the symptoms, the gushing female chatter about the tall Viking look, the sighs, 'He's such a heart-throb!' " Even though Alexandra was about to marry King Peter of Yugoslavia (another wartime exile who had been in Egypt), she still felt possessive over Philip. She recounts once sitting at his bedside in a suite in Claridges which belonged to a family who had lodged him there while he recovered from a serious bout of 'flu: "I . . . reproached him for not seeing enough of Mummy and myself, while he cheerfully plucked the grapes somebody else had given him and ejected the pips at me with blithe, naval accuracy." A version of the sailor's farewell?

A little later we learn that Alexandra, "Full of my thoughts of Peter . . . twice saw Philip lunching at Claridge's and merely nodded across the room." Clearly those grape pips had done the trick. Just before she married Peter, Alexandra and he went to tea with the King and Queen at Windsor. Elizabeth and Margaret were there.

"We talked of Marina [widowed in August 1942]. . . . We talked of Uncle Dickie and Uncle George [of Greece]. We skimmed the usual huge round of news of uncles and cousins. But Philip was never mentioned."

Was Philip, then, a taboo subject early in 1944? Elizabeth was nearly eighteen. She had been allocated a sitting-room of her own at Windsor and a lady-in-waiting to help her with her correspondence. Soon she was to get her way, despite the King's misgivings, and join the Auxiliary Territorial Service as "No. 230873, Second Subaltern Elizabeth Alexandra Mary Windsor", where she learnt to service motor engines and tended to converse earnestly on the subject of sparking-plugs.

The King, who identified closely with her as one shy person with another, could not bring himself to believe that his eldest daughter had fallen irrevocably in love with the first eligible male she had met. Yet the correspondence with Philip grew more intense; there were more visits to Windsor and Buckingham Palace ("I'd call in and have a meal" is how the Duke of Edinburgh has put it); all the signs of an increasingly serious attachment were there. At Alexandra's wedding to Peter of Yugoslavia, King George II of Greece (the "King of Claridge's") seized the opportunity of putting in a warm word for Philip's claim. George VI indicated that Philip should think no more about it for the present.

In March 1944 the King delivered an authoritative, though interim, private pronouncement: "We both think she is too young for that now," George VI wrote, "as she has never met any young men of her own age. . . . I like Philip. He is intelligent, has a good sense of humour and thinks about things in the right way." Born in a humbler social station, an eighteen-year-old girl might well have agreed that "now" had arrived. Still, the door had been left open, and despite guards officers being drafted in to private parties at royal residences to show the Princess more of "young men her own age", it was to remain open.

By August 1944 HMS *Whelp* was fully commissioned and ready to put into service. Nine months had elapsed since the *Wallace* had been put into dock for a refit, nine months which were crucial in allowing Elizabeth's relationship with Philip to progress from a distant, cousinly correspondence to the point where the King was considering, not without misgivings, the prospect of his daughter's marriage. It is interesting to speculate what would have happened if the *Wallace* had remained in service during this period.

Was Philip's posting to the *Whelp*, which was due for far-eastern service, the result of Lord Mountbatten's belief that it was better to remove his nephew for a time from too frequent contact with Elizabeth? Certainly Mountbatten had played a large part in getting Philip the commission, just as he had taken up the cause of his nephew's application for British citizenship. As it happened, *Whelp* sailed for the Mediterranean before British citizenship could be granted and Philip was obliged to drop the matter once more. The brand new destroyer's ultimate destination was to join the 27th Destroyer Flotilla of the Pacific Fleet, then fighting the Japanese navy off Burma and Sumatra, and working towards the eventual invasion and overthrow of Japan itself. As Supreme Allied Commander in South-East Asia, Lord Mountbatten was, to say the least, a useful relative for the First Lieutenant of the *Whelp* to have, a usefulness proved beyond reasonable doubt when Michael Parker was simultaneously assigned to HMS *Wessex*, a destroyer in the same flotilla.

While waiting for the *Whelp* to be commissioned, Philip had spent some time in Newcastle, making regular visits to supervise the work on the destroyer. He lived in a small hotel, paying six guineas a week for his room, which was a large slice of his lieutenant's pay of eleven pounds. He lived modestly, used public transport, and remained unrecognised, or rather unidentified, since few people in these parts knew of his existence until news of the presence in their city of some obscure Greek prince reached the *Newcastle Journal*. The editor promptly assigned a young girl reporter to track down the foreigner and interview him. Olga Franklin, later to become famous as a leading British journalist, certainly made the most of this intriguing subject.

When she found the prince she was disappointed and fascinated – he was not her idea of a dark, brooding, semi-oriental Greek, but a cheerful, down-to-earth cosmopolitan: "Few workers in a North-East shipyard", she wrote, "are aware that the tall, ash-blond First Lieutenant, R.N., who travels by bus to work among them each day, is a royal prince." Wartime secrecy prevented her from giving many details, but she did mention that the prince was living quietly in an hotel while "standing by" on a British destroyer. She added that he had "the looks of a typical Prince of a Hans Andersen fairy tale" and would have been noticed already by many a girl worker at the shipyard. She was surprised that he did not find the northern dialect difficult to understand: "I understand the local people perfectly," he assured her with some amusement, adding diplomatically, "and I am enjoying my stay." He then said, less than accurately that he had "been to England twice before – to school." Olga's piece, cut down to size from reams of enthusiastic copy, was the first interview with Philip to appear in the British Press. Though she could not have known it at the time, it was an intriguing scoop.

HMS *Whelp* and Philip left England only a few weeks before the war in Europe took a sensational turn. On the eastern front the *Wehrmacht*, its back broken at Stalingrad, was reeling back before the Red Army; Italy was being finally wrenched away from the Axis; the balance of air power had shifted in the Allies' favour; and the great assault on the Normandy beaches signalled the arduous, bloody, irresistible liberation of the Continent. As the final struggle to overthrow Nazi Germany began, the royal family, the British government and Lord Mountbatten must have been relieved to see Philip continue his naval service on the other side of the world.

Philip and Michael Parker were reunited at the Australian base of their flotilla. They set about exploring Parker's home ground. Philip met his friend's family and there were celebrations, some of them raucous. Sydney, Melbourne, wherever he went, the Greek prince, who, in some quarters, was confidently expected to become Princess Elizabeth's husband, was received with intense interest, though his popularity probably owed more to his social dexterity and spontaneous informality. It seems that he was never in greater form than on this Australian visit, almost as if it was his last fling before succumbing to the restrictions of royal etiquette – though that impression may owe much to the wisdom of hindsight.

Michael Parker was adept at organising parties, and assorted extravaganzas, and soon there were exaggerated tales of irresistible blondes and brunettes, daughters of publishers, sultry-eyed steel heiresses, girls with strings of huge department stores, and heiresses to farming fortunes yapping around Philip's heels. In the face of such tempting opportunities he was, in fact, remarkably restrained, behaving with quite extraordinary tact – a quality not always associated with him – and learning to live under constant observation. He had developed a capacity for non-involvement in these matters, though was still able to enjoy himself.

While *Whelp* was having a comparatively quiet time, the war in Europe was going well. Although Philip and his fellow officers were kept informed about the progress of the Allied armies, one piece of news that did not reach him until much later was the death of his brother-in-law, Christopher of Hesse, who perished while flying with the *Luftwaffe* over Italy. Hesse's death at least allowed Philip to avoid the grave embarrassment he would have faced as Elizabeth's suitor had Sophie's husband survived to bear the consequences of his association with some of the most reprehensible elements in the Nazi regime.

Allied military progress in two areas had a special meaning for Philip – the landings in the South of France and the return of British troops to the Greek mainland. He was once more able to communicate freely with his mother in Athens and his father in Monte Carlo, rather than rely on the sparse and garbled messages via Sweden by which the two sides of the family had maintained a tenuous contact. As he had predicted, the indomitable Alice of Greece had survived the German occupation unscathed. Prince Andrew, on the other hand, was in poor health and had developed a heart condition. He died on 3 December 1944, before Philip had the chance to meet him once more – his involvement in the war prevented him from returning to Monte Carlo at that point.

December 1944 was a month of contrasting fortunes in the war. In Europe, the *Wehrmacht* launched its final gamble, a counterattack in the Ardennes; nearer Philip's station, the Americans landed in the Philippines. At the Yalta Conference in February 1945, Churchill, Roosevelt and Stalin marked out their respective spheres of influence as German and Japanese power was slowly destroyed.

Lord Mountbatten had still not finally ejected the Japanese from Burma. He came to Europe for the Potsdam Conference (where Attlee sat in with Churchill) and left with instructions to complete the total defeat of the enemy within a month. On 6 and 9 August 1945 Hiroshima and Nagasaki were each devastated by an atomic bomb and Japan surrendered. Philip was in *Whelp* which, with her sister ship *Wager*, escorted the flotilla's flagship, *The Duke of York*, and joined the US battleship *Missouri* in Tokyo Bay to receive the final Japanese surrender on 2 September 1945. Ten days later, in Singapore Town Hall, Lord Mountbatten accepted the surrender of the 730,000 Japanese in South-East Asia.

The war was over. The *Whelp* and other warships were sent off to pick up and take home prisoners of war. Then the destroyer sailed back to Portsmouth to be decommissioned. During this two month period Philip was in charge – an odd way of getting one's first command. It was early in 1946, and he was back in Britain.

6

Betrothal

ONE OF PRINCE PHILIP'S FIRST ACTIONS when he was granted leave from his duties with *Whelp* was to dine with Princess Elizabeth in her sitting-room at Buckingham Palace. Margaret was there as a chaperone, but it appears that all three enjoyed themselves hugely, the still bearded Philip roaring with laughter as they chased each other along the Palace's long corridors – apparently a common sport among European royalty.

Philip had, however, another duty to fulfil. After consultations with the Greek royal family, he boarded a ship bound for Monte Carlo, where his father had died in 1944. "He was in a sombre mood," said the restaurant manager of the Hôtel de Paris who served him at the table his father had always occupied. Clearing up Prince Andrew's affairs was a melancholy task. The Prince had died penniless, owing a few francs here and there; only a few personal belongings remained intact. Of these Philip kept, and for a time wore, a couple of suits, and had the ivory handle of his father's old shaving brush freshly bristled. It gave him some pleasure to hear that his father had been buried with military honours, his coffin escorted by a French army unit to the cemetery in Nice. With the approval of King George II of the Hellenes, who was about to reclaim his throne, it was arranged for Prince Andrew's remains to be taken to Greece to be reinterred in the royal burial grounds in Tatoi. Philip wrote out the inscription for a simple headstone:

Andrea Vasilopais (Son of a King)
Prince of Greece
Prince of Denmark
1882–1944

In Germany, Philip's sister Sophie started a new chapter in her life. Two years after the death of her husband, she married again, this time to a man of very different calibre. Philip's new brother-in-law was his Salem contemporary, Prince George William of Hanover, son of the Duke of Brunswick, who had served in the German army in the war until discharged under a Nazi decree barring members of the German ruling houses from the armed forces. When Salem School, which had been closed down in 1944, was re-opened after the war, Prince George – although not a trained teacher, took over as headmaster of his old school; several of his, and Philip's, nephews and nieces became his pupils.

Back in Britain the question of Philip's nationality was again raised. Lord Louis Mountbatten was still pressing for his nephew to become a British subject, and it was rumoured that the Prime Minister and both his Home and Foreign Secretaries had been approached over the matter. There had certainly been discussions, if not at such a high level, but it may have been thought wiser not to involve the man who might well be Princess Elizabeth's future husband in public speculation and controversy of any kind. There were other foreign, dynastic implications – notably, the uncertainty as to whether the monarchy would be restored in post-war Greece. Might not Philip's naturalisation indicate a lack of confidence in the stability of the Greek monarchy? But for these various considerations there would have been no problem – foreigners serving in the British forces were liberally accorded British nationality and German refugee scientists working on the atomic bomb had even been naturalised in the middle of the war. But it required careful timing to smooth Philip's transition from one nationality to another, and from the Greek royal house to the House of Windsor.

Had it all been settled, then? Even a considerable time before Philip's well-documented visit to Balmoral in August 1946? The Duke of Edinburgh sees Balmoral as the turning point:

I suppose one thing led to another. I suppose I began to think about it seriously, oh, let me think now, when I got back in 'forty-six and went to Balmoral. It was probably then that we,

111

that it became, you know, that we began to think about it seriously, and even talk about it.

Perhaps not as crystal clear as one might like, but a rough and ready sort of date all the same. Is it, however, right? From the Dartmouth meeting, via "Chips" Channon's breathless revelation from Athens, right through the early 'forties – with letter-writing, Windsor pantomimes, photographs of bearded naval officers on dressing tables, and so forth – a relationship was clearly developing. Even if it had not been particularly serious at first on Prince Philip's side, it had undoubtedly been taken seriously by Princess Elizabeth. In any case, what possible purpose could he have had in feeding a rather shy and sheltered girl's fantasies, if not to bring her closer to him? It was, after all, rather different from flirting with eager and brassy heiresses to business fortunes. The King-Emperor's daughter was involved.

There is, moreover, a good deal of evidence to show that the relationship was a matter of serious consideration within the royal family, well before the significant step of inviting Philip to Balmoral was taken. In 1945, with the war drawing to a close and Philip's return growing more imminent, it seems that Princess Elizabeth was pressing, with more self-confidence, for her parents to recognise the true state of her feelings. One symbol of this growing assertiveness, always difficult for a naturally retiring person who was so closely linked to a possessive father, was the celebrated photograph of Philip in her room. The first photograph displayed brought about a rebuke from her father for her lack of discretion, but it was merely replaced by a photograph showing the beloved naval officer bearded and thus somewhat disguised. Nobody had been put off the scent, and it was at this time that the first rumours of the romance appeared in the press.

A further indication of how seriously Elizabeth's attachment to Philip was taken by her father lies in his attempts to put other eligible young men in her path. Earlier reference has been made to the rather forced gaiety of the parties organised at Windsor and elsewhere, when suitably blue-blooded young guards officers were positively encouraged to cluster round Elizabeth, and the King himself led congas round the ballroom.

Queen Mary was not hoodwinked for a moment. As formidable and upright as ever, Elizabeth's grandmother rather disapproved of the clumps of young men, referring to them as the "Body Guard".

She took Elizabeth's part with some vigour. Her lady-in-waiting, Lady Airlie, once said to her that she herself had fallen in love at nineteen, then Princess Elizabeth's age, and that it had lasted for ever. Queen Mary's own marriage had hardly been the result of spontaneous attraction: her intended first husband, the Duke of Clarence, Edward VII's elder son, had died in 1892 of pneumonia before she could marry him, a tragedy immortalised in a contemporary popular ballad:

> A nation wrapped in mourning,
> Shed bitter tears today,
> For the noble Duke of Clarence,
> And fair young Princess May.

With an admirable, and prudent, closing of ranks the royal family had handed Princess Mary on to the Duke of Clarence's younger brother, the future King George V. Although the resulting marriage had been remarkably successful, Queen Mary in her old age seems strongly to have approved of her granddaughter's "unarranged" choice of future husband. At any rate, she replied to Lady Airlie, "Elizabeth seems that kind of a girl. She would always know her own mind. There's something very steadfast and determined about her." On another occasion, fun was made of Prince Philip's education at Gordonstoun, "a crank school with theories of completely social equality where the boys were taught to mix with all and sundry". What sort of a background was that? Would it prove useful or useless for a future consort? Queen Mary "bestowed upon the questioner one of her most withering looks. 'Useful,' she said shortly."

If the "Body Guard" was not making much progress, it was entirely due to Elizabeth's preference for naval as opposed to military tactics. Nonetheless, rumours appeared, particularly in the American press as to her likely choice of marriage partners. There was Charles Fitzroy, Earl of Euston, and Charles Manners, Duke of Rutland, first mentioned in 1943, and both graduates of Eton, Cambridge and the Grenadier Guards. Really, what more could any girl want? Then there was the Prince Regent, Charles of Belgium, who despite hovering on the brink of middle age was unmarried. Philip of Greece, it is true, was mentioned once, but only as a second-ran to Charles of Belgium's first place.

Alexandra of Yugoslavia has left an account of Philip and Elizabeth's relationship at this time, as she perceived it. First, there is a glimpse, before the end of the war, of a meeting in Windsor Great Park: "Once we were a little astonished to find he had come home on leave, for we met him walking there with Lilibet and Margaret and their cousin Lord Elphinstone. We exchanged greetings but asked no questions: it was never polite to ask questions in wartime."

On another occasion, walking with her husband Peter:

Two of the royal corgis dashed through the bracken and when we looked round expecting to see Uncle Bertie and Aunt Elizabeth, it was Philip and Lilibet, walking alone. They were so intent in conversation that we decided not to bother them so we just waved and walked on. They seemed relieved to be left in peace. "Could be," said Peter, reading my thoughts. "But for goodness sake . . . they're only out for a walk." This, however, was the first of several encounters. We used to see them holding hands, disengaging themselves sometimes until we came closer and they could see it was only us. Few people wander in the Great Park and it formed an idyllic setting.

One of the few people with whom Philip discussed his feelings at this time was Marina, the widowed Duchess of Kent, a Greek cousin who had already been fully accepted into the royal family. At Coppins, her home in Buckinghamshire, Philip and Elizabeth could meet conveniently and without attracting public attention. At this stage, everything was done to avoid premature discussion of the relationship.

Cousin Alexandra discussed it, though, and with Princess Marina. The discussion reveals rather more about Alexandra than about Philip. Here is Alexandra's version in full:

"I only hope Philip isn't just flirting with her," I once told Marina. "He's so attractive he flirts without realising it."

Marina said soberly, "I think his flirting days are over. He would be the one to be hurt now if it was all just a flirtation or if — if it is not to be. One thing I'm sure about, those two would never do anything to hurt each other."

"Well, let's touch wood they don't have to wait so long for their engagement and wedding as we did," I replied.

"They will probably have to wait much longer than you did," said Marina. And she added with a smile, "I won't be able to influence Uncle Bertie for Lilibet nearly as easily as I did for you."

114

Uncle Bertie, King George VI, was indeed difficult to influence. In part, it was a genuine and admirable concern lest his daughter should make an unsuitable choice of husband – in fact, an irrevocable choice in those days when divorce was unthinkable for British monarchs and when a decade earlier a King-Emperor had been obliged to abdicate in order to marry a divorced woman. But there was also a kingly possessiveness that often passed for devotion. Lady Airlie indeed "wondered sometimes whether he was secretly dreading the prospect of an early marriage for her". Having behaved, on the whole, as an over-protective father to his daughter, George VI was reluctant to abandon that protectiveness finally by handing Princess Elizabeth over to another man.

While the King held back, Scotland Yard's Special Branch was making enquiries about the young man's background. Perhaps there was some unacceptable skeleton in the royal cupboard? There were certainly those at court who questioned the wisdom of the proposed marriage. It has been suggested that Peter Townsend was one of these. Group Captain Townsend, a handsome ex-fighter pilot who had fought with distinction in the Battle of Britain, had been an equerry to George VI since 1944. Townsend proved adept at coping with the irritation and unreasonableness that, as well as the stammer, were often the surface expressions of George VI's deep-laid insecurities. Calm, strong, reliable and discreet, Townsend became a close confidant of the King.

Why would Townsend wish, as some allege, to obstruct Philip's attachment to Elizabeth? There have been some unlikely suggestions: that the man who had fought with "the Few" despised Philip's war record – Matapan being a poor exchange for the Battle of Britain; that it was the result of RAF-Royal Navy rivalry – which sounds ludicrous; that Townsend, perhaps subconsciously, resented Philip's more or less open relationship with Elizabeth, while his own chances of building a similarly close relationship with the lively and strong-willed Princess Margaret were minimal – mainly because he was already, if unhappily, married.

There is, of course, another explanation: that Townsend was simply doing his duty by discussing the King's anxieties on the subject with him, and at the same time pointing out various obstacles that might hamper a marriage between Philip and Elizabeth. There was, admittedly, enough to worry about. Some of those at court drew attention to the danger that Philip might be compromised by his German relatives. Even though Christopher of

Hesse was dead, there were still two brothers-in-law who had only recently been fighting against the Crown. What if they became entangled in the investigations, then in progress, into German war crimes? Albert, the Prince Consort, had suffered periodically from the expression of anti-foreigner and particularly anti-German sentiments. Since such feelings were at that time running high among the British people, as they counted the fearful cost of Hitler's war, might not Philip's "German connections" prove inconvenient and embarrassing to the royal family?

Nor was the Greek connection much happier. The King of the Hellenes was back in Athens, but for how long? There was a Communist rebellion against the crown, and Russia was arming the rebels. If Greece rejected the monarchy yet again, would King George VI be obliged to save his future son-in-law's relatives from the firing squad, much as Philip's father had been saved by George V? Would the Attlee government approve of a Greek prince being taken into the royal family? Was the risk of diplomatic conflict worth taking? Did the Greek government want the marriage as a guarantee of British support? Moreover, Philip was a member of the Greek Orthodox Church, a grave handicap for one aspiring to become consort of the future head of the Anglican Church – though, no doubt, this problem could be taken care of.

These diplomatic and, to a far lesser extent, spiritual problems might have had more weight if Princess Elizabeth had been torn with doubt – but she clearly was not. Furthermore, if there were those at court intriguing against Philip, there was Lord Louis Mountbatten, one of the nation's war heroes, and very close to the King, strongly supporting his nephew's claim.

While the matter of his suitability to become Elizabeth's husband was discussed further, Philip went back to work. In view of his now intimate link with the royal family, it was decided to keep him at home stations for the time being. His first posting was to HMS *Glendower* of Pwllheli, a naval training establishment. In the early autumn of 1946 he went on to HMS *Royal Arthur*, a school for petty officers at Corsham. There his duties as an instructor were to bring the outmoded curriculum up to modern naval requirements, something of which he had much practical and recent experience. He was left to devise a programme and teaching method on his own initiative; according to a biographical pamphlet put out by the British Information Services, "Only officers with a high record of leadership are selected for these duties."

The camp on the fringe of Corsham was a dreary collection of Nissen huts. Philip has never pretended that he particularly enjoyed this period in his life. As second-in-command of a house of eighty (out of two hundred) trainees he was as conscientious an officer as ever, whether watching a physical training demonstration, marking his pupils' papers meticulously, or, with his hands behind his back in the now familiar pose, inspecting the members of his course. Then there were lectures on current affairs to give, each requiring a fair amount of mugging-up on political and naval history. During leisure activities he was a confident opening batsman on the cricket field.

In the evenings there were excursions to the Methuen Arms, the local pub, where he and his fellow instructors drank and played a game of darts or skittles. With his naval colleagues, Philip tested his skill against the local skittles team, "The Moonrakers". It was all very ordinary. It was a long time before some of the regulars knew who he was.

One of his fellow officers was Lieutenant-Commander P. R. G. Worth, who had been to Cheam with him, and they sometimes did some gardening together. Most evenings, apparently, eschewing the delights of the Methuen Arms and Nellie and Phyllis the barmaids, Philip went to bed early, sleeping in an iron bedstead with the flag of *Whelp* above his head. His personal belongings on the sideboard showed something about him; apart from his pipes and lighter fuel, they included a Greek royal medallion, a Bible, manuals on seamanship, "The King's Regulations", "Admiralty Instructions", and leather-framed photographs of his father and of Princess Elizabeth.

Philip's shore-based naval activities were punctuated by a highly significant event. He was invited to spend part of the summer holiday of 1946 at Balmoral Castle with the royal family. What could the purpose of the invitation be, other than to give the King and Queen a lengthy period of time with the man their daughter wished to marry and thus enable them to decide whether an engagement should be sanctioned? It has been suggested that Peter Townsend was the instigator of this plan, that he proposed it as a further piece of vetting of Philip. "What infernal cheek," the Duke of Edinburgh was supposed to have exclaimed in the presence of a friend when the matter cropped up years later, "for a man who was already heading for divorce to set himself up as a marriage counsellor."

In fact, it is possible to view the invitation to Balmoral in another light. The King and Queen knew that the Greek government, with the monarchy's restoration recently confirmed by plebiscite, was not keen to have a Greek prince renounce his nationality so inconveniently close to the plebiscite; this imposed a further delay on the announcement of an engagement. Why not, therefore, make use of the delay, to find out more about Philip and to observe his relationship with Elizabeth? It must have seemed perfectly natural.

Prince Philip seems unaware of any skulduggery or vetting, telling Basil Boothroyd that it was at Balmoral that, "We, that it became, you know, that we began to think about it seriously and even talk about it. And then there was their excursion to South Africa, and it was sort of fixed up when they came back. That's really what happened."

In reality, it must have been rather an ordeal. Balmoral was hardly a cosy country cottage where Philip and Elizabeth could enjoy hours of intimate solitude. There were the other guests, and the eyes of the King and Queen, and Margaret and Townsend, upon them – even if discreetly. At a later stage, the Duke of Edinburgh talked light-heartedly about Balmoral – the company, as he put it, was exquisite but the comforts were not so far ahead of Corsham. He had a brass bedstead and a brass washstand, painted white – with no running water; the bathroom and toilet were at the far end of a very long corridor. Only the hunting trophies, hides, antlers, stags' heads, paintings of Scottish landscapes and the tartan mats relieved these austere surroundings.

Some days were spent deer-stalking, described as follows by Alexandra of Yugoslavia (whose husband, Peter, had also had the "Balmoral treatment"): "the appalling deer-stalks when one trudges for miles and miles into the hills behind some dour and determined ghillie. Philip had to fight off the swarming flies and mosquitoes just like Peter. He, too, I think, borrowed Elizabeth's rifle to bag his first deer." Still, it was not all incredibly hard work. The slaughtered deer was normally carried by a pony until the road was reached, where "the visitor finds a chauffeur waiting, saluting, and he sinks filthy and exhausted into the plush luxury of a limousine to be driven home."

In the evenings there were the games and charades without which no royal holiday was complete. Dinner was at 9.15, with the King in black tie, jacket and kilt. After dinner, fiddles, piano and bagpipes struck up in the sitting-room and space was cleared for Highland reels. Whether Lieutenant Philip of Greece's expertise at Scottish dancing influenced the vetting we do not know.

Then there were the walks through gratifyingly beautiful coun-
tryside. At some point on such a walk, Prince Philip proposed to
Elizabeth. She, apparently without a thought for Greek plebiscites,
paternal possessiveness, or the state of sterling, unhesitatingly
accepted him. Many column inches have been spent portraying the
imagined scene. There is a general romantic insistence on the proposal taking place beside "some well-loved loch, the white clouds
overhead and the curlew crying". Maybe. Maybe not.

A popular account in *Elizabeth and Philip* by Louis Wulff, published a year later for the royal wedding, paints a more
unashamedly romantic picture:

> It was in the romantic setting of the Highlands, amid the great
> mountains and wide moors that stretch around Balmoral Castle,
> the King's home in Scotland, that the Princess and Philip really
> decided they were in love and would marry. In August 1946 a
> fair-haired, tall young man in well-fitting sports clothes went out
> with the King and other guns on the "Glorious Twelfth". . . . It
> was his first appearance at Balmoral, where he had been invited
> by the King and Queen to stay for a few weeks, and among the
> ghillies and keepers the news that "Philip's here" spread quickly.
> Princess Elizabeth holds a place of her own in the hearts of the
> proud and independent men who tend the King's Scottish estates
> . . . so when they found that this year her eyes seemed even
> brighter, her smile even readier, her happiness more infectious,
> because of the presence of the young naval gentleman, there was
> nothing too much that a ghillie or keeper could do for Philip.
> And, as anyone knows who has spent a shooting or fishing
> holiday in the Highlands, to establish that happy relationship
> with the men who know the forests and streams is to ensure a
> good holiday. For the deep hearts of the ghillies are not easy to win.

No, indeed. Apart from the ghillies, however, could the King be
won over? According to one version, Philip promptly went and
"talked seriously" to King George VI in his study. But "there were
still too many difficulties. The idea of an engagement was tacitly
accepted but Philip was nevertheless advised to wait, at least for six
months, and maybe more, before it could be made public." In other
words, there would be the essentially unsatisfactory and confused
pattern of unofficial engagement and the need to maintain strict
secrecy. Apart from the King's deep-seated inability to let go of his

daughter, there was another powerful reason why the engagement could not be announced officially. This centred on the proposed Royal Tour of South Africa which was scheduled to take place early in 1947, and which the King viewed as a repayment for Prime Minister Smuts' successful struggle to bring the Dominion into the war in 1939 against the feelings of many Afrikaner Nationalist members of parliament. Moreover, Princess Elizabeth would attain her twenty-first birthday while in South Africa, and it was planned to mark the occasion by some sort of ceremony of dedication – a radio broadcast to the Empire and Commonwealth as it turned out. It would have been extremely inconvenient to have this important royal tour diverted from its original purpose by a public announcement of an engagement that would grab the headlines and turn the world's attention to a forthcoming wedding.

Princess Elizabeth accepted the good sense of this. She was essentially an obedient and supportive daughter and conceived it to be her duty to set aside her personal wishes until the South African tour was completed. George VI recognised her forbearance when he later wrote to her, perhaps a little guiltily, "I was rather anxious that you had thought I was being very hard-hearted about it. I was so anxious for you to come to South Africa as you knew. Our family, us four, the 'Royal Family' must remain together with additions of course at suitable moments!!"

The next obvious "addition" had clearly got to wait – for the best part of a year as it happened. There had been a discreet celebration at Balmoral after Philip's proposal had been accepted, an unofficial engagement party. Also, instructions went out to various experts, constitutional, genealogical and otherwise, to ponder the matter of Philip's name (an alternative had to be found to the unwieldy and distinctly foreign "Schleswig-Holstein-Sonderburg-Glücksburg" – and possibly "Beck"), his future title, his religion, the couple's future residence, and a score of other problems.

He stayed at Balmoral for some time longer than had been planned, perhaps anxious to please the King and Queen and to prove his worthiness. He rode with Elizabeth, with Townsend and Margaret behind as chaperones. Was Townsend hoping for him to make some tactical error of judgement? In a sense he did. He outstayed his welcome, and George VI finally grew impatient, saying, "The boy must go south!" Philip's departure caused Elizabeth a good deal of unhappiness, but Margaret was apparently as supportive and sisterly as she had been from the outset.

Would news of the secret engagement leak out? Some had already observed that Philip's presence at Balmoral had been recorded in the King's Game Book, and that his name had appeared in the Court Circular on 16 August 1946. His next public appearance with the royal family in October gave little away. As Lord Mountbatten's nephew, he was one of the ushers at the wedding at Romsey Abbey of his cousin, Lady Patricia Mountbatten, Lord Louis' elder daughter, to the seventh Baron Brabourne. It was a lavish affair attended by the King, the Queen and the two princesses. Philip conducted the royal family to their seats. He was most helpful to the press and readily supplied one reporter with information about the identity and background of some of the guests. However, a newsreel film of him helping Elizabeth take off her coat clearly revealed affection jostling with discretion.

More openly he sometimes drove from Corsham's wind-swept huts to Buckingham Palace in a small car at speeds which were to cause a scandal when he skidded and twisted a knee a month before the wedding: "Philip: Take it Easy!" said the *Sunday Pictorial* in tones of motherly anguish. He was still a Greek prince, serving as a lieutenant in the navy and earning eleven pounds a week.

It was impossible, however, to stem the rumours. Early in September 1947 an official statement had been issued from Buckingham Palace, firmly denying the newspaper rumours of an engagement. Undeterred, one newspaper again dug up the Earl of Euston's name, and that of the Duke of Rutland. Others were not deceived, taking the official denial as tantamount to confirmation in the curious fashion of these rituals. Still, Princess Elizabeth was soon to embark for South Africa; that hardly brought a marriage any nearer.

At the end of January 1947 the royal family dined at Lord and Lady Mountbatten's house at Chester Street. Philip was there. Mountbatten's valet, John Dean, although he had previously come across Elizabeth's photograph among Philip's possessions when he slept at Chester Street, did not detect any particular bond between Philip and Elizabeth. It was, after all, a family gathering of considerable moment, and feelings were bound to be running high: the royal family were due to leave in two days' time for South Africa, and the Mountbattens were soon to sail for India and the testing duties of viceregal rule. Clearly Philip and Elizabeth were being as discreet as they had been at Balmoral, where several guests had failed to detect any special relationship between them. However, the Chester Street dinner was obviously of particular significance, with the diners drinking champagne – apart from George VI who drank whisky from a little decanter at his side. Was it a celebration or an occasion for mourning? One description states that "Lord Louis was in tremendous form, preparing to be Viceroy of India. Philip and Elizabeth were rather wet blankets."

The royal family embarked on 1 February, sailing in the new battleship, the 40,000 ton HMS *Vanguard*. The tour lasted until the middle of May. If one purpose of separating Philip and Elizabeth in this way was to test the strength of her feelings for him during a prolonged absence, there was no doubt about the result. The princess frequently seemed subdued and in low spirits during the tour. She waited anxiously for letters from Philip, once, according to a member of the touring party, only throwing off depression when several arrived in one post – as letters from overseas are apt to do. Yet she was also dutiful and considerate to her parents: she spent much of the sixteen-day voyage to South Africa closeted with the King working on the speech she was to deliver on her twenty-first birthday; when climbing in the Matopos Hills in Rhodesia she gave her footsore mother her shoes and went on barefoot.

Her birthday speech was both an act of self-dedication to her future subjects and an attempt to emphasise the binding qualities of the crown throughout an Empire that, with India on the brink of independence, was within sight of disintegration. Her girlish voice, carried by radio waves to all of her father's subjects who would hear it, pronounced a declaration of duty:

> I declare before you all that my whole life, whether it be short or long, shall be devoted to your service and the service of our great Imperial Commonwealth to which we all belong. But I shall not have strength to carry out this resolution unless you join in it with me, as I now invite you to do; I know that your support will be unfailingly given. God bless all of you who are willing to share it.

It was to be the first of many speeches.

When Princess Elizabeth stepped ashore at the end of the tour she "noticeably had an inner radiance", despite Philip not being there to greet her. He had at least achieved something profitable in her absence: he had obtained British citizenship, which incidentally enabled him to respond officially to the call for support of loyal subjects contained in the birthday speech. Early in 1947 Philip had appeared in a list of names of newly naturalised subjects: there were over eight hundred of them, many of them German Jews who had fled from Hitler, but also Poles and other Europeans who had fought in the British forces during the war. Like them, he paid a ten pound fee for the privilege.

The marriage, though, seemed no nearer. George VI was concerning himself with further insubstantial obstacles. What should Philip's surname be? "Oldcastle" was suggested by the College of Heralds as an anglicised version of Oldenburg – an ancient German ducal family from which the Danish royal house had sprung. Prince Philip was favourably disposed, but the Labour Home Secretary, Mr Chuter Ede, thought "something grander and more glittering" could be found. Perhaps he was seeking some relief for a Britain struggling through a post-war austerity era recently compounded by a bitter winter and fuel shortages. Moreover "Oldcastle" was somehow redolent of grim-faced factory owners in harsh northern towns: "There's trouble at t'mill, Mr Oldcastle" – that sort of thing.

Eventually, Mountbatten was suggested. At least it emphasised his mother's (British) side of the family rather than his father's. It was, moreover, his uncle's name, and all the more illustrious for that. Uncle Dickie was naturally "delighted" at the suggestion, all the more so because it was his idea! After all, it symbolised a dynastic come-back of prodigious proportions after the humiliation of Louis of Battenberg in 1914. Prince Philip was, in fact, "not madly in favour of the proposal. . . . But in the end I was persuaded, and anyway I couldn't think of a reasonable alternative." That sounds rather grudging, but is perhaps an indication of his strong desire to be his own man rather than the appendage of a rich and famous uncle. "Mountbatten", however, would hardly be a ball and chain to drag through life.

At the same time as he acquired British citizenship, Philip ceased to be a prince of Greece. From 1947 until 1957 he was either plain Lieutenant Mountbatten or, far less plain, the Duke of Edinburgh. In 1957 his wife bestowed upon him the title of the Prince Philip.

There remained the problem of his religion. Marriage to a future Head of the Church of England necessitated the dropping of the Greek Orthodox label. The Archbishop of Canterbury, Dr Geoffrey Fisher, came to the rescue in a letter written to the King:

Sir,

There is a matter upon which I think I should consult Your Majesty. There was a paragraph in *The Times* which said that while Lieutenant Mountbatten was baptised into the Greek Orthodox Church he appears "always to have regarded himself as an Anglican". The same paragraph also misrepresented the relations between the Church of England and the Orthodox Church, but I need not trouble Your Majesty with that.

In the Church of England we are always ready to minister to members of the Orthodox Church and to admit to the Sacrament. No difficulty therefore arises of any sort on our side from the fact that Lieutenant Mountbatten was baptised into the Orthodox Church. At the same time, unless he is officially received into the Church of England he remains formally a member of the Greek Orthodox Church, which, though on the closest and most friendly terms with us, is not able to enter into full communion with us. If it be true that Lieutenant Mountbatten has always regarded himself as an Anglican I suggest for Your Majesty's consideration that there would be an advantage if he were officially received into the Church of England. It can be done privately and very simply. It may be that you and the Princess Elizabeth would feel it more fitting and happy that he should thus have his position regularised as a member of the Church of England.

If Your Majesty agrees that the matter deserves consideration I will most willingly discuss it further with you, or, if Your Majesty thinks fit, with Lieutenant Mountbatten.

> I am, Sir,
> Your faithful servant,
> Geoffrey Cantuar

The primate's letter occasioned no prompt action from the King, who still cherished hopes of delaying the marriage. Eventually it was arranged that Lieutenant Mountbatten would "have his position regularised". But it was only in the month before the wedding that the royal press secretary intimated that Philip had become an Anglican. *The Times* was more specific: "It is understood that Lieutenant Philip Mountbatten has recently been formally received into the Church of England." So that was that. No great excitement, as in the days long ago, of Cardinal Newman's conversion from the

Anglican faith to Catholicism, but it was a "joining" rather than a "leaving" and all the more reassuring for that.

Not that an opinion poll conducted in 1947 was particularly reassuring, finding that forty per cent of those questioned objected to Philip marrying Elizabeth on the grounds that he was foreign. This was *after* he had been granted British citizenship. But the public was still, understandably, confused by his antecedents: were they Greek or Danish or German or British or what? Then there was his mother, pictured in the mysterious grey robes of some foreign religious order, and his father, who had remained in Monte Carlo amid the Nazi occupation and reordering of Europe – what did that imply?

These misgivings were soon to be overridden. George VI, by one stratagem or another, made his daughter wait for two months after the royal family's return from South Africa before consenting to an official announcement of the wedding. By the summer of 1947, "There could no longer be any question as to the wishes and affections of both parties and their pertinacity and patience were rewarded."

The exact timing of the announcement, according to one observer close to the royal family, depended on the production of the engagement ring. Philip wanted the ring to embody jewels of particular significance in his family. Indeed his mother, who was then staying at Kensington Palace, had brought a ring which Prince Andrew had once given her. It was planned that a large square diamond and some smaller stones from that ring were to be incorporated into the new engagement ring. Elizabeth had seen and approved the design, but before a proper measurement of her finger could be taken, Princess Alice walked into a jeweller's, "produced her own ring and asked for the stones to be re-cut and adapted to the chosen new setting".

The ring timed events, which is, in a way, reassuring when one considers the usually immaculate timing of royal procedure. On 8 July Philip knew it was ready. He telephoned Elizabeth, and later the King, with the news. That night he went to Buckingham Palace and went straight up to Elizabeth's sitting-room. When they entered the dining-room together, Elizabeth's right hand was covering the fingers on her left hand. The Queen, who had throughout been far more certain that the couple were well-suited to each other than the King, at once went and kissed her. Elizabeth then laughed and said, "It's too big," showing the ring. She then added somewhat anxiously, "We don't have to wait till it's right, do we?" The King, by now reconciled to the idea of losing his elder daughter, smiled and shook his head.

On 10 July 1947 there was an announcement from Buckingham Palace: "It is with the greatest pleasure that the King and Queen announce the betrothal of their dearly beloved daughter the Princess Elizabeth to Lieutenant Philip Mountbatten, R.N., son of the late Prince Andrew of Greece and Princess Andrew (Princess Alice of Battenberg), to which union the King has gladly given his consent."

The wedding day was fixed for 20 November, despite a last ditch effort by George VI to delay the ceremony until June 1948 when the weather would be kinder. Elizabeth, however, insisted that she had waited long enough. As it happened, the wedding ceremony was to cut a brilliant swathe of warmth and light through a dull November day and enliven a year of national and international tribulation.

7

Marriage

I can see that you are sublimely happy with Philip which is right
but don't forget us is the wish of
Your ever loving & devoted
PAPA

King George VI to Princess Elizabeth
a few days after the wedding

THE ANNOUNCEMENT OF THE ENGAGEMENT unleashed a flood of
world-wide speculation and publicity. Winston Churchill, leader of
the Opposition, spoke of a "flash of colour on the hard road we
have to travel", but that might have been partly a jab at the Labour
government's austerity programme. News agencies on every continent vied for good copy. The familiar, smiling face of Princess
Elizabeth, and the unfamiliar, but also smiling, face of Philip
Mountbatten, adorned the front pages of thousands of newspapers
and journals.

The couple made their first public appearance at Buckingham
Palace garden party in July, causing their cousin Peter of Yugoslavia
to comment, "They've wasted no time. It's rather like throwing
them to the lions." There was a lot of lionising to come. Within a
week Philip was launched on his first royal public duty, dutifully
applauding as Princess Elizabeth received the freedom of the city of
Edinburgh. Then there was an appearance on the balcony of Buckingham Palace, appearances at Lords, at Ascot, and so forth.
Wherever they went the photographers were there, with their flash
bulbs exploding and hissing.

Philip took it all in good part; the attention of the press was still a
novelty and, after all, there was something to celebrate. We have an
early image of him, hands clasped behind his back, bending forward
protectively over his fiancée, and ready to smile with the eyes as well
as the mouth. It is an image that has endured.

There followed an almost embarrassing change in his material circumstances. Although he was still a lieutenant at Corsham, commuting between its tin-roofed shanties and royal palaces, fringe benefits began to pour into his lap. First of all, a house of his own: Clarence House, in London, to be refurbished at a cost of £50,000 voted by the House of Commons. There was also Sunninghill Park near Ascot, a crown property and a "grace and favour" home for weekends; oddly it was burnt to the ground before it could be redecorated, causing Princess Elizabeth to consider, fleetingly, arson. All this was a far cry from Philip's nomad-like existence in exile.

Of course, these palatial homes could only be lived in after the wedding. Until then Philip lived in his Uncle Dickie's empty house in Chester Street, moving after a while to the Dowager Marchioness of Milford Haven's less than luxurious apartment in Kensington Palace. There he was helped in answering his mail by Miss Lees, the Mountbattens' secretary; their valet John Dean also attended to his needs. Since he was still only earning eleven pounds a week, the wages of secretary and valet, plus the extra money he must have needed for new clothes, tips for servants and the like, were doubtless provided by Lord Louis. Not that he immediately appeared in Savile Row suits. At the July garden party at Buckingham Palace he appeared, according to Lady Airlie, in a "shabby" naval uniform: "It had the usual after-the-war look – and I liked him for not having got a new one for the occasion as so many men would have done, to make an impression."

Parliament voted a £10,000 a year allowance for Philip when he married, and increased Elizabeth's sum to £50,000. There was also the matter of his style and titles to consider. The King, who was a stickler for such things, arranged the appropriate titles. They neatly reflected the monarch's claim to reign over a united kingdom: Duke of Edinburgh, Earl of Merioneth and Baron Greenwich. Edinburgh had earlier been a royal dukedom for several Hanoverian princes and for Queen Victoria's second son Alfred – who, interestingly, we have already met as a possible King of Greece, when he was offered the throne in 1863 before "Willy" of Denmark grasped the nettle.

The engaged couple were deluged with presents. Queen Mary, one of their strongest supporters in the family who had been delighted to see them looking "radiant" on 10 July, gave them jewellery. Miss Julie Aloro of Brooklyn, on the other hand, having broken into her money box, sent them a turkey because "they have nothing to eat in England". All in all, there were one and a half thousand gifts catalogued and eventually displayed. Among them was a piece of cloth made from thread spun by Mahatma Gandhi himself and sent at the suggestion of the Viceroy. Queen Mary, who viewed Gandhi as an evil and seditious man, insisted that the gift was an inspired insult, probably a loin cloth, prompting Philip to remark that Gandhi was a great man; she remained unconvinced.

All these preparations were set amid the grim realities of post-war Britain. Thousands were homeless, many were unemployed, there had recently been the worst blizzard of the century, there was rationing and severe power shortages; while in Europe, East and West faced the intensification of the Cold War. Yet the nation was financing two opulent royal homes and a whole variety of other perks for the King's daughter and her recently naturalised future husband.

There were hundreds of protests against ceremonial waste at a difficult time in the nation's fortunes. One of the most spirited, came for the Camden Town First Branch of the Amalgamated Society of Woodworkers. The radical traditions of Camden Town – Richard Cobden as MP, the red flag flying over St Pancras Town Hall – were distilled into a frank letter addressed to George VI and containing a lengthy resolution:

> It wishes to remind you that any banqueting and display of wealth at your daughter's wedding will be an insult to the British people at the present time, and we consider that you would be well advised to order a very quiet wedding in keeping with the times. . . . May we also remind you that should you declare the wedding day a public holiday you will have a word beforehand with the London Master Builders' Association to ensure that we are paid for it.

It is easy to see what the Amalgamated Woodworkers were driving at, and to sympathise. Some members of the Labour government held similar views. Aneurin Bevan, Minister of Health, told the Lord Chamberlain that "under no circumstances" would he wear evening dress at the Buckingham Palace wedding party to which he had been invited. George VI, who had an eagle eye for the correctness of dress replied (through gritted teeth one imagines) that, "His Majesty approves no further action be taken in this matter."

Should the government, though, sanction an "austerity" wedding or a reasonably lavish one? What, for instance, was the escorting soldiery to wear? Khaki battledress or plumes, breastplates and shining riding boots? The Minister of War, Emmanuel Shinwell, an erstwhile "Red" Clydesider, shied away from austerity – but then he had always had a keen sense of the public mood. He wrote to Sir Alan Lascelles, the King's Private Secretary:

> As you are aware, there is considerable agitation in the Press that, for the occasion of the wedding of Her Royal Highness The Princess Elizabeth, the Household Cavalry should be in full dress. I personally have some sympathy with this. I do not think it would be inconsistent with any of our principles, and I believe it would have public support. Until recently it was thought that there would be insufficient time for the Regiment to fit their clothing and rehearse for full dress. I understand now, however, that the Commanding Officer thinks he can get the Escorts ready in time. . . . Little or no extra expense will be involved, as clothing required by other ranks already exists in store, and those officers not in possession of their own full dress are able to borrow from ex-Household Cavalry Officers. . . .

Shinwell carried the day, to the approval, one imagines, of Clement Attlee, inscrutable behind moustache and pipe, but, above all, decent and fair-minded. The Prime Minister, however, drew the line at pronouncing the wedding day a public holiday, believing that, in the existing economic circumstances, a stoppage of work would be "unwise" and "open to misconstruction".

So the "brighter wedding" lobby won, to the pleasure, it seems, of most of the British people. There were many who tried to get in on the act: a woman in Wales was getting married, too, and wondered if Elizabeth had a dress to fit her: "I take W size 36 Bust and again thanking you from the Bottom of my heart"; a widow from Chigwell wanted "a small seat (I only weigh 8 stone) inside the Abbey"; the "Girls of Brompton Sanitorium" wanted some of the wedding cake; the London Passenger Transport Board offered to put the wedded couple's photographs on hoardings outside its tube stations, but did not, since their Majesties "would prefer that this scheme should not be proceeded with"; starry-eyed Americans, obviously finding President Truman an unglamorous Head of State, offered honeymoon accommodation in Florida and elsewhere; dreadful, patriotic poems arrived; an American broadcasting company sent over a disc entitled "Salute to Romance"; a Mr Whigham sent a gold sovereign to the King as a feudal "levy" in aid of the marriage of his elder daughter – but had it politely returned; and hundreds of pairs of nylons arrived from girls who knew how easily they laddered and how hard they were to get.

There were some scandals, not all of them of serious proportions. One such scandal involved Princess Elizabeth's wedding dress. It had reached Clement Attlee's ears that the garment was being made out of Lyons silk, a clear contravention of clothes rationing, especially since the designer, Norman Hartnell, had not, apparently, applied for a permit. There was an investigation and a report was hurried to 10 Downing Street. All, it seemed, was well. There *was* silk in the wedding dress, but it "originally emanated from Chinese silkworms" – Nationalist Chinese silkworms, presumably. Anyway, the silk had been woven in Kent and Scotland. As for the train, yes, it did contain silk which had been produced (almost unbelievably) "by Kentish silkworms and woven in London". The going-away dress contained four or five yards of Lyons silk, which Norman Hartnell happened to have, legitimately, in stock. The Palace made it clear that, as with other brides, Elizabeth had been allowed an extra amount of clothing coupons for the special occasion. In fact, her allowance had been supplemented by pieces already in her mother's and Queen Mary's possession, not to speak of many gifts from well-wishers.

Another scandal involved the presentation to the King of loyal addresses to mark the occasion. Roman Catholic bishops, it transpired, were debarred from presenting one under the dusty Ecclesiastical Titles Act of 1871. The *Catholic Herald* protested vehemently; the Archbishop of Westminster, Cardinal Griffin, got in touch with the Home Secretary; the Pope, it was said, was going to be "a little hurt". Eventually a way was found round the problem by allowing Cardinal Griffin to present an address on the strict "understanding that his bishops did not claim to be bishops of anywhere". So that was all right, and it at least gave the Catholic Church equality with the Methodist Church of Australasia, which had presented a loyal address without any trouble at all.

For Philip there were the final rituals to go through before the wedding. He did not have to buy a wedding ring, being presented with a sizeable chunk of Welsh gold, and saying kindly, "There is enough for two. We can save a bit for Margaret." On the eve of the wedding the King, in a brief family ceremony at Buckingham

Palace, created his prospective son-in-law Baron Greenwich, Earl of Merioneth and Duke of Edinburgh. He then invested him with the Most Noble Order of the Garter – having prudently invested Elizabeth eight days before to emphasise her precedence and seniority.

The day before the wedding Philip was "so touchy and jittery that David Milford Haven, who was his best man, found that he had to exercise every ounce of tact and diplomacy to marshal Philip through the rituals of his last bachelor days". There were two bachelor parties: the first one, which the press attended, was ritually "jolly" and ended at the Dorchester Hotel at 12.30; the second, more private and intimate party was with Lord Louis Mountbatten (now back in Britain having supervised the partition of India), David Milford Haven and a few more. In the early hours of the morning, Philip stubbed out his last cigarette, declared that he had now given up smoking for good (which turned out to be the case) and was driven to Kensington Palace.

A few hours later, at seven o'clock on the morning of 20 November, Philip was woken. According to his valet, John Dean, he was "in great form . . . extremely cheerful" – which was good going considering the lack of sleep. He breakfasted on toast and coffee and then dressed in his regular naval uniform with his war-time decorations (five rows, though admittedly short ones) above the star of the Garter. He chose to be married wearing his grand-father Louis of Battenberg's beautifully fashioned sword, lent to him by Dickie Mountbatten and thus provoking instant gossip to the effect that he was too poor to buy one of his own! In fact, it was a gesture of dynastic sentiment and solidarity.

David Milford Haven had more trouble in getting up. They each drank a gin and tonic. Then David had a craving for a cigarette. Failing to find any, he dashed out to buy some. When they eventually got into the car which was to take them to Westminster Abbey, they realised that if they mistakenly picked up each other's naval cap, David's "would have fallen over Philip's ears"; the solution was to mark the inside of the larger cap with ink.

Elsewhere things were going more smoothly. The King and the bride were due to leave Buckingham Palace at 11.16 am, and to arrive at the West door of Westminster Abbey at 11.28; Queen Elizabeth left a little earlier, at 11.03 am, at which time, on the dot, Queen Mary set out from Marlborough House.

It was a grey, gloomy, typical November morning – but fine.

Enormous crowds lined the ceremonial route, many having camped overnight in inclement weather.

The bride and her father alighted from the Irish State Coach. Richard Dimbleby described the scene for radio audiences:

> The doors of the coach are open. The crowds shout with excitement and love. The King, in the uniform of Admiral of the Fleet, comes forward to help his daughter alight carefully. Now she steps down. A great cheer arises to sustain her.
>
> She pauses for a moment and looks at the Abbey. And perhaps – perhaps she is a little nervous in her heart as she passes from the grey of the morning outside into the warmth and colour of the Abbey.

Vintage, tear-jerking Dimbleby, but where better to shed one's tears than at a wedding?

As the King escorted his daughter down the aisle, he experienced that mixture of pride and loss that is commonplace in fathers about to give away their daughters, but which in his case was particularly deeply felt. "I was so proud of you," he later wrote, "and thrilled at having you so close to me on our long walk in Westminster Abbey. But when I handed your hand to the Archbishop I felt that I had lost something very precious. You were so calm and composed during the service and said your words with such conviction."

Princess Elizabeth was certainly outwardly calm, triumphant even. She looked particularly pretty – "like an English rose" observers were to say predictably – yet, at the same time, unassuming, ordinary in demeanour. There was nothing ordinary, though, about her wedding dress which shimmered as she moved; it was embroidered with the white roses of York, with orange blossom, and with ears of corn and wheat, emblems of harvest and fertility.

The bridegroom, suffering from a cold according to Alexandra of Yugoslavia, looked composed and dignified. As his bride approached he looked towards Queen Elizabeth "and gave her his warmest smile". As Princess Elizabeth promised to "love, honour and obey", Queen Mary dabbed her eyes.

In keeping with these emotions Dr Garbett, Archbishop of York, said in his address:

> Notwithstanding the splendour and national significance of the service in this Abbey, it is in all essentials exactly the same as it

133

would be for any cottager who might be married this afternoon in some small country church in a remote village in the Dales. The same vows are taken: the same prayers are offered: the same blessings are given.

As Elizabeth and Philip prepared to lead the bridal procession from the Abbey, they turned towards the King and Queen and Queen Mary, and Elizabeth curtsied deeply to them, Philip holding her hand as she did so. According to one observer the King and Queen had "not expected such a gesture . . . and one could see the muscle in [George VI's] cheek working as it always did when he was deeply stirred". Then the bride and bridegroom left the Abbey to be greeted by the cheering crowds. There followed the progress to Buckingham Palace, appearances on the balcony, and the reception in the State dining-room where the dishes included *Filet de Sole Mountbatten* and *Bombe Glacée Princess Elizabeth*, and George VI, like a man liberated from both doubt and grief, moved among his guests, joking and chaffing.

The wedding had brought together an impressive array of foreign royalty – though by no means all of them had thrones. They included the Kings of Norway and Iraq, the King and Queen of Denmark, the Queen of the Hellenes, the Princess Regent and Prince Bernhard of the Netherlands, the Crown Prince and Princess of Sweden, the King and Queen of Romania, the King and Queen of Yugoslavia, the Prince Regent of Belgium, Queen Victoria Eugénie of Spain, the Count and Countess of Barcelona, Prince Jean and Princess Elizabeth of Luxemburg and the Duchess of Aosta. On the bridegroom's side of the Abbey there were, in contrast, Corsham villagers, old Navy friends, and skittles players from the Methuen Arms.

Was it all worth it? Queen Mary was quite sure: "Saw many old friends," she had written in her diary two days before the wedding. "I stood from 9.30 till 12.15 am!!! Not bad for 80." Lady Airlie thought that she had looked "supremely happy", perhaps not the description of Queen Mary that springs most readily to mind. Princess Margaret was also in high spirits, organising the wedding guests for photographs and calling out, "Come along, everybody!" The King was apparently reconciled to his loss, the Queen was quietly content.

As for the press and the populace, they seemed even happier. *The New York Times* spoke of, "this welcome occasion for gaiety in grim England, beset in peace with troubles almost as burdensome as those of the war". Another American journalist wrote: "The glamour of it all, in the midst of Britain's drab existence nowadays, has jerked millions out of their one-candlepower lives and tossed them into dreamland" – where many Americans, it should be said, were happy to join them, "one-candlepower lives" or not. The Poet Laureate, John Masefield, did his best to earn his keep in a poem published in *The Times* which ended, rather lamely:

To such a Crown all broken spirits turn:
And we, who see this young face passing by,
See her as symbol of a Power Etern,
And pray that Heaven may bless her till she die.

For the British people, the size and response of the crowds, the ten thousand telegrams of congratulation, the evident good will, and the intense interest, spoke for themselves.

The honeymoon began at the Mountbattens' house at Broadlands in Hampshire, where Louis and Edwina had also spent their honeymoon, and which was once Lord Palmerston's house before it had descended through the Ashleys to Edwina Cassel. It was nearly dark, and raining, when the bride and groom set off in an open carriage with four hot water bottles packed round Elizabeth under the blanket to keep her warm; her favourite corgi, Susan, went too. They next caught a two coach train and travelled with Elizabeth's maid, Miss "Bobo" MacDonald, John Dean and seventeen suitcases – fifteen for the bride and two for the groom. Eventually they arrived at Broadlands, were cheered by a large crowd at the gates, and passed inside. The honeymoon suite was decorated in pale grey and white, with delicate eighteenth-century furniture, and sketches by Salvador Dali on the walls – a far cry from the interior décor of Balmoral and other royal palaces.

The King, despite his better instincts, had looked depressed after the couple had driven off. Alexandra of Yugoslavia recalls: "I . . . tried to cheer up Uncle Bertie who was looking quite miserable. 'Now Philip's got you and Aunt Elizabeth, as well as Lilibet,' I said, 'he *belongs* now.'

" 'That's right, Sandra,' said Uncle Bertie, suddenly smiling. 'He does belong. *You're so right!* Come and have a drink!' "

Broadlands, however, was not exactly an isolated first abode for Philip and Elizabeth. Photographers and reporters lay in wait for them, sometimes hanging like monkeys from august and venerable trees to get a better view. Once (shades of things to come) Philip drove at high speed through the gates of Broadlands, scattering press men as his new Humber car brushed past them. To placate the press, they went for one official informal walk while the cameras snapped away. But Broadlands, within easy striking distance of London, was not a good place for a quiet and peaceful honeymoon, and they were soon en route for Birkhall, a small manor-house near Balmoral Castle, where they were, happily, left alone.

Stopping at London on their way, Philip dictated a statement for the press which contained more than a little irony. It read: "The reception given us on our wedding day and the loving interest shown by our fellow countrymen ... have left an impression that will never grow faint. We can find no words to express what we feel, but we can at least offer our grateful thanks to the millions who have given us this unforgettable send-off in our married life."

George VI, writing to his daughter a few days after the wedding, had a different view to express:

> Your leaving us has left a great blank in our lives but do remember that your old home is still yours and do come back to it as much and as often as possible. I can see that you are sublimely happy with Philip which is right but don't forget us is the wish of
> Your ever loving and devoted
PAPA

For the newly-created Duke of Edinburgh, however, a great blank had been filled, not created, though we may presume that he, too, was "sublimely happy".

8

A Career of one's own?

"I want to assure you that I have no intention of being a sitting
tenant in the post."
The Duke of Edinburgh on becoming
President of the Playing Fields Association, 1949

ARTHUR BALFOUR, UNIONIST PRIME MINISTER from 1902–5, and a
bachelor, was once asked whether it was true that he was going to
marry the dominating Margot Tennant, later the second wife of
Asquith. He replied, "No, I rather think of having a career of my
own."

Lieutenant Philip Mountbatten was faced in 1947 with a drastic
alteration in his circumstances. The "gilded cage" that encompasses
royalty was closing around him. How would it affect his way of life?
Could he, too, hope to have a career of his own?

Clearly, like every man who gets married, he would have to adapt
to new circumstances – circumstances, however, which were
unusually restrictive and challenging. There would be detectives
guarding him and the Princess wherever they went. Ears would be
cocked and eyes alert to catch every unguarded remark or facial
expression. He would be under close scrutiny whenever he
appeared in public.

He was fully aware that joining the royal family would prevent
him from doing many of the things ordinary citizens could do with
impunity. For a self-willed man with a strong character, spontaneous, often impetuous, it would not be easy to wear the strait-jacket
of royal etiquette. His position would be even more delicate when
Princess Elizabeth became Queen, though this prospect must have
seemed to belong to the distant future in 1947, when King George
was only fifty-two years of age.

That his position as the future Queen's husband would frustrate many of his resolutions had perhaps not immediately occurred to him. He had to take account of the time-absorbing functions he would have to attend with his wife, of the duties that would fall to him, of the visits to the Commonwealth and Empire and other foreign countries that would have to be undertaken. Like Elizabeth, he would have to be devoted to the service of the British people. He had still to learn a good deal more about the royal family's history and obligations. Above all, he would have to acquaint himself more intimately with the experience of one man – Albert, the Prince Consort – against whose conduct and work his own would inevitably be measured. He would, moreover, have to evolve a style that enabled him to be master in his own house while at the same time being lower in official rank than his wife. It was a daunting prospect.

In the first years of his marriage, his role as royal son-in-law was not a particularly easy or enjoyable one to play. The King was not an especially relaxed father-in-law, and was soon to exhibit signs of the illness that would eventually end his life. The decorum now expected of Philip is illustrated by an incident at Sandringham during the royal family's Christmas celebrations of 1947. As a member of the family he was expected to wear a kilt. Offered several that had once belonged to George V, he chose the Stuart hunting tartan. So far so good. Unfortunately George V had been a much shorter man than Philip, and the latter came down to dinner showing several inches of skin above his knees. Embarrassed, he chose to play the fool, dropping a curtsy to his father-in-law. George VI had an exaggerated respect for proper dress, and had even returned from the recent wedding ceremony irritated that an admiral in Westminster Abbey had failed to wear his sword. The curtsy did not amuse him and "he told Philip so in a roar of quarterdeck language."

The atmosphere at Buckingham Palace and at other royal homes tended to be heavy and rather formal. Even the family's favourite indoor relaxation of playing parlour games, charades and so forth, had some of the stilted formality of an Edwardian evening of self-entertainment, with Papa and Mama leading the sometimes self-conscious revels. Royal staff, recalling Philip during these early months of marriage, found him "difficult to deal with on occasions – prickly". Others remembered him as "arrogant" or "defensive". It was perfectly understandable that he did find the adjustment relatively difficult. He had led a life, from Salem onwards, which had been in marked contrast to that of his wife and his in-laws. He had actually been to school, rather than being privately tutored; he had been allowed a freedom of self-expression and experience that made the royal family look positively cloistered; he had not felt the weighty hand of a tyrannical father, as had George VI; he had seen a lot of the world, and as a more-or-less ordinary man; he had served in the war with distinction. Above all, he had not been trained or brought up to relish a largely ceremonial existence a step or two behind his wife.

The difficulties he experienced on first being married were compounded by the fact that Clarence House had not yet been renovated after its wartime damage from bombs. At first, Philip and Elizabeth lived in her apartment at Buckingham Palace. Later, when the Earl of Athlone left to be Governor-General of South Africa, they moved into his apartment in Kensington Palace. There were also weekends at the small white country house they rented at Windlesham Moor in Surrey. Here Philip made one of his first alterations, creating a cricket pitch out of the small golf course and grass tennis court.

Work on Clarence House gave him another early outlet for his organising talents. The Ministry of Works architects found that he studied their plans carefully, quickly spotted any drawbacks, and made sensible proposals. Here again the differences in background and experience between Philip and Elizabeth were evident: she tended to be passive, taking such activities as furnishing and redecorating for granted, or as problems for somebody else to solve; Philip, on the other hand, found an intense satisfaction (interfering some might say) in the planning involved in establishing their first home.

Eventually Clarence House was ready. Philip's sitting-room was hung with Laszlo portraits of his mother and father, and beside his desk "a panel opened to reveal a completely modern drawing-table." The dining-room had Chippendale furniture and carved, gilded lamp brackets made, on Philip's instructions, in a late Georgian style. Of the apple-green walls, Elizabeth "proudly" said, "To get the exact shade, I mixed the paint myself." There were portraits of George II and his family (hardly an inspiring sight at the best of times), Paul Nash drawings, Bateman cartoons, modern glass and Georgian chandeliers. The detailing was, largely, a tribute to the thoroughness of Lieutenant Mountbatten's planning.

Moving into Clarence House helped to give him a greater sense of security and privacy; it became a real home, and the more valuable for being his first as an adult. Prince Charles and Princess Anne were born during this period and the house was associated with their babyhood. Some people noticed that his prickly and defensive behaviour became less of a problem after he moved into Clarence House. Certainly the prospect of leaving it after Elizabeth's accession to the throne in 1952 filled him with "a black depression" – but that was also the result of contemplating the practical and immediate effects upon his own career of becoming husband of the Queen rather than of the heir apparent.

After his marriage Philip was anxious to continue his naval career. Peacetime work, however, could hardly be as exhilarating as active service. For the first few months of his married life he had a nine-to-six desk job at the Admiralty in the Operations Division: "I was just a dogsbody, shuffling ships around. It was quite interesting." Work did not, however, finish at 6 o'clock. He was now expected to devote certain evenings to acts of royal "duty": opening exhibitions, making (and writing) speeches, presenting cups and prizes, and so forth. All of it interesting at first, even good fun, but sometimes perilously close to the public "performing" that he finds such a waste of time.

Philip told the King of his anxieties that his naval career was being jeopardised by these "royal duty" interruptions. George VI, whose own naval career had been wrecked by his brother's abdication, sympathised with his son-in-law's legitimate professional ambition, and promised to help him as much as he could. Philip was duly relieved to be posted to a Staff course at the Royal Naval College at Greenwich (very handily situated for the newly created Baron Greenwich of Greenwich in the County of London). It was a demanding course, and as near to higher education as he had so far got. It was also a prerequisite for high rank, and at least showed that the Admiralty still had the confidence that he could make good progress in his career. He relished the course.

His public duties as the Duke of Edinburgh, however, did not cease, even though he was living in at Greenwich and only returning to Clarence House at weekends. Apart from a host of official visits and trips in Britain, in May 1948 Princess Elizabeth and he went to Paris to open an exhibition illustrating eight centuries of British life. What began as a semi-private excursion quickly assumed the proportions, though not the status, of a full State visit. Elizabeth was pregnant at the time of the visit, but on the Sunday, with a full day before him, it was Philip who felt sick. He struggled through a communion service at the British Embassy Church, attended a race meeting at Longchamps, and in the evening he and Elizabeth went to a very staid night club which had been taken over for the evening by the British Embassy. The Paris visit demonstrated firstly the need, in his new position, to grit one's teeth and carry on smiling even though one felt nauseous, and secondly, the impossibility of pleasing all of the people for all of the time. On their return to Britain after a notably successful trip, Elizabeth and Philip learned that a fiercely Sabbatarian minister had objected to their Sunday activities, bewailing "a dark day in our history". Philip had not heard the last of the Lord's Day Observance movement.

He was already developing a distinctive style as he carried out official functions. For one thing, he wrote his own speeches and consequently delivered them as if he had actually read them beforehand and even approved of their contents – something that was by no means guaranteed by royal speechmakers at that time, particularly Princess Elizabeth, whose oratorical style had much in common with that of a vicar's wife opening a church bazaar. When he first became Duke of Edinburgh speeches were sometimes written for him. The turning point came when he was about to make a speech which had been written for him by the comptroller of the Clarence household, Sir Frederick Browning. Rising to address the banquet, and with Sir Frederick preparing to listen to the speech he had "ghosted", Philip pointedly put the first set of notes on one side, pulled out an entirely different speech written by himself, and went on to deliver it with verve. Sir Frederick was never again invited to write a speech.

Philip's public speaking style was, perhaps not surprisingly, remarkably similar to that of Lord Louis Mountbatten: straightforward, deftly humorous and frequently graceful, with no turgid phraseology, nor long-winded platitudinous ascents or descents. It was not easy to nod off when he spoke, even after a multi-course banquet. Some early examples from his speechmaking show that a fresh wind was blowing through official royal attitudes. On receiving the freedom of the city of Edinburgh he made a relaxed reference to a previous occasion when he had dined with the Lord Provost: "He very kindly offered us one for the road. When somebody said the train was twenty minutes late, we had another. . . . We eventually decided that the train was six drinks late." Not perhaps the best joke in the history of British humour, but what a relief in a royal speech in the late 1940s. It upset the puritanical, all the same.

More seriously, during his first speech at the Guildhall, having received the freedom of the City of London, he asserted that he had accepted the freedom on behalf of the millions who had fought against tyranny during the Second World War: "The ideal that my wife and I have set before us is to make the utmost of the special opportunities we have, to try to bring home to our own generation the full importance of that contribution." On another's lips it would have sounded trite and ritualistic, but coming from him it was more like an affirmation, an act of self-dedication.

In time, Princess Elizabeth was to be partly liberated from those upright but dull conventions of the House of Windsor that had dogged her early speechmaking. Though never able to rival her husband in spontaneity, she became a little more lively in her delivery, even essaying touches of humour that audiences seized upon as eagerly as a starving man grasps scraps of food. And when they travelled together on official duties during these early days, Philip was able to enliven the boredom they sometimes both felt by his private asides and comments, many of which rather shocked her by their frankness and wit.

Early in his marriage the Duke of Edinburgh gave an indication of the prodigious energy that he could put behind "good causes". The cause that came to hand was the National Playing Fields Association which, in the postwar years, was short of money and in need of revitalisation. Philip's interest in its work was fired by his visits, while at Greenwich, to youth clubs in the poorer parts of London. Like Edward VIII, when he was Prince of Wales, Philip believed that "something must be done". Did Uncle Dickie, as it was rumoured, suggest this outlet for his energies? Or did the King, himself a dedicated supporter of boys' camps before his accession, press Philip to take up the challenge? Alexandra of Yugoslavia believes that, "It was Uncle Bertie who saw that the post could help forge civic links for Philip throughout Britain's intricate national life."

At any rate, Philip became President of the National Playing Fields Association in 1949. He told the NPFA's committee at his first meeting as President: "I want to assure you that I have no intention of being a sitting tenant in the post." He immediately went on to redraft an appeal that was due to go out in his name. It was an early sign that he was not prepared to be associated with any national body as the "statutory royal" who lent his name to the letterheads and promptly disappeared from view.

He launched a £500,000 appeal scheme and masterminded the elaborate publicity campaign to back it up. With the King's approval, he invited the NPFA's council and senior officers to a luncheon party at Buckingham Palace, which was good for morale and provided a suitably august setting in which to do a little arm-twisting. When he finished his course at Greenwich he worked regularly at the NPFA office, walking every day from Clarence House to Buckingham Gate and putting in a good morning's work before going off to afternoons of public engagements.

Promising that "I'll go almost anywhere to open a new playing field," he travelled to many parts of the United Kingdom, raising money and opening new playing fields and centres. He got Frank Sinatra to attend the Variety Club midnight matinée, and to donate the royalties from two of his best-selling records to the appeal fund, although critics at court were shocked to see him in the presence of the newly-divorced Sinatra, and dancing a samba with the film star Ava Gardner. He played benefit cricket matches with teams that included the Middlesex and England Denis Compton and Bill Edrich. He received a cheque for £7000 from a Butlins holidaymakers' reunion at the Albert Hall and accepted another from five thousand girl campers at Skegness singing "All the Nice Girls love a Sailor". To many traditionalists, it seemed as if he was going too far.

Despite his relaxed and good-humoured public style, these activities were not without their cost. He made an appeal film with apparent calm and poise. "You think he was calm?" one of the film's makers said afterwards. "That's why we sat him at a desk. His left leg was jumping with nerves."

Still, it did not show, and the money kept rolling in. By 1953 playing fields were being opened at the rate of two hundred a year. The Presidency of the NPFA became his "longest term of office. . . . He doesn't ordinarily believe in prolonged associations, thinks they make for ossifications at the top, but this seemed a special case." It was also the first area in which he had been able to employ his undoubted organisational talents to achieve an objective of some national significance – very like Prince Albert and the Great Exhibition a century before.

Two events in the autumn of 1948 were to have a considerable effect on Philip's public role. The first was the birth, at Buckingham Palace on 14 November, of a boy to Princess Elizabeth. The baby was born at 9.14 pm while thousands of the public stood before the railings awaiting the announcement. Two Harley Street consultants attended the birth, while the King, Queen Elizabeth and Queen Mary waited anxiously in an anteroom. Philip was not present for the birth of his son; it was, after all, not fashionable in 1948 for fathers to share the birth experience with their wives. Instead he found some relief from his anxiety in a prolonged game of squash with Michael Parker, who had been taken onto the staff as joint equerry for Philip and Elizabeth.

The King's private secretary, Sir Alan Lascelles, brought the news to Philip on the Buckingham Palace squash court, which Philip had had renovated soon after his marriage, and which had certainly fulfilled a useful function on 14 November. Delighted, Philip took the stairs leading to the Buhl Room three at a time. Elizabeth was under anaesthetic since the delivery had been by forceps. The baby was in the nursery where Philip saw him. When his wife regained consciousness, he was sitting at her bedside with some carnations and roses. Champagne was being drunk, telegrams were being sent off, and more of the public were swarming before the railings.

The boy, second in succession to the throne, was later christened Charles Philip Arthur George. Why those names? Philip was obvious. So was George, on both sides of the family. Arthur has been quite often used by British royalty. But Charles? Was it an unfashionable tribute to the troubled House of Stuart, which had produced Charles I and Charles II? (When the couple's second child was christened Anne it seemed to confirm this theory.) Or was it because the baby's godfather King Haakon of Norway had originally been Prince Charles of Denmark before he was invited to ascend the newly created Norwegian throne in 1905? Both explanations were plausible, but inconclusive. It seems, quite simply, that the baby's parents had liked the name Charles best – which, considering the Duke of Edinburgh's capacity to come to sensible and clear-cut decisions, sounds the obvious explanation.

While Princess Elizabeth was recovering from the birth and devoting herself to caring for her first baby, including breast-feeding him, her father suffered from the collapse of an artery in his left leg. The diagnosis was arteriosclerosis, an obstruction to the circulation in the arteries of the left leg, and thus a form of thrombosis. It did not bode well for the lengthy survival of the King, though he underwent an operation in the Spring of 1949 and made a reasonable recovery.

With his wife unable to play a full part in royal duties and with the King incapacitated, Philip was subjected to greatly increased demands on his time. The crippling of his naval career seemed once again to be a real possibility. Although it was not apparent, the prospect of slipping behind in his career must have taken the edge off some of the pleasure to be wrung from inspecting regiments, laying foundation stones (not that he ever got much pleasure from that), signing the vellum pages of civic visitors' books with gold pens, and eating predictably tasteless food at official functions. He still enjoyed the speechmaking, though, particularly since he was writing his speeches by himself, with some help from Michael Parker.

By the autumn of 1949, however, the King was sufficiently fit to allow him to return to sea. He took up the post of First Lieutenant in HMS *Chequers*, leading ship in the 1st Mediterranean destroyer flotilla. *Chequers* was based on Malta, still the premier Mediterranean base for the Royal Navy, and as yet undisturbed by nationalist agitation. The advantage of being based on Malta was that Princess Elizabeth could join her husband for quite lengthy stays.

This was the period of their married life which has been most commonly described as "normal", and "lacking in ceremony". Yet as it turned out they were simply not treated "like any other married couple": when Elizabeth flew to join Philip for their second wedding anniversary, the Governor gave a ball in her honour, crowds swarmed round her when she went shopping, and her personal detective was never far away. Nor could she escape from the sense of duty so earnestly subscribed to by the House of Windsor; soon, almost by reflex, she was offering to visit schools, hospitals and public works.

Still, the pressures were far less than in the United Kingdom, and the flow of royal mail from London was carefully restricted to allow them both a greater feeling of freedom. There were a great many pleasures and relaxations to be found on Malta and the small neighbouring island of Gozo. Staying with Lord and Lady Mountbatten in their rented house, the Villa Guardamangia at Pieta, Philip and Elizabeth were able to join in swimming parties, dances and excursions to unspoilt beaches on the island. Elizabeth "had the exhilarating experience of actually going out to get her hair done". She apparently laughed a good deal, and "looked blooming". The couple also entertained other officers and their wives. It was on Malta that Philip first caught the polo bug, the virus being encouraged by Uncle Dickie who was, it seems, a better teacher than player.

Elizabeth made several trips to Malta, which at least broke the royal family tradition of Christmas at Sandringham, summer at Balmoral, and so on. She discovered that she was pregnant again early in 1950; she returned to Clarence House and in July Philip came back to be present for the birth. "It's the sweetest girl," Philip told his grandmother, the Dowager Marchioness of Milford Haven after the birth on 15 August 1950 of his daughter, christened Anne Elizabeth Alice Louise.

Princess Anne's birth marked a dividing line in her father's naval career. Until his leave in July 1950 he had been the *Chequers* First Lieutenant, revelling in being back in naval harness; he was still a strict disciplinarian, responsible for the stores, welfare and general running of the ship. Apart from these duties he made sure that *Chequers* kept the string of sporting trophies her crew had won.

He had some difficulties over his royal status. The *Chequers'* captain felt obliged to call him "Sir", until he insisted that it was the captain who was "Sir" to all his officers, and he was "Number One" to the captain. Then there was the painful incident after he failed an examination paper in Torpedo and Anti-Submarine. Michael Parker, his equerry, was summoned before the Commander-in-Chief, Admiral Sir Arthur John Power who, clearly embarrassed, thought the paper was not a fail at all but "a damned good pass". Was he thinking of overruling the examiners? Any hint of special treatment, especially of this nature, infuriated Philip. His reaction to Parker's interview with the Commander-in-Chief was direct and predictable: "If they try to fix it, I quit the Navy for good!" He re-sat the examination and passed it comfortably.

Philip returned to Malta after his daughter's birth to take up his first command on the frigate HMS *Magpie*, a sister ship of HMS *Amethyst* of the Yangtze River incident. Gazetteered as Lieutenant-Commander, he was now twenty-nine years old, about the age when he might have expected such promotion. No sign there of favouritism or nepotism, though his unrivalled connections had hardly held him back.

Early in September 1950 he was piped aboard HMS *Magpie* and told the crew that he meant to make the ship one of the finest in the fleet: "It will be up to you, and up to me." Cousin Alexandra, quoting this unremarkable exhortation says, "It could have been

Uncle Dickie speaking." Well, yes – but also Captain Smith or Lieutenant-Commander Brown.

As it turned out, Philip meant what he said. He worked the *Magpie*'s crew hard, and she became "cock ship". Reactions to his style of command were not universally admiring. One of his crew later said he would rather die than serve under him again. Another claimed that, "He stamped about like a ----ing tiger." Yet another said, "He worked us like hell, but he treated us like gentlemen." Privately they called him "Dukey"; it could have been a lot worse. "Dukey" also drove them hard in the naval sporting competitions, practising his crew for the annual regatta so hard that their hands blistered. To be fair, he was in it with them, rowing stroke and stripped to the waist. *Magpie* won six out of the ten regatta events, with her captain leading one of the winning crews.

Although he commanded *Magpie* for less than a year, it was a full and active time. When she had finished nursing Princess Anne, Elizabeth went out once more to join him. On this occasion Admiral Sir Arthur John Power showed some favouritism and got away with it. He put his despatch vessel HMS *Surprise* at her disposal, one of the arguments being that *Magpie* did not have suitable accommodation. *Surprise*, with a destroyer, and escorted by *Magpie*, carried the flag prestigiously to various Mediterranean ports. With the heir apparent on one vessel and her husband on the other, some rather obvious jokes were exchanged by signal:

Surprise to *Magpie*: "Princess full of beans."
Magpie to *Surprise*: "Is that the best you can give her for breakfast?"

At that time there were biblical codings, apparently much favoured by British sea-dogs, who seem to have known their Old Testament as well as their King's Regulations: "Isaiah 33:23, Thy tacklings are loosed," for example. All harmless, jolly sort of stuff.

While Princess Elizabeth was in the Mediterranean, they visited Philip's relatives in Athens. King Paul and Queen Frederika greeted them. The Parthenon was floodlit for their benefit, and there were picnics and family gatherings. King Paul went aboard the *Magpie* where he was entertained in the ward-room. He found "with astonishment that Philip was still simultaneously carrying on a lot of his English office work including the preparations for the Festival of Britain and complicated plans for an overseas tour. There was no room on board for a secretary, and no officer could be delegated for

147

that task." Apparently Philip spent "hours drafting his own letters and memos in pencil". The King had imagined "that he would find a qualified commander acting as nominal First Lieutenant under Philip", but there was nothing of the kind.

By July 1951 it was all over. George VI's deteriorating health demanded it. Lieutenant-Commander Mountbatten was given indefinite leave and came home to do his duty. The gilded cage at last seemed to have snapped shut. Certainly an active naval career was impossible. "Indefinite" leave came to mean "permanent" leave.

Although the King had been well enough to open the Festival of Britain on 3 May 1951, he was obviously tired and ill. At the end of May he wrote to Queen Mary that his doctors had diagnosed "a condition of the left lung known as pneumonitis . . . I was X-rayed and the photographs showed a shadow. . . . The doctors think the cause of the cough . . . has now moved into the lung."

The shadow on the lung was, in fact, cancer, although this was not finally diagnosed until the middle of September. His doctors then advised the King that the whole of his left lung must be removed. As far as it is known, he never knew the true cause of the operation, accepting the official explanation that a blockage of one of his bronchial tubes necessitated such radical surgery.

On 23 September his left lung was removed. Despite the success of the operation, there remained the very real danger that the King might at any moment die of a coronary thrombosis. It was also feared that, because of the need to remove certain nerves of the larynx, George VI might never again be able to speak above a whisper – a cruel irony for one who had throughout his life struggled with a speech impediment.

These traumatic events threw a sombre shadow over the royal family. In particular, they promised to destroy the plans for Elizabeth and Philip to pay a state visit to Canada and the United States on the King's behalf. The date of departure had been fixed for 25 September 1951 in the *Empress of Britain*. Since this was so near to the date of the King's operation, the whole tour of North America seemed in jeopardy. In any case, how could Elizabeth leave her father at a time when he was so perilously close to death? Even when the operation was declared a success, the couple could hardly embark two days later for North America. Of course, they could wait until the King seemed well on the road to recovery and then fly across the Atlantic – but such a journey was then considered too dangerous for the heir apparent to undertake.

Enter a former naval person. With George VI's agreement Philip hatched a plot to break the flying embargo: first the tour would be called off, then, in the wake of protests from North America, the Prime Minister, Attlee, and the leader of the Opposition, Churchill, would be presented with a solution – flying. Churchill, despite his own inclination to risk life and limb on wartime travel, was the hardest to convince. But at last it was done, and on 7 October, with the King much improved, Elizabeth and Philip took off from London airport in a BOAC airliner bound for Montreal.

The tour was an outstanding success, and the first lengthy overseas visit of this sort to be undertaken by Elizabeth and Philip. In thirty-five days they crossed the North American continent twice and travelled nearly 10,000 miles in Canada alone. They were rapturously acclaimed almost everywhere they went, and even in Quebec there was warm appreciation. In the United States they were greeted with similar fervour. President Truman wrote a glowing note of congratulation to George VI; his aged and deaf mother-in-law, on being introduced to Princess Elizabeth, and knowing that Churchill had just been returned to power in the general election, greeted her by saying, "I'm so glad that your father's just been re-elected."

In truth, Elizabeth's father, if not re-elected, at least seemed much restored when they returned to Britain. As a mark of his gratitude for their services they were sworn in as members of the Privy Council on 4 December. Their next overseas mission was planned for January 1952 when they would undertake, on the King's behalf, a tour of East Africa, Australia and New Zealand.

On 31 January 1952 King George waved farewell to his daughter and her husband from the tarmac of London airport. He stood bareheaded, his hair ruffled by the keen, cold wind, and his face, as he at last turned away, seemed drawn with anxiety and perhaps grief.

He was never to see his elder daughter again. On the seventh day of the royal tour, early on the morning of 6 February at Sandringham, his valet entered his bedroom with a cup of tea and found that he was dead. He had died in his sleep from the coronary thrombosis that had for some years threatened his life.

Four thousand miles away in the Treetop Hotel in Kenya, Princess Elizabeth had succeeded to the throne while watching game at play below her in the hours before dawn. She was to return to England to a new way of life, long anticipated, but still awesome to contemplate. For the Duke of Edinburgh the change was even more far-reaching in its effects. His naval career was now finally over, and he was obliged to adjust to subtly different roles: consort and husband to a Queen, and father to children that were first and second in line of succession to the throne. His first reaction was to view the adjustment with despondency.

9

Consort

WITH A SMALL "c"

"Within the house, and whatever we did, it was together. I
suppose I naturally filled the principal position. People used to
come to me and ask me what to do. In 1952 the whole thing
changed, very, very considerably."

Prince Philip

PRINCESS ELIZABETH HEARD THE NEWS that her father had died at
2.45 pm local time, 11.45 am Greenwich mean time. Her husband
broke the news to her, after Michael Parker had received official
confirmation of the King's death. Despite her grief, the new Queen
had to set about drafting telegrams to Australia and New Zealand
apologising for the necessity of cancelling the royal tour. She was
asked to declare by which name she would be known as sovereign
and answered, "Oh, my own name, what else?"

To Michael Parker it seemed as if the Duke of Edinburgh was the
most obviously affected by the news: "He looked as if you'd dropped half the world on him. I never felt so sorry for anyone in my
life." According to his cousin Alexandra: "Philip for some days felt
stunned, as if he were anaesthetised and moving nervously in a
vacuum. He was consort to the Queen and in the first hours of
shock, could well have echoed Prince Albert's despairing entry in an
early diary, 'Oh, the future!' "

Queen Elizabeth and her husband left the Treetops Hotel as
quickly as possible. Parker recalls, "We got out of that place in an
hour." Then there was the drive to a small local airport, past crowds
of sympathetic and silent Africans, before flying to Entebbe and
boarding the plane that was to take them the 4000 miles to London,
via Libya. At the airport her uncle the Duke of Gloucester, and the
Prime Minister, Winston Churchill, tears rolling down his cheeks as
he bent to kiss her hand, Clement Attlee and Anthony Eden were

awaiting them. By four o'clock in the afternoon of 7 February the Queen and the Duke were back in Clarence House; half an hour later Queen Mary drove out from Marlborough House: "Her old Grannie and subject," she said, "must be the first to kiss her hand."

Nine days after his death, King George was buried at Windsor Castle, to the dull thud of drums and the wailing of bagpipes. The new Queen had been poised and controlled until now, but on the way back to Clarence House she broke down and wept in the back of the car; her husband tried to comfort her. Yet despite this natural, and perhaps too long repressed, expression of grief, Elizabeth II continued to cope extraordinarily well with the new duties and responsibilities that had so suddenly descended upon her. She had, of course, been prepared for them.

The Duke of Edinburgh, however, had not been trained from childhood for such a dramatic change of circumstances. A few days after George VI's funeral, ex-King Peter of Yugoslavia (he had been deposed by the Communists in 1945) had lunch at Clarence House and later told his wife his impressions of Philip: "You could feel it all underneath. It was as if a volcano had been stoppered up. . . . I don't know how long he can last . . . bottled up like that." Philip's elder sister, Margarita, also remembered his black depression during the two days after George VI's funeral. He could hardly be got to stir from his room, saying despondently, "You can imagine what's going to happen now."

What cataclysm did he imagine? Basically, being submerged, sunk without trace, amid a flood of constitutional and official business that would naturally flow directly to the Queen – a singularly disquieting fate for a promising young naval commander. Nearly two decades later the Duke of Edinburgh recalled his feelings: "Within the house, and whatever we did, it was together. I suppose I naturally filled the principal position. People used to come to me and ask me what to do. In 1952 the whole thing changed, very, very considerably."

What did he want from the new set of circumstances? To get his hands on those ubiquitous red boxes of official papers? To reign as co-monarch? To be another Prince Albert? These are flights of fancy, and one at least was later laid to rest by an American interviewer:

Interviewer: 'Your grandfather was a King, your great-great-grandmother was a Queen, your wife is a Queen. Have you

152

ever thought, maybe it would be nice to be King? Or have you thought, I'm glad I'm not King?

Duke of Edinburgh: "Oh, I'm glad I'm not."

Interviewer: "Why wouldn't you like to be King?"

Duke of Edinburgh: "Well, I'm not. It's a hypothetical question."

Interviewer: "You mean you are making the best of your present lot?"

Duke of Edinburgh: "Oh, yes. But I would anyway."

For a dominant man, who had come to believe that he knew best, his new status was clearly summarised in the Royal Warrant issued in September 1952 which stated that, "His Royal Highness, Philip, Duke of Edinburgh, henceforth and on all occasions [shall] have, hold and enjoy Place, Pre-Eminence, and Precedence next to Her Majesty." Not much different from before, one might argue, except that he was used to bearing the weight of most decisions and now became fearful that the Queen would have to shoulder the vast load of official matters unaided. The protective role that he had played, almost from the first, would be that much more difficult to fulfil: protocol, precedence, pre-eminence would all be obstacles to his offering practical support. Courtiers might well be resistant to any initiative that smacked of trespassing on the royal prerogative.

The Duke of Edinburgh later described his problems in this respect:

Because she's the Sovereign, everybody turns to her. If you have a King and a Queen, there are certain things people automatically go to the Queen about. But if the Queen is also the *Queen*, they go to her about everything. She's asked to do much more than she would normally do, and its frightfully difficult to persuade . . . Many of the Household . . . the fact that they report to the Queen is important to them, and it's frightfully difficult to persuade them not to go to the Queen, but to come to me.

Apart from these anxieties over his wife's new responsibilities (and perhaps over his own official exclusion from the innermost mysteries of the system), there were other stresses. Moving out of Clarence House, his first adult home, was a bitter blow. The gloomy grandeur of Buckingham Palace must have seemed a poor substitute. As it happened, at first he had nowhere appropriate to settle in;

153

Elizabeth, the Queen Mother, was, understandably, slow to move out of her quarters, and Philip was bedded down in a large, ground-floor room of the palace. Admittedly he had brought his bed and a television set from Clarence House, but he was surrounded by heavy, ornate, black and gold, marble-topped furniture, and the red silk walls were hung with the muted portraits of Spanish kings and infantas.

Significantly, he spent part of his first few weeks in this uninspiring room ill in bed. He had gone down with yellow jaundice and was obliged to stay in bed for three weeks. For one who prized good health so highly, even to the point of mildly disapproving of illness in others, this malady was a clear indication of the depression and strain from which he was suffering. There was obviously a good deal in his new circumstances that he found intolerable and difficult to cope with.

Another vexation was the matter of the family name. When she married Philip, Elizabeth had taken the surname of Mountbatten, and she began her reign bearing that name. Winston Churchill's government, however, objected, preferring that she should reign under her father's name of Windsor. It was an awkward and unprecedented proposal, the full significance of which will be discussed later, but on 21 April 1952, by an Order in Council, the Queen decreed that she and her immediate descendants should bear the name of Windsor. This was another rebuff to her husband's feelings, and the implications rankled.

The problem over his role was not imaginary. There was a substantial, and not too far distant, precedent to ponder over – that of Prince Albert and Queen Victoria. It is somehow reassuring to know that, before marrying Elizabeth, Philip read several biographies of "Albert the Good", who was his great-great-grandfather as well as his wife's.

What he learnt from them is difficult to know, for Albert aroused widely differing reactions, few of them particularly favourable. On the one hand, Victoria had loved him passionately from first sight (a good omen perhaps for Queen Elizabeth's husband?). She admired his "exquisite nose", his "delicate moustachios", his "beautiful figure"; after their wedding she came equally to admire qualities of a more private nature – certainly their nine surviving offspring indicate that their marriage bed was not a frigid one.

This queenly devotion to Albert both solved and created a problem. On the one hand, Victoria did not jealously guard state secrets from her husband; rather she welcomed the advice, and the support, which he was only too willing to give in such matters. She made him Prince Consort in 1857 (the only husband of a British queen to be granted this formal, though vague, title) in partial recognition of his services to the state, and to herself. Albert, in short, saw the "boxes", advised on policy, dabbled in statecraft. He was her confidant, her private secretary, her closest counsellor.

Herein lay the problem. British politicians resented Albert's influence, and the patriotic public distrusted him as a foreigner. During the Crimean War a popular ballad had claimed that:

> Little Al, the royal Pal,
> They say has turned a Russian.

Lord Palmerston, who had his own robust views of the constitutional proprieties, confessed his fear that had Albert lived longer he would have become a virtual dictator. Victoria's first Prime Minister, the paternal and still handsome Lord Melbourne, had, however, encouraged the young Queen to communicate all foreign despatches to her husband, being perhaps anxious to involve a more mature royal head in such matters. Albert had responded gratefully, writing in 1840: "Victoria allows me to take much part in foreign affairs, and I think I have already done some good. I always commit my views to paper, and then communicate them to Lord Melbourne. He seldom answers me, but I have the satisfaction of seeing him act entirely in accordance with what I have said." Some wishful thinking here, perhaps, but at least Albert had a role, albeit an increasingly controversial one. In the end his role turned out to be a far cry from his claim that he was "sinking his individual existence in that of the Queen"; rather the Queen sank her personality in his.

Were British statesmen perturbed that Queen Elizabeth might play Victoria to Philip's Albert? It seems unlikely. For one thing, Elizabeth was far more familiar with her official duties and responsibilities than Victoria had been at her accession, and Philip was perhaps initially less certain in these matters than Albert had been. For another, the function of the monarch had been far more clearly defined by 1952 than they had been in 1837. Victoria had begun her reign at a time when certain royal prerogatives were open to debate and closer definition. Elizabeth, and her father and grandfather, had virtually no room for manoeuvre, their constitutional duties and obligations being plainly understood on all sides. Nonetheless there were undoubtedly those in the British establishment who wanted to keep Philip Mountbatten's nose out of official business.

One of Albert's great and uncontroversial contributions to the British monarchy had been to ensure its respectability, after the excesses and scandalous behaviour of Victoria's Hanoverian uncles. He also helped to put its financial affairs in order, and he took an active and knowledgeable part in the encouragement of technological and scientific innovation. Here at least were examples which Philip might profitably follow.

Family respectability, of course, is a fragile flower: Victoria and Albert's firstborn, the future Edward VII, had led a life of determined debauchery, there had been the painful crisis over Edward VIII and Mrs Simpson, and Princess Margaret's activities were later to provide front-page copy for the world's newspapers. Still, to be the father of a close, loving and respectable family was a worthy ambition for the Duke of Edinburgh.

In the financial affairs of the monarchy, Philip was to play an important, though sometimes controversial, role. Soon after her accession, Elizabeth II made him Chief Ranger of Windsor Great Park, which sounds rather jolly, but was in effect a potentially demanding job in royal estate management. He was soon to bring a good deal of drive, and a keen sense of economy, to the management of the other royal estates. In this respect he has been at least as successful as Prince Albert, and has similarly taken another load off the Queen's shoulders. He has also brought a frankness to the public discussion of the state's financing of royal activities, and in 1969 he stirred up a controversy by remarking on American television that the monarchy would be "in the red" by 1970. This led to a wide-ranging, and sometimes wildly inaccurate, debate about the financial means of the royal family. At least there were fewer dusty, undisclosed secrets at the end of it.

The encouragement of science and technology had been one of Albert's greatest contributions to his adopted nation. His high-minded and earnest approach to these matters did not, however, automatically bring him popularity: once, when Palmerston observed in a speech to a learned assembly that no one could converse with the Prince Consort without having his mind improved, the remark was greeted by a stony silence. No modern Prime Minister has so far put a contemporary audience to a similar test, but it is reasonable to suppose that even if there were to be a silence, it would be less stony.

The Duke of Edinburgh had begun his special official relationship with the sciences and technology before Elizabeth's accession. In 1951 he was appointed President of the British Association for the Advancement of Science. Before he left the *Magpie* he was working on his presidential address entitled "The British Contribution to Science and Technology in the Past Hundred Years" – a fair undertaking for a man whose post-school training had been in the Royal Navy. He addressed a packed and learned audience of over two thousand at Edinburgh University, beginning with an arresting quotation (from Prince Albert, appropriately enough): "Your kind invitation to me to undertake the office of your president could not but startle me. . . . The high position which science occupies . . . contrasted strongly in my mind with the consciousness of my own insignificance."

From this disarming start, he went on to survey, as promised, the past achievements of British science and technology. He ended, however, with a more elegant version of his "pull your finger out" sentiments: "The rate at which scientific knowledge is being applied in many industries is too small and too slow. . . . Our physical resources have dwindled, but the intellectual capacity of our scientists and engineers is as great as ever, and it is upon their ingenuity that our future depends." He went on to point out, unremarkably perhaps, that man's scientific knowledge could now either free the world from drudgery, fear, hunger and disease, "or obliterate life itself . . . It is clearly our duty as citizens to see that science is used for the benefit of mankind. For what use is science, if man does not survive?"

The speech was greeted with tremendous applause, and the press the next day were equally approving. Why were these reactions so enthusiastic? Perhaps relief explains a good deal: relief that the Queen's husband could make a speech that contained some real meat; relief that the peroration had not been a dreary compilation of those platitudes so beloved of royal speech-writers; relief that something relevant had been said. Of course, Philip's speech was not a collection of totally original thoughts strung together in a shimmering oratorical necklace, nor, despite his gloomy forebodings over man's chances of survival, had he become a spokesman for the campaign for nuclear disarmament. What the address did show was a capacity to speak frankly and plainly about some of the unpleasant facts of life facing the British people as they entered the second half of the twentieth century. It was a theme he was to return to. It also gave the Duke of Edinburgh, almost overnight, a stature that he had not previously enjoyed.

Apart from Albert, there was another, and in those days, untarnished model for Philip's guidance. Prince Bernhard of the Netherlands, Queen Juliana's husband, as yet unscathed by the Lockheed corruption scandal, was "the greatest living expert on the subject". Philip consulted Bernhard, who apparently said, "You are new at this thing . . . and you probably don't realize what you are up against. Practically everything you do will be a subject of criticism. You can't ignore it because some of it may be justified, and even if it isn't, it may be politic to heed it. But don't let it get you down. In this job you need a skin like an elephant."

Essentially, the Duke of Edinburgh has tried to combine the best of the "Albert approach" with the best of the "Bernhard approach". He has not even tried to sink "his individual existence in that of the Queen" (as Albert put it); he has far too strong an ego and sense of worth to do anything of the sort, except where constitutional form demands it. On the contrary, he has devoted much of his energy to the promotion of science, technology, design, international cooperation, the conservation of the world's resources and sport.

He is under no illusions as to his official constitutional status: "Constitutionally, I don't exist." Albert would not have said that, but perhaps it is healthier for the Duke of Edinburgh to have acknowledged the fact. Of course, Albert was eventually made "Prince Consort", a title to which Philip has never aspired, though in 1957 the Queen created him *the* Prince Philip, which, to the outside world is even more meaningless – unless one assumes the existence of another and inferior Prince Philip. Although the Duke of Edinburgh is a Privy Councillor it is a privilege shared with quite a large number of others; in any case, he rarely attends its meetings, finding its formal proceedings, in which discussion hardly ever occurs, a waste of time.

His role in the procedural mystery that still surrounds the British monarchy is, therefore, not one to which a constitutional definition can be attached. It is, in fact, an "unwritten" role, rather like the British constitution itself, which relies largely upon the observance of precedent, bolstered by isolated pieces of statutory legislation. With customary determination and flair, however, he has carved out a role that makes his constitutional impotence irrelevant.

Quite simply Philip acts, in the words of Michael Parker, as a kind of super Chief of Staff who can give the Queen the complete "lowdown on absolutely everything". Whereas the Queen's life is circumscribed by the convention that the monarch must preside impartially over the nation's affairs and only indulge in a bland, non-sectarian pursuit of pleasure, her husband suffers far less from such restrictions. He can prod and pry, ask awkward questions, stir up people's consciences, issue a rebuke here and there, express opinions that are not mere bromides, and generally act with far more freedom. If his official relationship to the Queen often has to be measured by the protocol of the second handshake, the foot a step behind her own, his unofficial role is comparatively far-ranging and unfettered. To a certain extent he can see the world as it is, and bring this experience and knowledge to the service of the monarchy.

In 1970 Michael Parker summed up Philip's active role, and his early difficulties in finding his feet:

> With the job itself, starting from the very beginning, when there was nothing at all, he had to build it up brick by brick. Apart from the King, I was surprised, to be perfectly honest, that he didn't get a great deal of help – that there wasn't a collection of great men in the land who had suggestions to make. He had to think it out alone. I know that his prime object from the word go, was to be of service, and to help the Queen. Nothing's ever changed that, and nothing's stopped it, and he pitched into it with a vigour that was absolutely staggering. I don't think he's let up.

The Duke of Edinburgh's activities as another pair of eyes and ears for the Queen, as a "kind of super Chief of Staff", were still those of a second-in-command. He conceived the role, though, as being essentially a creative one: to boost her confidence and broaden her experience in private, and to act as a consistent support in public.

Over a year after she came to the throne, Elizabeth II's coronation service offered a neat illustration of the ambiguities of her husband's position. The coronation ceremony held at Westminster Abbey on 2 June 1953 included the act of homage whereby the senior peers of the realm knelt one by one before the newly crowned Queen to swear allegiance. At their head came the Duke of Edinburgh, who knelt before his wife and swore to become "Your liege man of life and limb and of earthly worship; and faith and truth I will bear unto you, to live and die against all manner of folks. So help me God."

On the day, the Duke performed the act of homage with high seriousness and not a little emotion. Many of those who witnessed the moment either in the Abbey or on television found it a moving experience. Yet at one of the final rehearsals Philip, "feeling a little foolish", had "mumbled the words at high speed, jumped up; gave the crown a mere flip of his hand, pecked at the air a foot from the Queen's cheek; and backed off rapidly. With the amused exasperation of a mother with a wayward child, Elizabeth said, 'Come back, Philip, and do it properly!' "

Yet it had been the Duke of Edinburgh who had thrown himself headlong into the intensive preparations for the coronation. If he did not take the rehearsal seriously, it was the one act of flippancy that he allowed himself. As Chairman of the Coronation Commission he proceeded, in his usual fashion, to make a full contribution to the planning of the arrangements. He stood on the balcony at Buckingham Palace, imagining that he was wearing the crown on his head, and studied the sky to see where the Queen might reasonably be expected to look for the RAF fly-past without hurting her neck. He insisted that the maximum opportunity for symbolising the unity of the Commonwealth should be found in the ceremony. He helped to track down a vial of four ounces of the sacred oil that had been used to annoint Queen Victoria. In short, although it was Elizabeth II who had stood, dazzlingly, in the limelight, her husband had played an important, but unsung, part in focusing the beam and stage-managing the performance.

19

20

9 Meanwhile, back at
e naval training
tablishment at
orsham, Lieutenant
Iountbatten's
deboard displays books
y Godfrey Winn and
rthur Koestler as well as
e Bible, *The King's
egulations*, and the two
olumes of *Manual of
eamanship*

0 Lieutenant
Iountbatten's petty
fficers put on, with some
fort, a balletic gym
isplay

1 The night before the
iorning after.
raditional, hearty stag
arty, with uncle Dickie
econd from right)
ading the revels

21

22 Not a scene from *Les Sylphides*, but bridesmaids arranging Princess Elizabeth's star-spangled train as she arrives on her father's arm at the West door of Westminster Abbey

23 Get me to the church on time! Kensington Palace staff speed the bridegroom and best man (David Milford Haven) on their way to Westminster Abbey

24 Marriage certificate: note Queen Mary's approving flourish

25 The Queen's wedding group: amongst the many guests are, *centrally*, above the royal couple, Queen Mary, the bride's grandmother; *front row, 2nd from left*, Princess Alice, Prince Philip's mother; HRH Princess Margaret; pageboy, HRH Prince William of Gloucester; 3rd Marquess of Milford Haven (best man); HRH Princess Elizabeth; HRH Prince Philip; pageboy, HRH Prince Michael of Kent; HRH Princess Alexandra of Kent; a pensive King George VI; Queen Elizabeth; the Duke of Gloucester, with his hands on shoulders of his younger son; standing slightly behind him, the Duchess of Gloucester. *3rd row from front, 2nd from left*, a contented Louis Mountbatten

ROYAL WEDDING

20 November 1947

23

24

25

26 Public
happiness on the
balcony of
Buckingham
Palace
27 King George VI
and Queen
Elizabeth lead the
procession of
European royalty
out of Westminster
Abbey following
their daughter's
wedding. Queen
Mary and Princess
Alice of Greece,
the bridegroom's
mother, follow as
they move from the
centre of the nave.
King Michael of
Romania, the
Queen of the
Hellenes, and the
twelve-year-old
King of Iraq walk
next followed by
King Frederik and
Queen Ingrid of
Denmark.

27

28

29

28 Private
happiness on
honeymoon at
Broadlands
29 The Duke of
Edinburgh behind
his desk at
Clarence House in
1951
30 Princess
Margaret seen
thoughtfully
puffing a cigarette
in a group
including Group
Captain
Townsend at
Badminton during
the 2nd day event
of the Olympic
Horse Trials

30

31

32

31 & 32 Family of four in
the gardens of Clarence
House, August 1951. All
the movement seems to be
coming from Princess
Anne.
33 A later addition. A
bonny Prince Andrew
(and corgi) at Balmoral in
September 1960
34 The family completed.
Prince Edward was born
in 1964. Prince Philip has
said: "I don't goo over
them. I think they're just
people."

35 The Coronation: Prince Philip apparently weighed down by his ducal coronet at Westminster Abbey
36 On the balcony of Buckingham Palace

36   35

10

Husband and Father

"I do not think that you can perform any finer service than
to help maintain the Christian doctrine that the relation of
husband and wife is a permanent one."

Queen Elizabeth II

IT IS DIFFICULT ENOUGH to gauge the quality of any marriage, let
alone that of a couple so surrounded by protocol and secrecy as the
Queen and the Duke of Edinburgh. That Elizabeth fell in love with
her future husband at their first meeting seems quite clear. When, or
how, he finally fell in love with her is a matter of speculation;
perhaps the "one thing led to another" school of thought holds the
key to the mystery.

Basil Boothroyd says, loyally, "No one should think, as some
chose to think at the time, that he saw marriage to the most eligible
of heiresses as a stroke of high gamesmanship. . . . If his was a hard
assignment, hers would be harder. . . . Perhaps all the crooning
about a love match, which arose from a thousand pages in the
summer of 1947, went overboard a bit. But a marriage either of
convenience or ambition it certainly was not."

But was it, and has it been, a marriage of passion, of intimacy and
of mutual trust? As with couples in humbler social positions the
answer is both "yes" and "no". Few can doubt the depth of the
attachment that built up during Elizabeth and Philip's courtship
and carried them triumphantly beyond their wedding. Despite
Philip's naval service in the Mediterranean the marriage had produced two children by 1950, and, more interestingly, went on to
produce another two in the early 1960s. Not that it should be
supposed that Prince Andrew and Prince Edward were the acciden-
tal by-products of uncontrollable passion: the Queen had always

161

wanted a fairly large family, and might well have produced her children in a more regular sequence if she had not ascended to the throne well before she expected to.

Comparison between Elizabeth's marriage and Victoria's is not necessarily very revealing, especially in view of the availability of the latter's diaries and letters and the complete non-availability of the former's private papers. Nonetheless, one is left with the impression that Elizabeth has hardly remained as besotted with her husband as did Queen Victoria – if, indeed, Elizabeth was ever as besotted. That they love each other, while being acutely aware of their partner's inadequacies and foibles, is widely accepted.

The main component of their marriage, apart from the shared experience of child-rearing and care of the family, is a mutual respect that has withstood thirty-three years of living together. They have a capacity to talk to, and listen to, each other that is more marked than in many couples. When separated, they frequently talk affectionately of the other – which is a good sign. The Duke of Edinburgh's capacity for laughter is evident and well-documented, and has rubbed off on to the Queen. At the beginning of their relationship they both shared a taste, apparently predictable in royal families, for jokes of a venerable and obvious nature. Since then the Queen's "latent sense of the comic, not given much chance in the sheltered days, has been brought much nearer the surface". Her eye for the absurd has been enhanced by Prince Philip's own keen perception of the ridiculous. She has developed a lively gift of anecdote, recalling minutely observed incidents for the amusement of her family and close friends. Laughter, in fact, has been a most valuable cohesive force between husband and wife, and something which those near to them unfailingly remark on.

Their marriage has had to accommodate, and may paradoxically have been sustained by, a certain separateness. They do not, for example, share the same bedroom, let alone the same bed. When they moved into their first home, Clarence House, they decided to sleep in neighbouring bedrooms and have kept up the arrangement ever since. At Clarence House, "The Princess's elaborately draped double bed featured a crown suspended from the hangings. The Duke's quarters were more spartan, and every morning they would sit at their respective dressing-tables talking and joking through the half-open connecting door between them."

In Buckingham Palace, too, their offices are side by side, with their respective staffs working together on the floor below. The list of their official engagements contains a certain proportion of joint visits as well as allowing them to operate as individuals. Their separate engagements do not always reflect stereotyped "male" and "female" roles. For instance, though in February 1980 the Duke of Edinburgh visited "the Safety Vessel MSV *Tharas* near the Piper Platform in the North Sea", two weeks beforehand it had been the Queen who had dined in the Officers' Mess, Royal Air Force, Marham. At Trooping the Colour it is, after all, the Queen who rides at the head of her scarlet-jacketed guards.

Within the domestic setting, however, there is little role reversal. The Duke of Edinburgh, though he is unwilling or unable to bully his wife, presides over "his home as an old-fashioned *pater familias*". Generally speaking, his word goes. He runs the estates and drives the car "where she has learnt to draw breath only silently". Though he is very much "a man's man", he does enjoy cooking, mostly in the open air and often something a little more exciting than sausages. Sausages, however, were for a time cooked by him for breakfast in a special electric pan; the Queen put up with it for a while, but eventually convinced him that the smell was still hanging about at lunchtime, and that perhaps it was not worth it. Despite these culinary activities, the Duke wears the trousers and his wife the apron – which is something of a reversal of their formal constitutional roles.

In times when divorce has become a commonplace in the United Kingdom, and has even involved members of the royal family like Princess Margaret and the Earl of Harewood, it is inconceivable that the Queen and Prince Philip might be tempted to contemplate separation. Even if both felt the need, there would be formidable obstacles, not least of which would be Elizabeth's position as Supreme Governor of the Church of England. In any case, the Queen's position is quite clear; she is for marriage and family life, and against divorce.

In a speech to the British Mothers' Union she once said, "When we see around us the havoc that has been wrought – above all among children – by the break-up of homes, we can have no doubt that divorce and separation are responsible for some of the darkest evils in our society today. I do not think that you can perform any finer service than to help maintain the Christian doctrine that the relation of a husband and wife is a permanent one." These sentiments were expressed well before Princess Margaret finally decided to separate from the Earl of Snowdon, but there are no grounds for believing that the Queen's views have changed. As for Prince Philip, despite, or perhaps because of, his own parents' separation, he also has a traditionalist view of such matters.

Divorce, like war, is a final solution to the incompatibilities, outrages, or treacheries that two parties have endured at each other's hands. There is no evidence that either the Queen or the Duke of Edinburgh have suffered in any way through their marriage: he has supported her with a zestful consistency, and she has provided a stability and domesticity that he greatly needed. To outside observers, and to those close to both of them, they seem a happily married couple, complementing each other's blind spots and shortcomings.They do quarrel, and it would be disturbing if they did not: "Voices are raised. 'Watch out, a couple of acid drops,' servants will whisper as the pair stride out icily silent to their limousine."

Prince Philip, however, has not escaped gossip and wounding innuendo. This is inevitable: he exudes masculine drive and self-confidence, and his royal status is both intriguing and seductive. He is, moreover, a man who is attractive to women. Basil Boothroyd quotes an American who saw him once in Chicago: "We were on some kind of bridge, and he waved from his car, and my wife said, 'He could put his shoes under my bed any time.' Get that. My own wife." The American's wife is not an isolated case. The press, and particularly the European press, have been hungrily searching for juicy tit-bits of gossip ever since he became engaged to Princess Elizabeth. Were there, in short, "other women"?

Two case studies illustrate with great clarity the difficulties which the Duke of Edinburgh has faced in this connection. To begin with there is the speculation that surrounded his relationship with a childhood friend from Greece, Hélène Foufounis, better known in Britain as Hélène Cordet, the hostess of the early television show *Café Continental*. That they had been close when adolescents was no secret. But foreign journals, particularly in France, West Germany and Italy, made a good deal out of any contact between the two, especially in the late 1940s and early '50s. Much was made of events which would have passed without provoking so much as a neighbour's comment in a British suburb or country town.

Upon what evidence were the rumours based? In 1943 Philip gave Hélène away at her wedding to an officer in the Free French forces, but he was also best man. He was later godfather (some said father) to her children Max Philippe, who became a pupil at

Gordonstoun in Philip's footsteps, and Louise. Although her mother, Madame Anna Foufounis, was invited to Philip and Elizabeth's wedding, Hélène did not receive an invitation; the nearest she got to the ceremony was to help her mother dress for the occasion. An Italian newspaper made a good deal of this, reporting that Elizabeth had forbidden Philip to invite Hélène. Philip also once tried to help Hélène to get started in British fashion modelling.

All of this is quite compatible with shared childhood experiences, an adolescent infatuation, a more mature love affair, a straightforward platonic friendship, or a mixture of any of these. Eventually Hélène published her memoirs, which, entitled *Born Bewildered*, probably left most of her readers equally bewildered. The memoirs are studded with protestations of injured innocence mingled with near-revelations. Some passages are worth quoting in full, if only to show the eagerness of Europe's newshounds to catch a whiff of scandal.

About the excitement and speculation that surrounded Philip and Elizabeth's wedding, Hélène wrote:

Just before the Royal wedding, I had noticed a few things in the French press that I couldn't understand . . .

Every paper for weeks was full of [Philip], and they quickly ran out of material. They talked about his last stay in Paris, and I was very surprised when they started asking questions about a blonde who had been seen with him then. They called her the mystery blonde, and a few days before the wedding one paper published the back view of a blonde with the caption, "the one who will *not* be invited to the wedding".

All this puzzled me, for I had seen Philip in Paris and I could swear that there was no question of a blonde, or a brunette for that matter.

Two or three years later when I became friendly with some journalists from the French magazine *Paris-Match* I discovered with amazement that the mystery blonde had been me! I put them wise on the spot and I got a feeling they were slightly disappointed.

At the time of the wedding, someone saw at my brother's flat a picture taken on my wedding day with Philip at my side. The day before the wedding, a magazine offered him a considerable amount of money for it, and he had to lock it in his safe. When my brother told me, I couldn't believe to what length some people would go, just to get an untrue story. It was frightening.

Then there was the time, later, in Britain, when she took her children to watch Philip playing polo:

> Sunday always was – and still is – our day of rest. I don't think I could have gone on without it. So when Philip invited me and the children to go and watch polo whenever we wanted to, I thought this was a very good way to get the fresh air I needed so much. But after one Sunday I never dared go back. I hadn't thought of the interest my visit would arouse, and I am sure Philip hadn't thought of it either.
>
> On the day we went, he chatted with us between chukkas. I suddenly noticed cameras focused on our group, and we were followed around by journalists. We said goodbye to Philip and left early because of all this fuss. On our way home we stopped at Staines and decided to see a film. When we got home, quite late, we were told that newspapers had been telephoning all evening asking why I wasn't back yet, although the polo had finished hours before.
>
> I decided there and then I wouldn't watch polo again – I'd find my fresh air elsewhere.

In other words, the press was behaving as if Philip and Hélène were having an affair, and was trying to catch them in a compromising relationship to each other.

These rather coy protestations of Hélène's rub shoulders with more ambiguous passages. We learn, for example, that Hélène, now famous through the success of *Café Continental*, "was approached very discreetly by the BBC, who asked me to appear on a very special programme they were planning for the Queen and Prince Philip's visit to the television studios at Lime Grove". "Very discreetly" is the suggestive phrase. Then Hélène remarks, rather mysteriously, "For some time now I had been a bit embarrassed at the way the newspapers always said 'Prince Philip is godfather to her children' when they wrote about me. This was quite reasonable, of course, but I never wanted to cause any embarrassment to the royal family." Of course. It also appears that Hélène had "been told several times by Prince Philip that they never missed *Café Continental* if they could help it". The Queen Mother "said the same thing". The Queen's comments are not available to us.

More mystery: Hélène was asked to appear "on the royal TV show", but "I hesitated [why?]. . . . Then I wrote to Philip and asked his and the Queen's permission. The answer came like a shot, by telephone from Balmoral. . . . I was told to get on with it, so I did." And one final, spontaneous piece of self-revelation: "As I was writing this, my television set was switched on to a circus performance and quite incredibly, one of the spectators was Philip himself! For one moment I went back years and got quite hot under the collar."

The second case study of damaging gossip concerns Philip's lengthy trip through the South Atlantic after opening the Olympic Games in Australia in 1956. The trip covered nearly forty thousand miles, part of the distance being covered by air, and part in the new royal yacht, the *Britannia*. It took several months to complete from October 1956 until early in 1957. Immediately the tour was announced there was speculation as to its significance. Why so long away? Why was the Duke going alone? Had there been a colossal row, a rift even, with the Queen? There was undoubtedly some divergence of interests at this point in their marriage. Robert Lacey in his biography of Elizabeth II has said, "Her husband's resentment at the truncating of his naval career took the form of long hours in the *Britannia*, like his expedition . . . in the winter of 1956–7 when he could exploit the chores of his role as consort to recapture something of his carefree days at sea. His wife's reaction was to retreat into the privacy of her family and tight little circle of friends."

The storm did not break until early in 1957, as the Duke of Edinburgh was sailing homewards from Gambia (where he had been greeted with astonishing shouts of "Welcome, Duke, and Jesus keep you for the Queen!"). It was then that the press learned that Mrs Michael Parker was about to divorce her husband, who was aboard *Britannia* as Philip's secretary. Rumour then had the Queen, whose views on divorce were well known, demanding that Parker should be dismissed. There was gossip of Parker and Philip having attended "wild parties" – obvious echoes of reports from over a decade previously. Parker decided to resign before *Britannia* arrived home. Philip was deeply upset at his friend's fall from grace. The "row" between him and the Queen was reported in the *Baltimore Sun* as having escalated into something really serious. A British reporter phoned a press officer at Buckingham Palace who promptly issued an official denial. The home press proceeded to print the denial and what was being denied. Now speculation ran riot, and the Queen's long-arranged flight to Lisbon to meet Philip

in the *Britannia* acquired all the melodramatic overtones of a reconciliation set-piece.

What had really happened? Parker had not been sacked on
prurient royal demand. He had recognised the scale of the scandal
that was about to engulf him and had decided, in Prince Philip's
words, that "he had to go". Indeed, according to inside information, "The break was sad for all three, and was entirely his own
decision. They both urged him to stay (the Queen by radio-
telephone to Gibraltar, where Philip's world tour in *Britannia* was
ending. . . .)"

When the Queen eventually joined the Duke of Edinburgh at
Lisbon, she did indeed find an embittered man; a man who deeply
resented the banner headlines that had attended the whole business
and who felt that his best friend had been thrown to the journalistic
lions to satisfy their hunger for salacious morsels. The hullabaloo
had also rendered the real achievements of the tour insignificant.
Was there a dramatic reconciliation? One authority thinks not,
"just a joyful reunion". But the popular press chose to see things
differently and front-page stories bore bold captions like "Radiant
Queen" or "Smiling Prince". In fact, Philip's smiles were not for the
press, for whom his feelings were decidedly hostile.

The foreign press, in particular, has been a heavy cross for both
Philip and Elizabeth to bear. European editors especially are less
squeamish than the British press when it comes to speculation of a
private nature, and, moreover, they cannot be muzzled by patriotic
press barons or by sympathetic Prime Ministers. In 1972, in fact,
the Paris newspaper *France Dimanche* calculated that in the previous fourteen years there had appeared in the French press sixty-
three reports of Elizabeth's abdication, seventy-three reports of her
divorce from the Duke of Edinburgh, and ninety-two reports of
pregnancies. The Queen sometimes reads *France Dimanche* and is
known to admire its writers' powers of invention.

The proper perspective in considering these tides of speculation
and rumour is obvious: in 1972 the Queen and the Duke of Edinburgh celebrated their Silver Wedding, with more than adequate
satisfaction. They have shown no signs of any rift since; rumours of
Prince Philip's extra-marital adventures seem to have faded away;
the bonds of love, mutual respect and caring are as strong as ever.
The marriage, put simply, stands solidly and shows no sign of
withering away.

Above all, their relationship encompasses their four children.

One of Elizabeth's first protective instincts was to ensure that they suffered as little from exposure to the public and the mass media as was consistent with their status. Rather arch, posed official family photographs were one thing, a photographers' free-for-all was another. When Charles started at Cheam School in 1957, he was so harassed by newsmen that the Queen's press secretary had to summon the editors of the London newspapers and point out that if there was no let-up the prince would be taken away and educated privately. Quite apart from it being their father's school, one advantage of the Queen and Duke's three sons being sent on to Gordonstoun was its distance from Fleet Street. Even so, Prince Charles' first days there were made a misery by the activities of pressmen.

Apart from trying to ensure the family's privacy, Queen Elizabeth has been insistent that her children should grow up "as normally as possible". For princes and princesses, growing up "normally" might be supposed to entail not breakfasting off caviare and smoked salmon, nor having cringing servants tying up their shoelaces and generally attending to their every whim. Compared with almost every other child in the United Kingdom, of course, the royal children have colossal built-in privileges – not the least of which is the rock-like security of their background, barring a bloody, revolutionary assault on the monarchy.

What Elizabeth II meant by as "normal" a childhood as possible was: "bread and sandwiches to be finished at tea before the cakes were attacked, hems let down, elbows patched, 2s. 6d. a week pocket money, and servants instructed to call the children by their first names when young and not 'Your Royal Highness'." Laudable aims, but hardly a startling experiment in social engineering.

The Duke of Edinburgh's influence on his children's development and education has been the more obvious, though not necessarily the more constructive in the long run. They call him "Papa", and he has always played the role of a traditional, yet benevolent, father figure. Finding the time to be an effective father has been one of his problems and lengthy overseas tours, with or without the Queen, cannot have helped his early relationship with his children. In the tradition maintained by George VI, and going back to Prince Albert, he has tried to spend as much of his free time as possible with his four children – in contrast to the fitful presence of his father, Prince Andrew, during his own childhood.

Although he managed to dig out some of his old baby clothes when Prince Charles was born, the Duke of Edinburgh's main contribution to his children's upbringing has come after the nappy, breast and bottle stage of their development. He played with them a good deal and introduced them to a wide range of physical and sporting skills (the Kurt Hahn ethic again). Eventually he taught them swimming, sailing, shooting, fishing, riding, go-karting and, inevitably, polo. He also tried to interest Charles in his own love of painting, in which, perhaps surprisingly, he is extremely proficient. The philosophy behind this teaching of certain skills has been clearly explained by Prince Philip, though the philosophy is hardly revolutionary: "I've always tried to help them master at least one thing, because as soon as a child feels self-confidence in one area, it spills over into another."

Like the Queen he believed that, whenever possible, his children should not escape ordinary chores. For instance, he "was similarly keen on Charles making his own bed and getting to breakfast punctually every morning. Without these basic disciplines, the Duke would ask, how could the boy tackle the life he was in for?" At the same time, Philip was realistic about the chances of his children living a "normal" life, telling Basil Boothroyd:

> People talk about a normal upbringing. What is a normal up-bringing? What you really mean is: was I insisting that they should go through all the disadvantages of being brought up in the way other people are brought up? Precisely that – disadvantages. There's always this idea about treating them like other children. In fact it means they're treated much worse, because they're known by name and by association. . . . It's all very well to say they're treated the same as everybody else, but it's impossible. I think what is possible, and in fact necessary, is that they should realise they're not anonymous. This has got to come at some stage.

Prince Philip has given his children a firm lead, but he has not expected them to follow it automatically. Although occasionally severe, he has not been an over-strict disciplinarian or a stickler for details. In this he contrasts favourably with the Queen's grandfather, George V, who tended to treat his children as if they were the potentially mutinous crew of an unseaworthy vessel. George VI, also, for all his diffidence and personal gentleness, tended to expect too much in the way of good behaviour from those close to him. The Duke of Edinburgh has expressed other, liberal, views, though more about his children when older: "It's no use saying do this, do that, don't do this, don't do that. You can warn them about certain things – that's about the most you can do – or you can say this is the situation you are in, these are the choices, on balance it looks as if this is the sensible one, go away and think it over, and come back and let me know what you think."

This is hardly the style of command to which the Duke aspired in his naval career, and, of course, there were occasions when he was obliged to say "no" to his children's demands. Even so, at least in retrospect, he preferred a more flexible response: "It's very easy, when children want something, to say no immediately. I think it's quite important not to give an unequivocal answer at once. Much better to think it over. Then if you do eventually say no, I think they really accept it." An interesting point of view, but sometimes difficult to put into practice with a screaming toddler or a child issuing insistent requests for the immediate gratification of some whim.

The Duke of Edinburgh has set a high store upon the honesty of his children, "by which I mean that if you ask them a question, they must give you an honest answer". Dishonesty, in fact, is considered to be the major crime that can be committed in the family. One obvious advantage of an honest relationship is that it lessens the need to prod and pry: "There are often questions you'd like to ask, but it's much better not to unless it's really necessary."

He moreover has no illusions that childhood development takes a straight, steady path from the cradle to adulthood:

Children go through enormous changes. For a time they're in phase with life around them, then they go out of phase and become unliveable with, and everything they do is wrong and cross-grained and maddening. Then suddenly it all comes right for a bit. Then they go off on another tack. It's impossible at any point to say, "This is what they're going to be like." The pendulum's got to swing a lot more before it settles down.

One of Philip's most positive contributions to his children's development has been in helping to choose the sort of education they should have. It is popularly supposed that because Cheam and Gordonstoun have figured so largely in the education of the royal princes they were automatic choices, a mere following in father's footsteps. It was not quite as simple as that. The Queen, while believing that her children should have a much more public education than she or her sister had ever had, was not sure of which schools to choose. Neither, it seems, was Prince Philip dead set on Cheam and Gordonstoun. The royal couple visited a good many schools and talked to various headmasters before the choice was made.

In 1956 Philip gave an indication of what he and his wife wanted for Prince Charles: "The Queen and I want Charles to go to a school with other boys of his generation and learn to live with other children, and to absorb from childhood the discipline imposed by education and others." Clearly a private preparatory boarding school was the prime objective; they ignored the possibility of finding a suitable state school – something which certain critics and friends of the monarchy felt to be mistaken tactics.

On 28 January 1957 Charles joined Hill House School as a day boy, but spent only two terms there. The big step came in September, when he was sent to Cheam prep school. He had no say in the matter and had already expressed his misgivings at having to live away from home. That it was Prince Philip's old school, though on new premises since his schooldays, was obviously significant. Understandably, like many fathers he must have found the prospect of his son attending his old school irresistible.

Similarly Charles, and Prince Andrew and Prince Edward after him, went on to Gordonstoun. The Queen and the Queen Mother would have preferred Eton, which was after all a mere stone's throw away from Windsor Castle. In the end it was Philip who got his own way, though he did not impose it crudely from above, choosing, rather, to let a rough and ready democracy prevail. Prince Charles was certainly closely involved in the decision:

> From the beginning I [Philip] was careful not to make a rigid plan – I haven't for any of them – until some sort of foreseeable situation arose. I said, "Well, here are the alternatives: you've seen Eton, you know the place, it's right on our doorstep [at Windsor], you can more or less come home every time you like. It's disadvantages are that every time you hiccup you'll have the whole of the national press on your shoulders. Also, Eton is frequently in the news, and when it is it's going to reflect on you. If you go to the north of Scotland you'll be out of sight and they're going to think twice about taking an aeroplane to get up there, so it's got to be a major crisis before they'll actually turn up,

and you'll be able to get on with things. . . . And we had a general discussion and I said "Well, it's up to you."

Prince Charles, who was at that time particularly close to Prince Philip, has admitted that, "My father had a particularly strong influence, and it was very good for me. I had perfect confidence in his judgement." At the same time he acknowledged the democratic framework within which the decision was made: "My parents were marvellous in this way. They'd outline all the possibilities, and in the end it was up to you."

When it came to Prince Charles' higher education, a number of august opinions were sought, including those of the Prime Minister, Harold Wilson, Dr Ramsey, the Archbishop of Canterbury, and Lord Mountbatten. The Duke of Edinburgh wanted to keep his son's options open, saying, "I don't think his course should be constrained by the absolute need to take a degree." Was he afraid of failure, or, at one level, resentful that he had never gone to a university? At any rate, Charles opted for Trinity College, Cambridge, where he gained an average BA Honours degree in History.

Princess Anne, Prince Andrew and Prince Edward have also trodden the path of a private school education, though Anne has not attended a university. At the end of it all, they will at least have been more broadly educated than any other British sovereign's children in this century. If none of them turn out to be academic high-flyers, they will be in good, royal company, and, in any case, their father does not rate such achievements all that highly. He rarely recriminated over their school reports, later admitting, "I really don't take them frightfully seriously. I say: 'Look, I'm only going to bother if you're permanently bottom. I really couldn't care less where you are. Just stay in the middle, that's all I ask.' " Nor did he believe that his children could be formally trained for the official responsibilities that would one day be theirs: "Training isn't necessary. They do on-the-job training, so to speak, and learn the trade, or business or craft, just from being with us and watching us function and seeing the whole organisation around us. They can't avoid it. What is much more difficult is bringing them up as people."

How are Prince Philip's and the Queen's children turning out as people? The Prince of Wales is nearing thirty-two years of age: he is affable, humorous, rather gentle, still somewhat shy, and none too happy with his chin or his protruding ears. Although he started off by hero-worshipping his much more aggressive and extrovert father, and conceding to him in argument, he now feels much closer to his mother, with whom he shares many traits of personality. He has in fact followed his father on to the polo field and has also won his flying "wings", but he prefers the arts to the sciences and is not especially keen on sailing.

Princess Anne has much in common with her father, including a tendency to be brusque with photographers. She is stubborn, strong-willed, and is not afraid of giving offence. She has several times been voted the royal family's least popular member. Her choice of a husband did not improve her relationship with Prince Charles, who privately calls Captain Mark Phillips "Fog" – because "he is thick and wet". The birth of Princess Anne's son Peter in 1977, not only made the Queen and the Duke of Edinburgh grandparents, but also helped to reconcile Charles to the brother-in-law (and sister) that fate has bestowed on him.

Prince Andrew is twenty years old, notably good-looking, and causing female hearts to flutter in every continent. Charles may feel in danger of eclipse, and has said of him, "Ah, the one with the Robert Redford looks." His career at Gordonstoun and his obvious liking for the more vigorous of trainings (from parachute-jumping to marine assault courses), mark him out as a son close to his father. Prince Edward, sixteen years younger than the Prince of Wales, is at Gordonstoun where English Literature, History and Geography are his favourite subjects. He is said to be the more contemplative and artistic of the royal children. He describes his favourite food as "Balmoral butties" (rolls filled with barbecued meat or fish) and names Pink Floyd as his favourite pop group. He enjoys photography and cricket, and believes that his career will be in the Royal Air Force.

Inevitably, all four children bear the physical imprint of their father, as well as some of his mannerisms and tastes – though Charles would sometimes consider himself to be more sympathetic to liberal, even left-wing, opinions. The Duke of Edinburgh says of them that their behaviour has been average to good: "I think they do silly things occasionally, but it's nearly always satisfactorily resolved, more by discussion than anything." Certainly family decisions are taken on a joint basis, with each member having one vote. It seems, on the whole, to be a happy and united family.

Basil Boothroyd recorded a scene, a decade ago, which sums up a lot of it:

Buckingham Palace, a car for Heathrow waiting at the King's Door. He [Philip] comes down the stairs, laughing, with Prince Charles, Prince Andrew and Prince Edward. He peers at Charles' tie and scratches at a stain on it, while Edward rolls head over heels down the last few red-carpeted steps. They call him "Papa", and all kiss him goodbye.

Philip,
The House of Windsor,
and the 'Margaret Problem'

"Probably the only cloud on the horizon lay in the appalling
storm of publicity that thundered . . . around the friendship of
Group Captain Townsend and Princess Margaret. Philip disliked this midsummer storm of speculation and rumour
intensely, just as he disliked anything that could diminish or
threaten the dignity of the Crown."

Ex-Queen Alexandra of Yugoslavia

IF THE MARRIAGE OF PRINCESS ELIZABETH and Lieutenant Mountbatten was charged with the uncritical and sugary symbolism of the
"good, demure, princess" swept off her feet by the "strong, handsome young-man-of-the world and war hero", the private life of
Princess Margaret has offered no such easy satisfaction to the
British public. In fact, from the time of Elizabeth's accession to the
present, the deportment of Princess Margaret has been a cause of
vexation and sadness to many of her close relatives, while at the
same time providing the press and the public with an unrivalled
opportunity for salacious and scandalous gossip.

Princess Margaret Rose was born four years after her sister, and
was soon to emerge as a very different personality. Although both
sisters were treated rather similarly in their early years together –
similar outfits and closely parallel nursery disciplines – George VI's
accession to the throne in 1936 altered this. Princess Elizabeth, as
the heir apparent, had to be prepared for the enormous responsibilities that would eventually be hers, if, as looked more and more
likely, the King and Queen failed to produce a male heir.

As the nature of her future role slowly dawned upon Elizabeth, it
had the effect of accentuating characteristics that had already been
bestowed upon her by heredity and environment. Elizabeth tended
to be solemn, shy and gravely aware of the need to maintain her
poise in public; she needed "drawing out" and was, indeed,

eventually to be drawn out by an ebullient Greek prince with a penchant for jumping over tennis nets!

Princess Margaret, on the other hand, had a much more vivacious and extrovert personality. By the age of six she was demonstrating a gift for music and mimicry which greatly appealed to the rather repressed personality of her father. He encouraged the mimicry and sense of fun, in a sense licensed a childish naughtiness. Courtiers were soon to remark, discreetly, "What a good job Margaret is the *younger* one!"

As they grew up, the differences between the two sisters became more obvious. Margaret was less conscientious and less well-mannered. In his biography of the Queen, *Majesty*, Robert Lacey quotes a neat illustration of the dichotomy in sisterly approach when Elizabeth was heard to say, "If you see someone with a funny hat, Margaret, you must *not* point at it and laugh. . . ." On the occasion of Elizabeth's first meeting with Philip at Dartmouth, the latter initially found it easier to relate to the younger sister: "He was quite polite to Elizabeth, but he did not pay her any special attention. He spent a lot of time teasing plump little Margaret." In other words, Elizabeth's reserve made it difficult for him to establish contact, while Margaret looked a likely recipient for banter. *Private Eye*'s nicknames for the two sisters also makes a plain and irreverent distinction between them: the Queen is "Brenda", which sounds rather solid and dull and worthy, whereas Margaret is "Yvonne", which has a tawdry, suburban glitter about it.

Margaret Rose is also the victim of her curious standing in the order of succession. If Elizabeth had failed to produce children, then Margaret would have inherited the crown after her and would have passed it on to her own offspring, if any. Once Prince Charles was born, to be followed by three siblings, Margaret's significance to the succession ceased. Short of a holocaust involving her sister and the whole of her family, she had become, from a constitutional point of view, irrelevant. This could not have been an easy thing to realise and accept – there was enough scope for sisterly rivalry as it was. This extra dimension may have contributed to Margaret's final decision to kick over the royal traces and strike out for a style of living that owed nothing to contemporary family convention. At least she became able to lead the sort of life that gave her a better chance of personal fulfilment.

Her liberation, however, was a long time in coming. Indeed, from her adolescence to the time of her marriage in 1960 to Antony

177

Armstrong-Jones, she remained a basically staunch supporter of the royal family's concept of "duty"; a duty which, in her case, led to a self-sacrificial act of particularly traumatic nature. It says a good deal for the close relationship that she had enjoyed from childhood with her sister that the stresses she brought into the family, both before and after her marriage, caused so little evident disharmony and dislocation.

Put very simply, the "Princess Margaret problem" has centred on her search for a permanent and satisfying relationship with a man. At the time of writing, after the stresses of the Peter Townsend affair, the divorce from Lord Snowdon, and the well-publicised cavortings, on Mustique and elsewhere, with Roddy Llewellyn, it is by no means certain that she has found such a relationship. Certainly a marriage to Llewellyn would not receive the Queen's approval.

Prince Philip has played an important part in the royal family's attempt to contain and cope with Princess Margaret's personality and needs. He became involved, though without any real chance of altering events, during the Second World War.

In 1944 George VI appointed a new equerry. He was Group Captain Peter Townsend, a thirty-year-old war veteran who had flown with "the Few" (of whom there were, in fact, quite a lot) during the Battle of Britain. Townsend was awarded the Distinguished Flying Cross and the Distinguished Service Order. He was an attractive man with blue eyes, fine features, wavy hair and a slim, graceful build. He was also married – to Rosemary Pawle, by whom he had two sons.

Princess Margaret was fourteen when Townsend was taken on to the King's staff. He thus became closely involved with the royal family at a time when Margaret's adolescent and romantic fantasies were in full flood. Her admiration for him grew, in a sense, more respectable as King George came to rely increasingly upon Townsend's advice and support. There is even evidence that the King saw his equerry as the son he had never had.

As her infatuation for Townsend deepened, Margaret was doubtless resentful, at some level, of her sister's growing involvement with Prince Philip. On the surface she was a caring and supportive younger sister, sympathising with Elizabeth in the face of the King's reluctance to treat her attachment to Philip seriously. She was also something of a nuisance, frequently joining the couple when they would have preferred to have been alone. Miss Crawford noticed that, "The constant presence of the little sister, who was far from understanding, and liked a good deal of attention herself was not helping the romance." Neither Philip or Elizabeth, however, harboured any lasting resentment on this score.

Margaret's involvement with her sister's courtship – the "constant presence", the not always welcome teasing, the intense interest – was partly a displacement of her own feelings for Peter Townsend. Her infatuation was certainly not respectable; was, indeed, of a semi-adulterous nature. What would her father and mother make of that? Where did the doctrines of the Church of England stand on such matters? Divorce seemed unthinkable for Townsend, and in any case, the royal family and divorce did not mix – witness the self-imposed exile of the Duke and Duchess of Windsor.

If Margaret was jealous of her sister's comparatively open relationship with Prince Philip, her relationship to them both was complicated by a further factor. Townsend and Philip did not apparently get on well together. One of Margaret's biographers, Willi Frischauer, has written, perhaps over-dramatically, "When Peter and Philip brushed against each other it was like ice floes passing in the arctic. Difficult to say how these things start but perceptive, experienced palace staff could already discern a clash of temperaments of two men who ... were ... incompatible and jousting in a narrow space big enough only for one."

Any rational explanation for this alleged incompatibility must lie chiefly in Towsend's intimate relationship with King George VI. As we have already seen, the King's reluctance to sanction an engagement, official or otherwise, between Princess Elizabeth and Prince Philip was supported by Townsend. This must have been a source of friction between Philip and Townsend. Did Townsend, however, have much choice in the matter? The King was unmovable on the issue. In any case, it was quite reasonable to support George VI's contention, as the war drew to its close, that Elizabeth hardly knew Philip and must be given time to make sure of her feelings. With his own hastily arranged marriage already suffering from the long hours required by his duties as equerry, Townsend had every reason to counsel caution in such matters.

Townsend, in his autobiography *Time and Chance*, published in 1978, has vigorously denied that he was " 'the King's adviser', 'closest confidant' etc.", saying, "That is rubbish. The King's closest confidant was obviously his wife, Queen Elizabeth, and on political matters, his private secretary Tommy Lascelles. Nor was there any question of my 'advising' the King. He was just about old enough to be my father and had no reason, on important matters, to ask my advice, nor had I any to give him. The relationship, I repeat, was a simple one, motivated as it was by sympathy." Not all commentators would agree with so uncomplicated an assessment.

There is no escaping the impression that when Philip was invited to Balmoral in 1946 to be more thoroughly appraised by the King and Queen, Townsend was employed as an extra pair of eyes and ears. Next, the royal tour of South Africa must have been doubly galling for Philip: not only was it seen by the King and probably Townsend as a final testing time for his affection for Princess Elizabeth, but Townsend, as George VI's equerry, sailed with the royal family on HMS *Vanguard*. The time Townsend spent with Margaret during the South African tour undoubtedly strengthened the growing bond between them.

Later that year, Philip and Elizabeth were married, and there is no need to doubt the affection and support that Margaret showed at this important event in her sister's life. Nor indeed did they show any lack of affection for her.

The next few years of Margaret's life were taken up in a hectic pursuit of pleasure. She became a stock subject of the gossip columnists who solemnly noted the names of her large number of "suitors" or "escorts" and described the night life of which she had become so fond. When she holidayed on Capri, press photographers with telephoto lenses struggled to take pictures of her in a swimsuit – the assumption apparently being that princesses do not have real legs under their dresses, unless proved otherwise.

When Elizabeth succeeded to the throne, Margaret's position became both simpler and more complex. Having widened her experience of men, she was now convinced that she wanted to marry Townsend: that, at least, was plainer. More complicated were the implications of Townsend's decision to divorce his wife. He had separated from her in 1951, and his divorce went to court in December 1952; he was granted a decree *nisi* on account of his wife's adultery. Being the innocent party, however, did not remove the contemporary stigma of divorce and made it particularly difficult for the new Queen, as Supreme Governor of the Church of

England, to sanction the marriage her sister desired. A further complication lay in the King's death itself. Townsend's close attachment to George VI had seemed to Margaret to offer a possible solution to her problem. Fanciful though it may appear, Margaret believed that "Papa would have found a way." The King, however, was now dead.

In the aftermath of Elizabeth's succession there was a subtle shift in Margaret's official status. Under the Regency Act of 1937 Margaret was designated to act as Regent, and hence to be on the Regency Council if Elizabeth, when Queen, should die before her eldest child came of age. Now that Elizabeth had become Queen it was suggested that Margaret should be replaced on any future Regency Council by Prince Philip; the Queen Mother would also sit on the Council. Margaret's special status as "next in succession" was swept away in an amendment to the Regency Act. Philip was given precedence next to the Queen. In a word, Margaret was out and Philip was in.

There is no need to see any sinister plotting behind this move; it seemed, overall, logical and proper – a tidying up in the light of new circumstances. On the other hand, there has undoubtedly been disquiet in political and court circles over the prospect of Margaret retaining her privileged position in the event of her wishing to marry a divorced man, and thus unleashing a public and religious controversy that would cause the royal family profound embarrassment. In effect, she was now freer to marry Townsend.

Was Philip one of those who pressed for the change? It is clear that he dreaded a scandal and, bearing Townsend no particular love, thought it best that he should be removed from royal employment – he was now Comptroller of the Household of the Queen Mother. His cousin Alexandra, writing of the period leading up to Elizabeth's coronation, confirms his misgivings:

Probably the only cloud on the horizon lay in the appalling storm of publicity that thundered at this time around the friendship of Group Captain Peter Townsend and Princess Margaret. Philip disliked this midsummer storm of speculation and rumour intensely, just as he disliked anything that could diminish or threaten the dignity of the Crown. On the other hand, the unpleasant undesired furore must have clashed with the tolerant philosophy he once held that everybody must lead the life he or she thinks best.

181

During the coronation, Margaret gave the clearest public indication of her feelings for Townsend. In the annexe of Westminster Abbey a reporter saw her flicking a speck of dust from the lapel of Townsend's uniform; it was an instinctive, intimate gesture which revealed far more than most official statements do. Another reporter, Donald Edgar, noticed with astonishment the familiarity with which Margaret and Townsend treated each other after the ceremony: "At first I thought this slight man in RAF uniform was a member of the royal family"; he saw "the officer holding out his hands, Margaret almost falling into his arms, a half-embrace".

The scandal broke shortly afterwards. A fortnight after the coronation it was filling the pages of the British press, often in the traditional "righteous indignation" style of home-grown popular journalism. The *People*, for example, led with a headline, "Stop These Scandalous Rumours", proceeded to repeat them, and then concluded: "The story is, of course, utterly untrue!" In July the *Daily Mirror* had gone so far as to come out with an eight-inch tall, single word headline – YES; it was the readers' answer to the question, "Should Princess Margaret be allowed to wed Peter Townsend?" – a 96.81% "yes" vote, against 3.19% for the "noes", but on a small sample.

The *Daily Mirror*'s readers did not, however, form part of the British establishment. Most senior Anglican opinion disapproved of the proposed match, and the Prime Minister, Winston Churchill, though once a strong supporter of Edward VIII during the Abdication Crisis, said quite bluntly that Townsend must go. Sir Alan "Tommy" Lascelles, the Queen's Principal Private Secretary, had been equally discouraging when Peter Townsend told him that he loved Princess Margaret. According to Townsend, he was "visibly shaken", and could only say "You must be either mad or bad." The Queen and her mother felt much more sympathy with Margaret. Philip, who had been obliged to wait for several years before he could marry Elizabeth, apparently favoured Margaret going away for some time. In the end, it was Townsend who went away. He was posted as air attaché to Brussels. It was part of a plan. The couple, though they might correspond and telephone, should not meet for one year. If after two years they were still determined to marry, their case would be reconsidered.

Two years later, the problem re-emerged. On 21 August 1955 Princess Margaret attained the age of twenty-five; she still wished to marry Peter Townsend. She was now quite free to give notice of her intention to marry whoever she liked, since she no longer needed her sister's permission under the terms of the Royal Marriage Act. As it happened, the Queen had remained warmly sympathetic to her sister's needs, though the Queen Mother seems to have had second thoughts during the two years of the couple's separation.

Townsend was encouraged to return. He and Margaret were reunited at the Berkshire mansion of the Queen's friends Mr and Mrs John Lycett Wills. The press bayed in pursuit of them. The cabinet, led by the new Prime Minister, Anthony Eden, conveyed to the Queen the message that if Margaret married Townsend she would, in their opinion, be obliged to leave the country for several years at least.

The Duke of Edinburgh threw his weight against the marriage. This might seem surprising in view of the appeals to the divorced Michael Parker to stay on as joint equerry just over a year later, and of the recent tolerance shown to Townsend after his own divorce had been announced. But, according to one authority: "His sense of propriety was outraged, his belief in discipline flouted, and his strong sense of loyalty betrayed. He felt that Margaret was letting the side down. . . . ."

Was this all? Or was he recalling Townsend's earlier apparent opposition to his own marital ambitions? This is an uncharitable explanation, but should not be dismissed as a possible motive lurking somewhere in Philip's conscious or subconscious reactions to the crisis. It is interesting, and perhaps significant, that one of Prince Philip's most authoritative and benevolent earlier biographers, Basil Boothroyd, found nothing to say on the subject and ignored the "Margaret problem" altogether. There are only three page references to Margaret in his book, all of them dealing with the early meetings between Philip and Elizabeth. Peter Townsend's name does not even appear in the index, and an unwary reader would not suspect his existence. Lord Snowdon is mentioned once.

Peter Townsend's autobiography does little to clear up the matter of his relationship with Prince Philip. The latter is mentioned in the text only six times, and four of these six mentions are inconsequential. Townsend does, however, devote a paragraph to a tantalisingly incomplete assessment of the man who might have become his brother-in-law. He writes that, "Before I ever met Prince Philip I was prepared to like him." The main reason for this seems to have been that when Philip had served on the destroyer *Chequers*, the captain had been Townsend's brother, who "had often extolled to me the Prince's virtues as a sailor". We next learn that Peter Townsend's "admiration for him increased when he became a pilot". Although these are favourable impressions they are based on evidence of professional competence in the armed service rather than on intimate traits of personality.

Indeed, Townsend goes on to admit that, "I never, however, got to know Prince Philip well, though we often fought each other to a standstill in the squash court at Buckingham Palace and on the badminton court at Windsor Castle." This statement is in itself odd. To play another man regularly in a fiercely competitive game like squash can frequently reveal a great deal about the characters of both players – unless both were keeping a particularly tight rein on their feelings. In addition, the opportunities for Townsend and Prince Philip to have contact, apart from sporting contact, were considerable. That this contact led to what was apparently only a superficial understanding of Philip is surely significant. In fact, Townsend's final judgement of Prince Philip is based upon the "sporting affrays" that "left me with the impression, which remains indelible, of the Prince as a genial, intelligent and hard-hitting extrovert". This is a very conventional, and perhaps guarded, assessment.

Townsend has left one account of Prince Philip's reaction when Princess Margaret told her sister of her love for him. Townsend was impressed by "the Queen's movingly simple and sympathetic acceptance of the disturbing fact of her sister's love for me". But "Prince Philip, as was his way, may have tended to look for a funny side to this poignant situation." Townsend adds, charitably, "I did not blame him. A laugh here and there did not come amiss." All this does not give the impression of a sympathetic and serious response to Margaret and Townsend's dilemma. On the other hand, it was clearly not an openly hostile reaction.

A recent biographer of Margaret has claimed that when, two years later, she agonised as to whether she should marry Townsend, in order "to avoid a total break with the Queen, Margaret shifted the weight of her attack towards Philip and blurted out some tittle-tattle about him, and a car accident in which he was supposed to have been involved with an unnamed lady, which had no substance in fact." According to this version she also "repeated some silly rumours about Philip's lively friend Baron, the photographer, their get-togethers at Baron's Brick Street . . . studios", and about the " 'Thursday Club' of which he and Baron were members, meeting at Wheeler's Oyster Bar in Soho every Thursday for a private lunch and some harmless frolics".

Whether Margaret undertook this counter-offensive is difficult to know, and in any case the argument presupposes an imminent break between her and the Queen – of which there is little evidence. Rather Elizabeth II seems to have been "helpless . . . All that she could insist was that [Margaret's] mind was made up quickly, for the public controversy had now gone on for a fortnight."

Obligingly, Margaret came to a decision, and on 31 October 1955 a statement was released to the public:

> I would like it to be known that I have decided not to marry Group Captain Peter Townsend. I have been aware that, subject to my renouncing my rights of succession, it might have been possible for me to contract a civil marriage. But, mindful of the Church's teaching that Christian marriage is indissoluble, and conscious of my duty to the Commonwealth, I have resolved to put these considerations before any others.
>
> I have reached this decision entirely alone, and in doing so I have been strengthened by the unfailing support and devotion of Group Captain Townsend. I am deeply grateful for the concern of all those who have constantly prayed for my happiness.
>
> MARGARET

So that was that. "Respectability" had won, and of the nation's daily newspapers, only the *Manchester Guardian* and the *Daily Mirror* declined to applaud the decision. The royal family had decided, in the end, that it did represent certain traditional values in a shifting world – and Prince Philip had strongly supported those values. If Margaret had gained no personal happiness from the whole affair, at least she still remained a fully integrated member of the royal establishment, with all the material advantages that went with it. She had also, belatedly, won a good press, and public opinion had swung her way. She had, at a stroke, combined perks and sympathy – a most sustaining brew for someone of her tastes.

By 1959 the private lives of both Princess Margaret and Peter Townsend had been revitalised. In that year Townsend married a twenty-year-old tobacco heiress, Marie Luce Jamagne, by whom he was to have one son and two daughters. Margaret had also met and fallen in love with a well-connected and talented photographer, Antony Armstrong-Jones.

On 26 February 1960 the princess and Armstrong-Jones announced their engagement to be married. He seemed a curious recruit to a royal family that had only recently found a Battle of Britain hero unacceptable: he was amiable, suave, unconventional, arty and cosmopolitan, working in a show business *demi-monde* which was a far cry from the solid familial virtues so highly esteemed by the House of Windsor. An early whiff of scandal came when it was revealed that the bridegroom's first choice of best man had, in 1952, received a conviction for homosexual offences. A substitute best man was hastily found.

The royal family had, however, moved with the times. They also realised that Armstrong-Jones's interests and style fitted in very well with those of Princess Margaret. Moreover, he had never been divorced. The Duke of Edinburgh, in fact, was responsible for introducing Armstrong-Jones to the Queen. After the death of Baron, it had seemed appropriate for his erstwhile assistant to be invited to take his place as a court photographer. He had already taken family photographs of the Duke of Kent's family. His first photographs for the Queen, of Prince Charles and Princess Anne, were received with great pleasure. He had made his entrance, and his relationship with Margaret thereafter developed steadily and discreetly.

On 6 May Margaret and Armstrong-Jones (not yet elevated to the Earldom of Snowdon) were married. The Duke of Edinburgh gave the bride away. An act of reconciliation? Or simply because there was no other male member of the royal family sufficiently closely connected to the Queen's sister? It was a visible token of support all the same. When the engagement had been announced, Philip had been delighted and had telephoned Margaret from Windsor Castle to congratulate her personally. He later spent time giving Armstrong-Jones some coaching in the deportment now expected of him: how to walk purposefully into a crowded room and make straight for the person to whom you wanted to speak; what to do with one's hands when on public display, and so forth. Observers were interested to see that Armstrong-Jones adopted, in almost comical fashion, one of his brother-in-law's most characteristic postures – his hands-behind-the-back, inquisitorial stance. All the same, despite his love of field sports, Armstrong-Jones was hardly Prince Philip's sort of man. This impression was subsequently strengthened when Prince Philip made an apparently offensive reference to his brother-in-law's bohemian qualities at a

"Saints and Sinners" lunch. In front of television cameras he said at one point, "unlike my brother-in-law", and added with a smile ". . . well, he isn't really, but you know the chap I mean." Enigmatic, but hardly complimentary.

The Snowdon's marriage produced two children: David, Viscount Linley, born in 1961, and Lady Sarah Armstrong-Jones born in 1964. But by the late 1960s the marriage had run into serious difficulties. According to one authority: "Margaret had proved a possessive wife. Intensely in love with her husband, she smothered him. Her emotional life was keyed to a neurotic pitch. Psychiatric help was called in. Marriage had not resolved but had intensified her problems of identity." She envied her sister's close relationship with Prince Philip: "She wanted her husband beside her . . . as her sister had Philip." Snowdon resented the demands made on him by his wife. There were "blazing rows" and an increasingly separate social life.

Although the Queen and Prince Philip hoped that matters would improve, this was not to prove the case. When the Snowdons carried out public engagements together there was often embarrassing evidence of disharmony and antipathy. There was gossip about other "men" and other "women". On 19 March 1976 it was announced that the couple were separating. It was part of a strategy agreed between the Queen and the Snowdons: if absolutely necessary, a separation; a two-year wait; and then a dissolution of the marriage whenever they chose.

It seemed inevitable that divorce would follow. Scandalous stories of Margaret's holidays on the West Indian island of Mustique became commonplace. Roddy Llewellyn, son of an Olympic equestrian gold medal-winner, emerged as her none too tactful lover. There were accusations of a depravity that might have shocked her male Hanoverian ancestors. In 1978 Margaret and Snowdon were finally divorced.

Her sister's misfortunes made the Queen and her family face up to the problem of divorce in a more constructive way than ever before. There was little inclination to apportion blame, and there has been an attempt to maintain contact with Lord Snowdon. The couple's children are closely involved in the royal family's activities, and Lady Sarah Armstrong-Jones has said that the person she admires most is the Queen. Whether Philip and those who opposed the Townsend marriage ever have misgivings over their stand is unclear; certainly the argument that what Princess Margaret

needed was the controlling influence of an "older man", like Townsend, has been often made.

In keeping with the times, the House of Windsor has, admittedly
rather late in the day, shown its capacity to accept the hitherto
unacceptable, and in that sense the vagaries of Princess Margaret's
personal life have helped to identify the royal family more closely
with the contemporary attitudes and problems of many in British
society.

12

The Mountbatten
Connection

". . . the House of Mountbatten only reigned for two months,
from 8 February to 9 April 1952, but historically it takes its
place among the reigning houses of the United Kingdom."
Earl Mountbatten of Burma,
in The Mountbatten Lineage

PRINCE PHILIP'S CLOSE CONNECTION with the late Lord Louis Mountbatten has been misunderstood, wilfully misinterpreted, and the
subject of criticism. To begin with there was, and still is, a good deal
of confusion as to their precise family relationship. Did Lord
Mountbatten adopt Philip? Was he an older brother? Was he, in
lieu of any other obvious candidate, really his father?

The Duke of Edinburgh has tried to put the record straight:

I suppose they know I was born a Prince of Greece, but one
impression that I think needs to be corrected is that the whole of
my life has been spent here, and that I was brought up by Lord
Mountbatten, neither of which is true. This impression that I've
lived here all my life, and that I'm a Mountbatten, which of
course I'm not. I mean, I'm a Mountbatten in exactly the same
way that everybody else is half mother and half father, but
normally speaking you're concerned with the father's family. I
don't think anybody thinks I had a father. Most people think that
Dickie's my father anyway.

Interestingly, Philip's physical resemblance to his father has
become the more marked as he has grown older. In 1946 when he
went to his sister Sophie's wedding in Germany, her second, to
Prince George of Hanover, his sister was powerfully struck by the
likeness: "I hadn't seen him for nine years, not really grown up at

all. My father died in 1944. He was so like him. I shall never forget that moment when I saw him again." Philip had the same mannerisms, movements, ways of standing, walking and laughing – "the colossal sense of humour, really seeing the funny side of things, always, and making everybody else laugh".

These shared characteristics make it difficult for those who prefer to see Philip as a Mountbatten, conveniently forgetting the existence of Prince Andrew of Greece. The Duke of Edinburgh, as we have seen, tends to be defensive about his father and his father's family: "I grew up very much more with my father's family than I did with my mother's. And I think they're quite interesting people. They're the sort of people that haven't been heard of much." Prince Philip's insistence on this point is perhaps an attempt to defend a father who, in effect, deserted the family. Yet it was not a complete desertion by any means: there was the period when they lived together at St Cloud; later on, Andrew sometimes joined family holidays, and Philip visited him quite often in Monte Carlo. At least Philip's parents had been united and apparently happy when they had been rescued from Athens in 1922. The commander of *Calypso* left an impression of that time: "Well, we slipped off all right and picked up their 4 daughters and baby son from Corfu next day. . . . Princess A. has two brothers in our Navy (she was a Battenberg). The Prince is delightful, and so English. . . . They were rather amusing about being exiled, for they so frequently are." Exile and separation, however, did not diminish Philip's love and admiration for his father.

One of the difficulties in assessing the importance of the Duke of Edinburgh's relationship with Earl Mountbatten is that it seems obvious that almost every important early turning point in the former's career bears the mark of his uncle's influence: his settling down to an education in Britain; entry into the Royal Naval College; the first meeting with Princess Elizabeth; his steady promotion during the war; his betrothal and marriage; his choice of a surname; his post-war naval career in the Mediterranean. The list is a lengthy one and could be extended.

Many of these points have been considered in earlier chapters. What is clear is that the Duke of Edinburgh is resistant to suggestions that the fact of his being Lord Mountbatten's nephew has profoundly shaped his life and career. It would, of course, be foolish to deny the help that so wealthy and well-connected a relative has inevitably given. On the other hand, Prince Philip has been quick to assert his independence, to make it known that major decisions and achievements have been his own, not anybody else's.

The decision to send him to Gordonstoun did represent the triumph of the British branch of the family over the German branch. But, in a way, they were filling a vacuum. It is interesting to speculate on what might have happened if Hahn had somehow managed to stay on at Salem, perhaps by keeping a low profile when the Nazis came to power. Then Philip might have stayed on, too, and been drawn even closer to his sisters and their German husbands. And after Salem? Service in the German navy? Marriage to a German princess? It could have happened. That it did not, was largely due to the Mountbattens.

Once in Britain, service in the Royal Navy seems a clear case of Uncle Dickie's influence. But to say this is to forget the more constant role of surrogate father played by the elder brother, George of Milford Haven, during Philip's schooldays. Uncle George was an ex-naval officer, and cousin David Milford Haven was just embarking on a career in the Royal Navy. As we know, Prince Philip has denied that either George of Milford Haven or Louis Mountbatten was particularly influential in his choice of a career, though he says the latter "may have persuaded me. Or said that it was easier to get in. I just sort of accepted it. I didn't feel very strongly about it." Then the final counter-attack: "I really wanted to go into the Air Force. . . . Left to my own devices I'd have gone into the Air Force without a doubt."

So there had been persuasion, a dangling of career carrots, otherwise why use the phrase "Left to my own devices . . ."? Perhaps again, the Duke of Edinburgh was reacting to the easy preconception that it was his British, naval, relatives who had fashioned his career. After all, he had been wooed by the Royal Hellenic Navy before he decided to enter Dartmouth, though his father had not seemed especially keen to commit him to the Greek service.

An interesting illustration of Prince Philip's feelings can be seen in his amendment of a short biographical hand-out issued by the British Information Services. The original version included this paragraph:

> In choosing a naval career he was following the tradition of the Mountbatten side of his family. Prince Louis of Battenberg was an Admiral of the Fleet and First Sea Lord; his son, the second

Marquess, served in the Royal Navy, like Prince Philip's cousin, the third Marquess, and his uncle, Admiral Lord Mountbatten of Burma.

The Duke of Edinburgh preferred to present this following version, which does not mention the Battenbergs by name and brings in both his father and his father's brothers:

In choosing a career in one of the services he was following a tradition of both sides of his family. Both his grandfathers served at sea. His father was a career officer in the Greek Army, and both his father's and his mother's brothers served in the Navy.

Once in the Navy, of course, the Mountbatten connection can hardly have done his prospects much harm. Some of those who served with the Duke of Edinburgh have expressed similar views. Prince Philip's comments on the subject are not recorded. He certainly spent a good deal of his wartime service in close proximity to his uncle, in the Mediterranean and finally in Far Eastern waters. After his marriage he was also attached to units commanded by Lord Mountbatten and based on Malta. It would be grossly unfair, however, to put his rapid promotion simply down to nepotism or the impeccable connections of his wife. He had shown great promise in the Navy from his time at Dartmouth onwards – the prize for the best all-round cadet of the term came before anyone had heard much of him, and his subsequent wartime and peacetime naval career is marked by a healthy compound of zeal and efficiency.

More intriguing is the idea that Lord Louis Mountbatten master-minded the marriage to Princess Elizabeth, and that it represented "a moving in on the monarchy". It is tempting to dismiss the idea as pure fantasy, at the most a product of political and press animosities felt for Lord Mountbatten of Burma, or possibly the last subterranean rumblings of the anti-German agitation that had driven Louis of Battenberg from office in 1914.

Yet a case can be made out to support the "moving in on the monarchy" theory. When naval cadet Prince Philip of Greece was sent to entertain the royal princesses at Dartmouth in July 1939, it was Lord Louis, King George VI's personal aide-de-camp, who "certainly presided over his nephew's historic meeting with Princess Elizabeth. . . ." The next day, according to Alexandra of Yugoslavia, Lord Louis "steadfastly procured his nephew an invitation to

7

7 Cook and father. Prince
Philip and Princess Anne
tend a barbecue at Balmoral.
A photograph released for
the Queen and Prince
Philip's Silver Wedding
celebrations in 1972
8 Prince Philip apparently
trying to interest the Queen
in a book. A photograph
taken for the Silver Jubilee
celebrations in 1977

39

40

41

PASSION FOR POLO

9 Wife and son are reasonably attentive, daughter and dog inattentive, during a break in a game at Windsor in 1956

0 Prince Philip in action in 1963, despite having had three stitches in an injured arm at Cowdray Park the day before

1 Fatherly advice. An eloquent and apparently despairing Prince Philip giving tips on polo-playing technique to a thoughtful and crestfallen Prince Charles

42

BOWLER AND VICTIM

Above, Prince Philip in action, bowling in the nets in 1947, and *left*, out first ball, l.b.w., during a village match in Kent in 1949

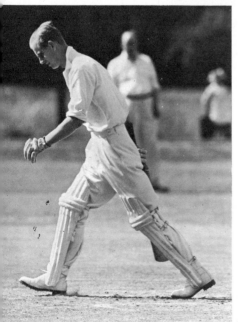

43

44 Another tiger-skin rug. Prince Philip killed the 8 ft 9 in long male tiger with a single shot through the head during the 1961 royal tour of India.

45 Prince Philip even played bicycle polo in 1967 and was involved in a crash with a member of his own side at Smith's Lawn in Windsor.

46 Sailor prince, seen here with Uffa Fox when they won 3rd place (and a prize of 15 shillings) at Cowes in 1968

47 Royal pilot. Prince Philip's passion for flying sees him at the controls of the Australian-built Victor Airtourer.

46

47

48 The Prince as competitive carriage driver, expressing his feelings after finishing a soaking fourth at the 1978 Royal Windsor Horse Show

49 Not necessarily the sport of consorts. Prince Philip, who does not share his wife's passion for horse-racing, steps rather self-consciously on to the Epsom turf to view the 1966 Derby

50 If you can't beat 'em, join 'em. Prince Philip, looking rather like our man from the Mafia, studies a race card at Newbury in 1966

49

50

51 Rapt attention as members of the royal family watch the cross country event on a portable television set during the 1973 Badminton Horse Trials. Alongside better known faces is Princess Margaret's son Viscount Linley (*far right*), instamatic in hand, and finger and thumb in mouth.

lunch on the royal yacht". That a flame was kindled at the Dartmouth meeting there is no doubt, though whether Philip consciously kindled it is more debatable.

It is clear that Lord Louis went on to press his nephew's claims during the war, and as a cousin of the King and eventually one of the most illustrious of Allied commanders, he was superbly placed to do so. On the other hand, Philip's Greek relatives were also aware of the possibilities of an advantageous dynastic match. Moreover, once Greece fell and they went into exile, they were able to make direct, over-the-table representations to George VI. King George II of Greece, as we have seen, did propose the match to Elizabeth's father during the latter part of the war, but received no encouragement. If the exiled Greeks were getting nowhere, there was always Princess Marina, the Duchess of Kent to promote Philip's cause: a sort of Trojan horse safely within the confines of the British royal family.

That the royal house of Greece was also pressing Philip's case does not disprove the "Mountbatten" theory, though it may somewhat weaken it. As for Prince Philip, his own recollections of this important episode in his life are vague – some might say deliberately vague. His capacity for honest self-appraisal is, however, remarkably well developed. If he thought at all about the pubescent Princess Elizabeth as a marriage prospect in 1939 it was probably in a rather vague fashion; something to be filed away and looked up later.

Once the war was over, Lord Louis Mountbatten worked diligently towards the granting of Philip's British citizenship. When this was eventually granted, the surname which the young naval officer adopted was that of Mountbatten. Lord Louis had even softened up the Beaverbrook press, his most persistent critics in the newspaper world, a month before Philip officially became a British citizen. In February 1947 he invited the chairman of Beaverbrook newspapers and the editors of the *Daily* and *Sunday Express*, Arthur Christiansen and John Gordon, to Chester Street for drinks. There, with uncharacteristic humility, he asked for their valued opinion as to how the public would respond to Prince Philip's naturalisation. Philip was there, "amiably self-effacing in a corner". The three Beaverbrook men were impressed by the young officer's Englishness and by his war record. They were flattered by Lord Louis' respectful enquiry. They felt that there should be no problems. When the announcement came, their newspapers could hardly object. It is said that Lord Beaverbrook "when he heard of the meeting, was more amazed than enraged. Three tough old war horses out-manœuvred like that?"

Prince Philip, however, though gratified that he had been granted British citizenship as a prelude to his marriage, appears not to have been overwhelmed by joy at the proposal that he should adopt Mountbatten as a surname. We have already seen that, in his own words, "I wasn't madly in favour. . . . But in the end I was persuaded, and anyway I couldn't think of a reasonable alternative." Why so grudging an acceptance of the surname? Residual loyalty to his father's side of the family? The determination to be his own man? An attempt to minimise Uncle Dickie's influential role in the making of his fortune?

There was no doubt as to the feelings of Lord Mountbatten. He was delighted. Philip's marriage to the heir presumptive represented a dynastic triumph: a resounding retaliation after the shabby events of 1914; an act of ultimate and comprehensive revenge against a British establishment that had driven his father from high office. Philip's adoption of his surname only sweetened the triumph.

Even before Philip's marriage to Elizabeth, Lord Louis had prepared and had published for private circulation *The Mountbatten Lineage* which proved, at a singularly appropriate time, the antiquity and nobility of his house. A revised version of this work of genealogy (some might say self-aggrandisement) was published in 1958. It contains some interesting references to Prince Philip.

On the subject of Philip's British citizenship, Lord Louis wrote:

> His father, ANDREW, wished him to have a less disturbed career than he had suffered himself with two long periods of exile from Greece, and in 1939 urged that he should become a naturalised British subject. PHILIP had become an enthusiastic sailor [!] and decided to become naturalised and finally did so on 28 February 1947, renouncing his succession to the throne of Greece, and his Greek and Danish titles and taking the new name of his mother's family in England, Mountbatten.

There is no hint here of any influence or pressure exerted by the author. Rather the moving forces are, apparently, Prince Andrew and the "enthusiastic sailor" himself.

In a later, rather breathless paragraph, Lord Louis clearly relishes the fact that for two months the House of Mountbatten took its place among Britain's ruling houses:

> Princess Elizabeth legally took her husband's name, Mountbatten, on marriage for there was no legal provision for any female, not even as an heir presumptive to the Throne, to retain her maiden name on marriage. So she succeeded to the Throne as a Mountbatten, but on 9th April, on the formal and insistent advice of the Prime Minister [Winston Churchill], she changed her name and that of her children, but not that of her husband, to Windsor, the name her grandfather had taken in 1917, when he had renounced the Prince Consort's name of "Saxe-Coburg". So the House of Mountbatten only reigned for two months, from 8th February to 9th April 1952, but historically it takes its place among the reigning houses of the United Kingdom.

Why was it considered necessary to revert to Windsor in April 1952? Queen Victoria's successors had contentedly borne the cumbersome Saxe-Coburg-Gotha surname until the anti-German hysteria of the Great War had forced the adoption of the artificially contrived family name of Windsor in 1917. One explanation is that, "It was a change the King had set afoot before he died, in discussion with Winston Churchill and Sir Alan Lascelles [the King's Principal Private Secretary]." Another explanation is that, "Most likely it was due to that underground agitation about 'the Mountbattens moving in on the Monarchy'." Winston Churchill, according to one authority, advised the Queen "that the feeling of his Government reinforced by public sentiment was that she should drop the Mountbatten and reign under her father's name of Windsor".

Whatever the background pressures, Prince Philip accepted the scrapping of the Mountbatten surname in 1952 without putting up much resistance. His one counter-attack was to suggest that an alternative could be the "Family of Windsor of the House of Edinburgh". This proposed compromise was a more rambling surname even than Saxe-Coburg-Gotha, though easier on the English ear. It did not win approval.

The "Mountbatten" cause was not lost yet, however. In 1960, some time before Prince Andrew's birth, a Declaration in Council of 8 February ordered another prospective change of surname: "While I and my children shall continue to be styled and known as the House and Family of Windsor, my descendants . . . shall bear the name of Mountbatten-Windsor." Prince Philip was not the inspiration behind this further change, though clearly it was meant to express gratitude for his contribution to the life and work of the House of Windsor. The palace press office simply said that the Queen had for some time wanted her husband's name to enjoy perpetuation. According to the declaration, only the Queen's grandchildren and their descendants should bear the surname "Mountbatten-Windsor". These matters, however, are not always as simple as they seem. When Princess Anne was married in 1973 she signed her marriage certificate "Anne", without a surname. Even more confusingly, the official inscription read "Anne Elizabeth Alice Louise Mountbatten-Windsor, 23, spinster", which pre-empted the Declaration in Council by a generation.

In reality, there was no confusion. Subsequent to the Declaration of 1960 the Queen had asked "Rab" Butler, "who was acting for the Prime Minister, to consult the Lord Chancellor and confirm that *all* her children in fact have the name of Mountbatten-Windsor". Having consulted the Lord Chancellor, Butler replied: "The effect of Your Majesty's Declaration is that all the children of Your Majesty who may at any time need a surname have the surnames of Mountbatten-Windsor." As for Princess Anne's surname in the marriage register at Westminster Abbey, an official statement from Buckingham Palace in October 1975 explained the position:

> This was the first time that the surname "Mountbatten-Windsor" was used on an official document by any of the Queen's descendants. It was The Queen's decision that this should be done as Her Majesty wished her husband's name to appear on the Marriage Register of their daughter. (The Queen did not seek the advice of her Ministers in this matter.)

Put very simply, the family surname is whatever the Queen and her husband want it to be. The Mountbatten element in the name has been strengthened as a result.

The surname change in 1960, and subsequently, also ensured that, since he had no son, Louis Mountbatten's surname would survive. As a double insurance, he was granted a Special Remainder as a result of which the name could descend, in his own family, through the female line. At least it finally put to rest "the spectre", as the *Daily Express* put it, that his family name would die out. In a curious way, the "Mountbatten-Windsor" surname seems to belong more to Lord Louis than to Prince Philip, although it represents a compliment to both. Lord Mountbatten said, some time before his death, "My greatest happiness is that in the future royal children will be styled by the surname Mountbatten-Windsor."

What accounted for the hostility felt towards the Mountbattens, uncle and nephew, by the Beaverbrook press, and in certain political circles, and was it this hostility which largely fed the "moving in on the monarchy" agitation? The hostility of the *Daily* and *Sunday Express* towards both Lord Louis and Prince Philip was at one time very pronounced. It is fair to say that Philip was a target largely because he was Earl Mountbatten's nephew, though later he gave provocation enough on his own account:

> A car-carrying raft is being added to the yacht's equipment so that the Duke can play commandos.
> *Sunday Express*, 1956

> SHOULD PHILIP DRIVE THE QUEEN?
> *Daily Express*, 1957

> After one bad miss at polo he shouted, "Oh, Damn it!" and the shout was so loud it could be heard across the field.
> *Daily Express*, 1957

> PHILIP RAPS PRESS AGAIN
> *Daily Express*, 1963

Lord Louis' main crimes in the eyes of Lord Beaverbrook were his involvement in the disastrous Dieppe landing of 1942, and his part in handing independence to India. These failings were no doubt compounded by his alleged sympathy with the Labour party.

The Dieppe landing of 19 August 1942 was an attempt to seize and hold the French port to the embarrassment of the Germans. In the event the raid was easily repulsed with heavy losses, especially among the Canadian troops involved. Lord Beaverbrook, originally Max Aitken, was a Canadian by birth and a staunch advocate of opening a "second front" in Europe. Not only was he deeply upset by the slaughter of his fellow Canadians, but he also believed that the raid had been deliberately arranged to discredit the "second front" campaign. At a private gathering shortly afterwards he "allowed his bitterness to outrun his discretion to the extent of launching an ill-tempered attack on the chief of combined operations, Lord Louis Mountbatten. . . . Beaverbrook accused him in unmeasured terms of faulty planning leading to the needless sacrifice of human lives. Lord Louis replied that the plans were his, but that in execution they were not carried out."

From that moment it appeared to many that Beaverbrook pursued a vendetta against Mountbatten. Beaverbrook's biographer, A. J. P. Taylor, thinks: "That is an exaggeration, Beaverbrook's relations with Mountbatten, as with other men, went up and down. Privately his view hardened over the years that Dieppe had been a deliberate massacre of his beloved Canadians." Unreasonable though this view was, Beaverbrook still held it in 1958, telling his son Max Aitken on 20 April: "Print these statements, simple statements. Don't Trust Mountbatten in Any Public Capacity. Together with a further quotation from Mountbatten's speech in Canada where he said he took full responsibility for Dieppe. Four thousand set forth and three thousand did not return."

As we have seen, Beaverbrook's antagonism for Lord Mountbatten could only have been increased a year or so after Dieppe by the supposed insult, mentioned in an earlier chapter, contained in the film *In Which We Serve*, which was based on the story of Mountbatten's ship HMS *Kelly*. The ironic close-up shot of a copy of the *Daily Express* lying in a gutter and bearing the pre-war headline, "There will be no war this year or next year", could hardly have reconciled Beaverbrook to a man he then saw as an enemy.

This hostility was reinforced by Mountbatten's service as the last Viceroy of India in 1947. The Beaverbrook newspapers were firm and strident opponents of any dismantling of the British Empire. Although the granting of independence to India had been accepted in principle in 1942 by Churchill's wartime coalition cabinet, Mountbatten was reviled by the *Express* newspapers as the man "who had given away India".

It was an eccentric and unrealistic campaign, but one which continued in one form or another until 1963. In 1955 Beaverbrook defended his hostility to Mountbatten by arguing that: "He is subject to the same measure of attack as any other public man who may transgress the high principles which the *Express* sets in all matters concerning the British Empire." Four years later he ascribed his dislike to "what I believe to be the betrayal of Burma, refusal to let the Dutch back into Indonesia. And over everything the sack of India. The bright jewel in Queen Victoria's crown."

Despite these comprehensible explanations, "It is difficult", in

A. J. P. Taylor's words, "not to feel that more lay behind. None of Beaverbrook's friends could discover what it was. Something about Mountbatten touched Beaverbrook on a raw nerve."

In 1963, however, a year before Beaverbrook's death, they were reconciled. It happened at a dinner party given by Roy Thomson (later Lord Thomson of Fleet), another Canadian newspaper magnate. With new-world gaucheness, Thomson had invited the old enemies to dinner, though they sat at opposite ends of a long table. As the guests made their way out of the dining-room, Mountbatten realised that he would come face to face with Beaverbrook at the door. When they met he said courteously, "It's a long time since I've seen you, Max. I want to thank you for the way your paper handled Edwina's death." (Lady Mountbatten had died in 1960.) According to Randolph Churchill who was close to both men, "Beaverbrook seemed greatly touched – almost confused" by Mountbatten's words. Perhaps it was Mountbatten's courtesy that did the trick; perhaps Beaverbrook, within a year of death himself, was moved by Mountbatten's loss. At any rate, the Beaverbrook group ceased their predictable attacks on Lord Louis from that moment.

Apart from the feud with Lord Beaverbrook, there were others in the Establishment who resented Lord Mountbatten's influence. One explanation may lie in his reputation for radical views – though liberal might be a more accurate term. Certainly he opposed the Tory establishment over Munich, India and the Suez crisis of 1956. There were stories that seemed to confirm this reputation. For example, during the 1955 election campaign it was said that a Conservative fund-raiser called at Broadlands, the Mountbattens' house in Hampshire. Lord Louis' response to his request was to say amiably, "We're on the other side you know. You'll have better luck in the servants' wing. They're all Tories."

Prince Philip, on the other hand, could not be accused of holding socialist convictions; indeed, his private views on certain trade unionists and "third world" leaders are fit only for off-the-record conversation. His intimate proximity to the monarchy, therefore, would hardly afford Lord Louis some sort of untoward, radical influence – a favourite fantasy of various detractors and supporters of the "Mountbatten conspiracy" theory. Yet Philip has been the recipient of one of the most consistently critical press coverages of recent British history. Even when the Beaverbrook papers eased up on his uncle, they still reserved the right to gun for him, especially since he supported Britain's entering the Common Market. It is fair, however, to say that their hostility at least diminished after the Lord Louis-Lord Beaverbrook *rapprochement* of 1963. Before that, as we have seen, he gave as good as he got, in revenge calling the *Daily Express* in 1962, "a bloody awful newspaper . . . full of lies. . . . It is a vicious newspaper." He particularly resented the Beaverbrook press criticisms of overspending on royal occasions. Of course, he is deliberately provocative, which accounts for a good deal of the press's critical attitude towards him, but there are very probably still some reverberations from the war waged by certain sections of the newspaper world against both his Battenberg grandfather and his uncle Louis Mountbatten.

At a more personal and private level the Mountbatten connection has been a fruitful and sustaining link between the Queen's family and that of Lord Louis. Broadlands was one of the half dozen private houses the Queen has stayed at regularly. She has also often stayed with his daughter Patricia at Mersham le Hatch in Kent. Patricia, Lady Brabourne, is one of the few prepared to argue to the bitter end with Prince Philip, sometimes to encouraging cries from the Queen of "Go on Patricia, you tell him!"

A few weeks before his assassination in August 1979 by Irish Republican terrorists, Lord Mountbatten gave an interview to Audrey Whiting of the *Daily Mirror*. In it he paid tribute to that close and loving relationship with the royal family which gives him a unique place in recent history. Of the Queen he said:

> I don't think many people realise just how curtailed her private life really is. That is why she loves Balmoral so much when she is away from crowds.
>
> When she comes to Broadlands she really relaxes and goes out riding on her own. When she comes back after a good gallop she doesn't seem to me to be all that different to the time when she and Philip honeymooned here.

Of Prince Philip, the nephew who has come nearest to being the son he wished he had had, he said:

> He can be a little stubborn with me sometimes but I think I brought him up on the right lines. He is always direct and honest — and those are fine qualities in a man.
>
> I suppose his great regret is that he always wanted to have a

career in the Navy like I did – but that just wasn't on when his wife became Queen.

I often think people underestimate his job today. I can think of few men who work as hard as he does. He has been a marvellous father to his four children.

Of Prince Charles, Lord Mountbatten believed him to be "the finest man I know today. I don't think I can fault him on anything. He is kind but he can be tough when it is necessary to be tough. I asked him to promise never to smoke and always be true unto himself. He has kept those promises. He deserves a very good wife. . . ."

At Lord Louis' funeral at Westminster Abbey on 5 September 1979 the service was punctuated by proud, rip-roaring hymns that he had carefully selected, four years before, for the event. The profound grief shown by the royal family was the plainest possible expression of the very close bonds between them and Lord Mountbatten. The wreaths placed on the grave at Romsey Abbey in Hampshire where Lord Louis was then taken to be buried were equally revealing. The wreath from the Queen and the Duke of Edinburgh carried the message, in the Queen's hand, "In loving memory, from Philip and Lilibet." Princess Anne and Captain Mark Phillips wrote, "In loving memory of a great uncle and a great friend." Princess Margaret wrote, "In loving memory of darling Dickie."

The wreath from Prince Charles, however, carried the most intimate message of all. The Prince of Wales' affection and admiration for his great-uncle had been one of the mainstays of his childhood and early manhood. He revered him, and his admiration was warmly returned. They had tried to see each other at least once every month. Apart from the Queen Mother, Lord Mountbatten was the only person with whom Prince Charles would share his deepest secrets. The Prince of Wales played a major part in the ceremonial attending his great-uncle's funeral: he marched, beside his father, set-faced behind the coffin; he read the lesson at the service in Westminster Abbey, and when the service ended he wiped tears from his eyes with his white-gloved right hand.

At the burial at Romsey Abbey, Prince Charles' wreath, made up of red roses and carnations, bore the message: "To my HGF and GU from his loving and devoted HGS and GN." It was a private code. As he grew up Prince Charles saw Earl Mountbatten as "His Honorary Grandfather" as well as great-uncle. After all, his maternal grandfather, George VI, had died when he was only four years old, and he had never known Prince Andrew of Greece. For his part, Lord Louis cherished his honorary role, and in return called Prince Charles "His Honorary Grandson" as well as great-nephew. These exchanges illustrate beyond doubt the very special relationship that was involved in the Mountbatten connection.

13

Private Pastimes

". . . the arts world thinks of me as an uncultured polo-playing
clot."

Prince Philip

PRINCE PHILIP IS NOTHING if not an active man. The immense pressures of his working life do not, however, leave him listless and idle during his off-duty moments. He has always pursued a number of private pastimes with all the zest and efficiency associated with the execution of his public duties.

His love of sport is well known and probably brings him closer to the British people than any other of his interests. From his schooldays at Cheam and Gordonstoun, through his naval career, his early association with the House of Windsor, his responsibilities as husband and father, and right down to the present, he has been deeply involved in the sporting world, as player, patron, and spokesman for sporting interests.

At Cheam School he became passionately fond of cricket. At Gordonstoun it was hardly possible to pass through the school system without undertaking a tremendous variety of orthodox and unorthodox sporting and out-of-door activities. In the Royal Navy he was the officer who drove his men hard, and by example, in the pursuit of coveted sporting trophies. As an aggressive man, sport has always provided him with a socially acceptable form of emotional relief. He is also highly competitive.

Shortly after he married Princess Elizabeth, he turned their weekend home at Windlesham into a sporting arena where "he could unleash his full extrovert energy in furious exercise". Alexandra of Yugoslavia noticed how he kept trim during these days:

"He was no longer the hungry old Philip I knew; he was trimming down, watching his diet with evident anxiety . . . when Lilibet had a full English breakfast, Philip contented himself with coffee and toast. When she nibbled sandwiches at afternoon tea, Philip took only tea without sugar."

Although golf is not normally associated with him, Prince Philip borrowed clubs to try out the small course set in the grounds of Windlesham. Golf did not stick, however. But:

> Cricket especially struck the responsive chords he felt for every-thing in the English way of life. Within a few weeks at Wind-lesham the soft tennis court was adapted as a cricket pitch, and friends, chauffeurs, detectives and gardeners were mobilised into a cricket team to play against other local teams. When a match was not forthcoming, Philip practised batting or bowling with a secretary or chauffeur.

When he could find no sporting partners, he put on three or four sweaters and, to his wife's amusement, ran round the grounds. At Buckingham Palace, as we have seen, he revived the old squash court and regularly used the swimming pool. His early involvement with the National Playing Fields Association was another indica-tion of concern for healthy out-of-door activities.

His sporting passions include not only cricket and squash, but also (and most notoriously) polo, shooting, sailing, riding and driving horses, and swimming. There is also flying which is argu-ably a sport of some kind, albeit an expensive one, and walking – which is perhaps more of a pastime. Horse-racing is definitely not an enthusiasm he shares with the Queen.

Cricket has proved a particularly satisfying sport, especially since it has led to involvement in the affairs of the cricket establishment. He has been President of the Marylebone Cricket Club and Patron of the Middlesex County Cricket Club. He has also been Patron of the Lord's Taverners, the exclusive philanthropic cricket dining club, and in 1971 he was acknowledged by the publication of *The Twelfth Man*: a book of original contributions brought together by the Taverners "in honour of their patron". There was a foreword by the Prince of Wales, and among the contributors were Prince Bern-hard of the Netherlands, the novelist Mary Renault, cricket writer E. W. Swanton and writer Nicholas Monsarrat.

If horse-racing is, for reasons that are not altogether clear, the sport of kings, then polo, in the recent British experience at any rate, has been the sport of princes. Prince Philip's enthusiasm for polo has communicated itself to Prince Charles, who is now the royal family's most active participant in the sport, despite a recent collapse while playing in Florida. Though the Duke of Edinburgh no longer plays polo, it was once his favourite sport. It was also his most expensive and exclusive sport and provoked a good deal of controversy on that account. Polo ponies had to be bought, stabled, fed, groomed, given medical attention and so forth. The grooms' services weren't simply "on the house", either; Prince Philip had to pay, house and feed them, too. It was no wonder that "the cry of 'Bloody Animals' " sometimes rang "out over Windsor Great Park".

The expense of playing polo was apparently once a real deterrent to any request for a pay rise from Prince Philip; after all, the Treasury could easily point to a simple cut in expenditure that would keep the princely budget nicely balanced. It was, in addition, one of the most socially exclusive of games, and for that reason it could hardly be justified as bringing the Duke of Edinburgh closer to even a substantial number of the Queen's subjects – let alone the man, or woman, on the Clapham omnibus. At least he was a good player: "Out of the four hundred or so in the country, experts put him in the first eight," or in the top 2%.

Driving a four-in-hand team at the Windsor Horse Show has replaced polo as the competitive sport that is most open to public scrutiny. Top-hatted, in a dark coat with tails, a carnation in his button-hole and a whip in his hand, Prince Philip has become a familiar sight in the nation's newspapers and on television screens. Again it is not an image with much of the common touch about it. Even driving a four-in-hand team has recently caused press concern, though mainly on account of the Duke's advancing years. In May 1979 the *Daily Mail* asked, "Will Philip lay down the reins?" It continued:

With his 58th birthday looming next month, there are rumours that Prince Philip is about to bow to age and give up his passion for driving around in a top hat with his four-in-hand team.

He may be looking quite fit; but he did have to give up his beloved polo because arthritis was nagging at his wrists.

Being the fighter he is . . . I am assured that he will be competing in the coming Windsor Horse Show.

205

After his birthday, though, the word is that he will choose his events carefully and will in no way risk his health.

Shooting, at least, only endangers the health of the creatures that are shot at. George V, the Duke of Windsor, and George VI were exceptionally good marksmen, and the bag of pheasants at Sandringham sometimes exceeded two thousand. Prince Philip is also an excellent marksman ("one of the best shots in the country"), though the prodigious daily slaughter of birds that sometimes stirred even the conscience of George V is no longer attempted; the biggest day's bag at Sandringham during the 1979–80 season, for example, was nine hundred cock birds – though even this is nine hundred too many for the anti-blood sports lobby that vociferously criticises the royal family's continuing predilection for killing wild animals and birds.

Paradoxically, though he would deny the paradox, the Duke of Edinburgh is deeply involved in the World Wildlife Fund and is a keen bird-watcher. He recently described for David Mitchell, the public affairs director of the World Wildlife Fund, his efforts to persuade local officials in Western Australia to abandon plans to develop a new town that would threaten the habitat of one of the world's rarest birds. The bird went by the unlikely name of the "noisy scrub bird". Prince Philip's words were as follows:

I heard about this through Peter Scott and went to see the then State Premier, who looked at me in astonishment.

I could almost see his mind working: "Do I take this man seriously or is he pulling my leg? Is there such a thing as a Noisy Scrub Bird? And does he really think that plans for a new development should be shifted because of it?"

Then, to his eternal credit, he suddenly thought, "Perhaps he's right." And they moved it [the site of the new town] a short distance."

Not content with this diplomatic triumph, Prince Philip went off to try to see the bird: "It was raining and there was a force eight gale, and the bird only lives in thick scrub. We crawled about in these bushes and I got to within about two yards of the thing and noisy is absolutely right. It made a hell of a racket – but I failed to see it."

At least he has drawn the constructive and sensible conclusion from his interest in bird-watching: "It's only a matter of a short time of bird-watching and photography before the question of survival of species begins to dawn on the mind." He has published a book of his photographs of birds, entitled *Birds from "Britannia"*. His favourite photograph from the book, and one which illustrates his particular brand of humour, was placed on the inside of a lavatory door at Sandringham, showing "a bird squatting low with an expression of great strain".

The three elements of land, water and air also provide him with pleasure when he travels on, or through them. His penchant for driving a car fast is well documented and requires little further comment. Sailing is a much more respectable pastime and one which does not generally threaten the safety of the public. As with slaughtering pheasants, it is a pastime firmly established in the royal sporting calendar from Edward VII onwards. In 1952 Prince Philip became Admiral of the exclusive Royal Yacht Squadron at Cowes, and Commodore in 1961. As Commodore he soon flexed his official muscles: he set about redrafting its constitution, contributed a hefty amount to its building fund, and had strong views on the appropriate design for its changing rooms. He enjoyed sailing with Uffa Fox, one of those hardy seafaring characters who appeal to his love of the independent and the adventurous. Sailing has remained one of the sports which he can enjoy despite arthritic wrists or less flexible limbs.

Given his confession that, left to himself, he would have joined the Air Force rather than the Navy, it is not surprising that the Duke of Edinburgh broke down official resistance to win his flying wings in 1952. A year before he had campaigned successfully for Princess Elizabeth and himself to be allowed to fly across the Atlantic to Montreal for the royal tour of Canada and the United States. Opposition to the royal family flying was based on the straightforward assumption that it was a far more dangerous form of travel than any other. When, for example, Winston Churchill heard in 1953 that Philip had been travelling by helicopter, he summoned Michael Parker to 10 Downing Street and, having kept him standing for some time, growled, "Is it your intention to wipe out the royal family in the shortest possible time?" Similar sentiments were expressed to Caryl Gordon, the man selected to be Philip's flying instructor, by his C.O. in October 1952: "If you kill him, you realise what it will do to the Queen?" Gordon's response is not recorded.

Early in 1953 the Duke of Edinburgh won his wings. He now felt able to appear with a clear conscience in the full ceremonial dress of Marshal of the Royal Air Force. He went on to train in a variety of aircraft, including helicopters, and to pilot the family to Aberdeen for the Balmoral holidays, and even to fly Prince Charles to school for the new term at Gordonstoun. He has flown to many overseas destinations – including Athens, Oslo, Chicago O'Hare, Luxor, Bangkok, Katmandu, Acapulco, Rio de Janeiro, Caracas, Ascension – and in many types of aircraft. The callsign "Rainbow" was attached to any plane he piloted. He has often taken the controls of aircraft of the Queen's Flight, the small private royal airline financed by the Ministry of Defence, or of the larger, more glamorous planes that carry the Queen on official overseas tours. He still pilots himself as often as he can. Despite the initial misgivings by politicians and courtiers, he smashed through a significant barrier when he won the right to pilot aircraft, and even established a royal precedent: the Prince of Wales has also won his wings, received glowing compliments in his report from RAF Cranwell, and went on to essay a parachute jump.

Why did the Duke of Edinburgh insist on qualifying as a pilot? One answer is that he quite simply enjoys the challenge of flying: the accurate calculations demanded, the mixture of daring and precision. For one who is known to love gadgetry, to sit at the controls of such a marvellously engineered piece of technology as a modern aircraft must be deeply satisfying. Moreover, there are no fines for speeding. It must also help to smooth out the tensions and frustrations of his official routines. Flying is also quick and efficient, an appropriate means of getting around for a man with many public engagements and a lot of energy to work through. Not that flying fast necessarily saves him much time; if he were to get to his destinations any faster, officials at the other end would simply fill the gap with more hands to be shaken, more things to be seen.

Sport aside, the Duke of Edinburgh has a wide range of pastimes. Photography is one of these. He does his own dark-room developing, and some of the prints and enlargements that result from this are occasionally displayed in exhibitions – mostly for good causes. The photographs are often of wildlife, hence the publication of *Birds from Britannia*. Though photography is expensive, he is not a photography buff, surrounding himself with incredibly costly cameras and equipment.

There is also painting. It seems an oddly contemplative pastime for a man who leads so energetic and active a life, but, then,

Winston Churchill also dabbled in oils – and perhaps for the same reason: to unwind. Prince Philip has said, "I don't claim any exceptional interest or knowledge or ability. It's strictly average." His canvases are not wild expressions of the imagination, but depict flowers or the occasional still life, and many show a pleasant appreciation of landscape, nothing more or less. Neither portraits nor even self-portraits figure much among his collected works (or, rather, dispersed works: "I rather think I've given the best ones away"). Once, however, while sitting for Edward Halliday, he did a drawing of the painter, under the pretence of toying with the notes for a speech. Halliday did not have the presence of mind to ask for it as a payment in kind.

As a patron of the arts Prince Philip has a good deal more to contribute than as an artist. Despite his reputation, not wholly justified, for philistinism, he gets on with artists – his friendship with Feliks Topolski being a case in point: "It isn't just that their skills fascinate him; their honesty and directness strike an answering chord. No fundungus which is his word for meaningless trappings." He also buys their paintings, which is at least a well-established royal tradition – indeed the accumulated art treasures owned by the House of Windsor are one of the reasons why the Queen is sometimes called the richest woman in the world. It is, however, an unrealisable source of wealth, for, so far, the monarchy has not had to pawn the Rubens and Van Dycks to stay in business.

Not only do Prince Philip and the Queen commission paintings and drawings from well-known or aspiring artists, they continue to purchase whatever takes their fancy during their tours of newly opened exhibitions. Prince Philip's official visits to galleries are sometimes followed by a call from his office saying he would be interested in buying number so and so from the exhibition. To critics of the royal life style, such patronage suggests that the rich are still able to get richer, in one way or another. Partly to counter accusations of the royal family hoarding millions of pounds' worth of art treasures, Prince Philip was instrumental in getting the Queen's Gallery opened at Buckingham Palace in 1962, where, for a modest entrance fee, the public can view the royal art collection. If not exactly calculated to assuage the envy of the less fortunate, it at least brought the monarchy down to the level of, say, the Duke of Bedford. At Windsor, too, there is a public display of drawings by the Old Masters, and the entrance fees go towards the castle's upkeep, which is good news for the tax-payer.

Collecting works of art is not quite the same thing as appreciating them, and the *avant-garde* continue to regard Prince Philip with a mistrust bordering on despair. He is hurt when portrayed as "a total Philistine", and has perhaps suffered from the royal family's well-established reputation for sub-middle-brow cultural tastes. A preference for Rodgers and Hammerstein rather than Beethoven's quartets, however, at least associates royalty with the mass of the population.

Prince Philip has also been a modest patron of music of the more serious kind. This has involved putting up money for an organ or music scholarship at St George's Chapel, Windsor, and getting Benjamin Britten to compose for the chapel in 1958. Britten was apparently "extremely excited" by the invitation and eventually produced a *Jubilate* and a *Te Deum*. Such patronage does not put the Duke of Edinburgh in the same league as some of the Habsburg Emperors or King Ludwig of Bavaria, but it does provide some evidence that the royal taste in music extends beyond *South Pacific*.

Matters of design are perhaps of more genuine interest to Prince Philip. He pays attention to the landscape of the royal residences – though sometimes, as at Sandringham, with an eye to improving the shooting as much as the vista. At Windsor he redesigned the East Terrace gardens, though since his study overlooked them there was some self-interest in the reform. It was, however, "a singularly unattractive garden. We tore up the previous pattern and made every kind of model, until we arrived at the present form, a kind of spoke system, with beds round the fountain." He also objected to the fountain which apparently depicted "a sort of huge black figure of a man strangling a snake" – which sounds like a design based on an example drawn from classical antiquity. Anyhow he produced an alternative, a lotus leaf design. There were official doubts over the acceptability of his design, so he had it made up of Roman cement and painted in bronze. After three years, when officialdom "found there wasn't a riot of disapproval they eventually had it cast properly in bronze".

Industrial design is an area where Prince Philip has had an unquestionably constructive impact: an example of his private concern with function and the quality of life overflowing into public activity. While Edward Halliday was working on a portrait of Prince Philip to be hung at Gordonstoun, he introduced his subject to the designer Gordon Russell, who was then busy organising an exhibition called "Design at Work". In 1948, with Britain struggling by means of the austerity programme to make good the material losses of war, with battered cities and drab, overworked, factories, the need to associate good design with everyday life was starkly apparent. Itching to get involved in some useful work, the newly-created Duke of Edinburgh leapt at the chance of associating himself with Russell's modest but significant crusade. He was soon deeply involved, giving advice (never in short supply when he takes up a cause), time and, above all, putting the weight of his position behind the project.

Russell recalls that, "Most important of all, he gave me his personal support publicly, at a time when I was much harassed by sniping from outside." The publicity generated by Prince Philip's involvement went a long way towards making British manufacturers more design conscious during the post-war years of economic recovery. Later Russell received more enthusiastic royal backing when the establishment of the Design Centre in the Haymarket, London, was proposed. The Design Centre was opened in 1956, despite some initial opposition, and continues to give its approval to a bewildering variety of artefacts. Prince Philip's name is still firmly associated with its work and his influence is given tangible form in the presentation of an annual prize: "Wednesday, 20th February 1980, 11 am. The Duke of Edinburgh will chair the Selection Panel for the Duke of Edinburgh's Design Prize at the Design Centre, Haymarket." An enduring memorial to influence well used, if ever there was one; most people would settle for that, or even less.

Prince Philip went on, however, at a dinner in Sydney in 1965, to offer a similar prize to Australian designers, proposing that it should be given the reassuringly straightforward title of "The Prince Philip Prize for Australian Design", which must have sounded sweeter to antipodean ears than the earlier, convoluted suggestion of "His Royal Highness The Duke of Edinburgh's Australian Design Award". It was his idea that the first prize should be designed by the first winner. He continued to keep a sharp eye on the whole business, suggesting ways of improving arrangements – something he seems unable to resist, no matter which project he is associated with, but which he continues to see as very much part of taking on any patronage.

His views on design, art and the environment have been expressed on several occasions, but nowhere more cogently than in a

211

speech given before the Convocation of the Royal College of Art on 8 July 1955:

There is no excuse for unattractive design in anything that is likely to be seen by human eyes, even less if it has a function to perform as well. With all due respect to that august body, it will be a great day when it is considered as important to have something shown in the Design Centre of the Council of Industrial Design as it is to have a picture hung in the Royal Academy. This day is bound to be some way off, as the Design Centre is only to be opened next spring!

To put it kindly, you are lucky if you own a picture painted by an R.A., but most people have got to live with furniture, domestic objects, cars, shops, pubs, and everything else which surround our daily lives. It is inevitable that we should see more advertisements than old masters.

Some people bewail the passing of the artist craftsman, others have no time for anything unless it is made by hand. Of course the artist craftsman is still there but he cannot possibly meet the needs of any but a small section of the public. It may be very sad that things are not made by hand, but the fact remains that to make anything in sufficient quantity it must be made by machine, and there is no reason why the machine should not make nice things if it is given half a chance. What we lack is not artist craftsmen but artist engineers. There is no reason whatsoever in this day and age why we should be palmed off with second-rate stuff on the excuse that it is machine-made.

Prince Philip's own capacity for design is frequently expressed when he is asked by this organisation or that to present a cup or some sort of prize – not just to hand the trophy over, but to produce it. Although not keen on providing the traditional cup (he calls them "Victorian pots"), he is good at making appropriate suggestions and seeing them through. When the show business philanthropic organisation the Grand Order of Water Rats proposed a Prince Philip Greyhound trophy, his first, and perhaps predictable reaction was to ask, "What about a silver lamp post?" Eventually he drew and specified a silver dog collar.

As the patron of tiddlywinks enthusiasts he was asked by the Scottish Tiddlywinks Association what he thought a proposed trophy of a Silver Wink might look like. Much diverted he replied, seriously, "It might be a plain silver coin of about crown size, with 'The Silver Wink' engraved on one side and my arms or badge on the other, with the words 'Presented by HRH the D. of E.' round it. "It could", he went on to suggest, "be set either as a mobile or firmly fixed in a solid glass support in some sort of flowing, rather than cut, design."

When in 1966 he offered, to the anticipated distress of his Treasurer, to provide a trophy for the Argentine Polo Association's thirty-goal tournament, he was quite clear what was needed: "We could get a nice miniature polo stick made, about three feet long, ebony and silver, and then each winning team could add a thing like a wine label with their names on. . . ." He then drew the stick and the labels, inscribing on the latter, "1. James Snitch, 2. Augustus Bull, 3. William Clot", adding a cautionary note for any over-respectful engravers, "These names NOT to be engraved." There were to be inscriptions in Spanish and English, and the stick enclosed in a satin-lined case.

What does such attention to detail mean? That he has got too much free time on his hands? Quite untrue, though there are those who insist he has not done a day's work in his life. That he is too much in control? The desire to be in reasonable control is well enough documented. That he is obsessional over details? Well, he certainly likes to get things right and has very clear ideas as to what is right. A thirst for efficiency and improvement is one of his most marked characteristics. If it is so important to the enjoyment of his private pastimes, it is even more plainly on display when he undertakes his public duties before a watchful and not uncritical nation.

14

Public Duties

"You might ask whether all this rushing about is to any purpose. Am I just doing it to make it look as if I'm earning my
keep, or has it any national value?"

Prince Philip

PRINCE PHILIP's PUBLIC LIFE is, at first sight, amazingly varied and
exciting. If the ambition of most aspiring beauty queens is "to
travel", he out-travels them all, averaging something like 75,000
miles a year. He also delivers sixty to eighty major speeches and
gives an even larger number of shorter talks, many of them off the
cuff. The number of hands shaken, smiles smiled, thanks expressed,
chicken legs chewed, schedules met, and crowds gratified make up a
programme that is as exhausting and daunting as that of any
American presidential candidate on the stump – and the Duke of
Edinburgh is not running for office. The programme must also be
essentially repetitive and potentially dulling of the senses, despite
the apparently endless variety of human contact and venue.

It is, of course, part of the job for which British royalty is paid by
the nation. Prince Philip, however, construes his public duties as
something more than being seen to be performing adequately in a
quasi-presidential role. Not only is he another pair of eyes and ears
for the Queen, but he believes he has a creative mission as well: to
present the monarchy as a dynamic, involved and responsive
institution that will address itself to some of the problems of contemporary British society. This means being seen to react to certain
situations, to produce alternative proposals, to exhort, advise,
warn, and sometimes to rebuke. In short, to act as watchdog in the
national, and royal, interest; a watchdog, moreover, that will sometimes shake off its muzzle and bark.

The Duke of Edinburgh's twice-yearly programme meetings organise his personal engagements for the next six months. The idea is to sift through the various invitations to open, dine, speak, attend and so on, and to produce a list based on some sort of merit rather than on the order in which the invitations are received. There are naturally some immovable dates which have already been written in: joint engagements with the Queen, overseas visits and tours, Order of the Garter services at St George's Chapel, Windsor, Maundy services, the chairing of the selection panel at the Design Centre – the full list would be daunting enough.

Over and above these engagements, many of which fall into the "morally bound to go" category, there is space every year for some three hundred out of over twelve hundred possible engagements. Impossible engagements have already been weeded out before the programme meeting, largely on the grounds of clashes with the points that are already fixed in Prince Philip's programme, but also because they seem unworthy of royal time.

The whittling down of the EPs (engagements possible) into a final list of EAs (engagements accepted) is an exercise which combines reason with instinct in creative juxtaposition. Prince Philip chairs these meetings assisted by members of his staff, his principal equerry perhaps (equerries tend to be middle-ranking officers, majors for example, on short-term secondment from the services), his chief clerk and accountant, and a couple of his secretarial staff, who sometimes have a better grasp of the logistics of the proposed operation than the military men present.

The main task is to discard enough of the EP cards. The Duke will often ask, "Who's pushing this?" Famous names may be greeted with a dismissive "Oh, him," and the cause is lost. Invitations with pompous overtones tend to earn a ribald reception: "Institute of Public Cleansing? A paper will be read on the Purposeful Uses of Solid Waste?" Laughter, but then a silence as the invitation is seriously considered; after all, an avowed environmentalist ought to look carefully at such thing.

There are lots of reflective pauses punctuated by "rapid mutterings of telescoped thoughts, sometimes a squeak of private mirth . . . 'I've been trying to miss this since 1966' . . . 'They must be out of their minds' . . . 'I can chopper from Goodwood, should be quite easy – an hour? Start the thing, lunch, chop back' . . . more pencil-tapping and rifflings from the desk, mutterings of semi-exasperation, silent probings of possibilities, sudden outbursts of

215

'crazy', 'lunacy', and other expressions of reluctance. An atlas is needed: 'Where's Ipswich? I don't seem to have anything here but south-west Russia.' "

According to Basil Boothroyd, "The girls are practised interpreters of his verbal shorthand, half thoughts, groans, mutterings and sudden reflective silences:

> HRH: Let's see, didn't we – ?
> 1st Girl: Yes, Sir. In September.
> HRH: What about the – you know – ?
> 1st Girl: There's a list, Sir. (*Blows nose*)
> HRH: I say, you've got a stinker, haven't you? But shan't we be – ?
> 2nd Girl: No, Sir. Cumbernauld isn't until the twenty-ninth.
> HRH: Good. All right, then."

In such mysterious ways are princely programmes formulated. It seems to work. An EP is promoted to an EA. The transport has been worked out; if he is going alone to speak overseas, the host organisation is expected to pay for the cost of travel. State visits are different, and funded accordingly. Helicopters whirling up from Buckingham Palace and Windsor Castle have made an enormous difference, giving the modern royal visitor a mobility and flexibility undreamed of even in George VI's reign.

Once an engagement is accepted, a letter goes out from Prince Philip's office asking for an outline of arrangements and reminding the recipient that the whole business must remain confidential until HRH has approved the programme and a date has been fixed for the press release. Plenty of room for negotiation, here, and eventually all is neatly filed away in a blue leatherette, gold inscribed ringbinder. There are draft programmes and amended draft programmes: the hosts "would be honoured if His Royal Highness would deliver an address" – answer "No". If HRH's speeches are to remain the pearls that many believe them to be, they cannot be scattered around too liberally.

Then there are the final arrangements over transport and the function's timing. Minutes are weighed with scrupulous care: "Arrival is now to be at 15.25. Prince Philip's pennant must fly. . . . Standards, 1, 6" × 3", sent. . . ." The hosts are informed: "Prince Philip may leave at any time from 18.15 onwards, half an hour being about the right time for tea." The police have to be informed

and so do the Lords Lieutenant of the counties involved. The fact
that an engagement has been sandwiched between two others is not
revealed, as it might take off the gilt. At any rate, everything is now
arranged, and the mayor's wife can buy her new hat and dress.

None of this background bustle is apparent to the public, and is
not meant to be. As onlookers they see a superbly smooth, well-
orchestrated show, with a dash of pomp here, some high ceremonial
there, and with a touch or two of the mundane as well. One of the
chief purposes of royal visits, after the secular anointing and blessings are over, is to show that the royal personage is also a human
being with limbs and facial muscles that function like those of an
ordinary person. Thus relieved by the visible proof of their shared
humanity, the subject goes (mostly) happily away.

The Duke of Edinburgh is particularly good at meeting the
public. Although he wears his Garter robes or his various ceremonial uniforms with poise and dignity, he is understandably
more relaxed in suit and tie and with the chance to see, hear and say
something interesting to members of the public.

Two recent royal engagements admirably illustrate his public
"style". The first is the visit undertaken with the Queen to the *Daily
Mail* Ideal Home Exhibition at Earls Court on Monday 3 March
1980. It was the day before the exhibition opened to the public, so
the onlookers crowding round the route the royal couple would
take between the stands were almost all exhibitors.

A couple of policemen sauntered in, there was a discreet flurry of
dark-suited VIPs, a doorman straightened his hat, and suddenly the
Queen was there – diminutive, looking rather shy, and dressed in
the rather unexceptional clothes normally associated with her. It
was almost as if she were trying to look as inconspicuous as possible. She walked straight ahead, without, it seemed, much interest in
the exhibits or the crowd straining to see her. All the comments one
could hear were about her, not Prince Philip: her "porcelain com-
plexion", her clothes, her skin (again), her size. She was, however,
hardly an animated visitor in these early moments.

A little behind her walked the Duke of Edinburgh, wearing a
beautifully cut dark grey suit, a striped shirt, and a reddish-brown
tie. He looked a little thinner, and shorter, than one might have
thought from his photographs; his face was tanned, and the skin
seemed to be drawn tightly over it, emphasising the beak-like
contours of his nose; his hair, lying so close to his skull that it might
have been sprayed on, was still recognisably blond; he looked

exceedingly fit and relaxed; the only indication of his true age was to be seen in his neck which is wrinkled and corded with veins and muscles.

In contrast to the Queen, he was full of movement and life: he talked, apparently incessantly, to the man walking beside him, smiling repeatedly; his hands were very busy, either gesturing sideways, or pointing to objects of interest. If he was *not* enjoying himself he was giving a performance of award-winning quality. The royal party flowed past as smoothly as a river in spring flood and the banks of onlookers dissolved and scattered in its wake.

Later, a little further along the route between the stalls, another part of the crowd awaited the passage of the royal visitors. Two charladies heralded their coming, carrying brooms, curtseying in mock respect to the onlookers, and calling out, "They won't be long!"

More ripples along the route and there was the Queen, her entourage flowing steadily behind her. The Duke was still talking. They stopped at a stall exhibiting examples of the craftsmanship of Dorset woodworkers. The Queen and the Duke were face to face now. She looked up at him and smiled; it was a brilliant smile, one almost of relief that support was at hand. He took over the conversation with a practised efficiency. He remembered that he had once visited the school for craftsmen in Dorset and had been presented with a small wooden cabinet. Did he still have it? Of course, it was on his work desk. The woodworkers looked gratified. There was uproarious laughter. He had recognised one of the craftsmen from his previous visit and cracked a joke. It was not a joke that would demand inclusion in an anthology of *The Wit of Prince Philip*, but it did very well: What, he asked the woodworker, Derek Christison, were you doing before making wooden furniture? The bearded Christison admitted he had been a boat-builder. "Renegade!" said the former naval person. Collapse of those within earshot. The Queen laughed too. The royal party moved on. The woodworkers glowed with pleasure. The whole encounter had lasted less than three minutes.

Afterwards a black Rolls-Royce without a numberplate waited at the end of a short, canopied walk. The Queen and the Duke drove off. Their departure was not observed by many.

Eight days later, Prince Philip, as President of the Central Council for Physical Recreation, opened the British Sports Exhibition at the Stock Exchange. The exhibition was in the gallery overlooking the floor of the Exchange over which soberly clad brokers walked purposefully, the sombre uniformity of their clothes broken by the occasional blinding flash of a brown suit.

It is very much a man's world, and the Duke of Edinburgh, when he appeared in the gallery, fitted into it effortlessly. Two Press photographers awaited him at the front of the small crowd. He gave them a warm smile of acknowledgment as their flash bulbs exploded – the hatchet seems well and truly buried nowadays.

A brief introduction was made. The Duke waited and smiled the smile one recognises on the Prince of Wales. He pulled his fingers and then played with his lips with the finger and thumb of his right hand. He was handed the microphone, looked down at it, and smiled again – as if recognising an old friend and a potential enemy.

He delivered a short graceful speech, and somehow made a joke out of the Central Council for Physical Education's reputation as the "Trades Union Council of the sporting world" and the fact that former Labour Sports Minister Denis Howell had once been its chairman. He concluded, "In case anyone is in any doubt, this exhibition is now open."

The exhibition was then viewed. He appeared to take a minute interest in every stand, even those of the most basic and uninspiring design. The questions came steadily as he moved among the exhibits. At the Sereena Sports stand he admired some large coloured photographs of girls wearing football shirts and very little else. He said "I didn't know so many pretty girls played football!" The two Yorkshiremen attending the stand enjoyed the joke. It was not a moment to be savoured by Women's Lib.

Hundreds of similar scenes, questions, remarks, even jokes, are part and parcel of Prince Philip's yearly work-load. He does the job well and apparently without resentment. His constant attentiveness is taken at face value and, indeed, could hardly be feigned, so close is the scrutiny to which he is subjected.

Apart from engagements like these within the United Kingdom, there are the overseas tours that have been so marked a characteristic of Queen Elizabeth II's reign. That these tours have become so relaxed in structure, with walkabouts to meet the people, is largely due to the influence of the Duke of Edinburgh.

Why are the tours undertaken? They are exhausting for the royal tourists and cost a large amount of money, though much of the expense falls upon the host nation. Prince Philip has said, "February and March are usually good times for overseas visits. There's

219

nothing much going on here and in any case the weather's usually better abroad." Just the sort of comment to enrage the critics of alleged royal extravagance. In any case, 1980, for example, was not like that at all; February and March were crowded with domestic engagements for the Queen and the Duke, and their major overseas trip was scheduled for 24–28 May – a quick dash to Australia to open the new High Court building in Canberra and to pay one-day visits to Sydney and Melbourne.

Royal tours overseas are the equivalent of a mediaeval monarch's progress round his realm: citizens of the Commonwealth have the opportunity to see the person who is Head of that disparate but still surviving organisation, while in foreign states the royal tourist is simply a glamorous super-ambassador, a purveyor, it is hoped, of abundant good will.

Certainly Elizabeth II saw her duty to the Empire and Commonwealth as one of her major responsibilities when she acceded to the throne in 1952. It was a view that Prince Philip strongly supported. In the winter of 1953–54 she and the Duke of Edinburgh undertook a vast overseas tour of over 40,000 miles, encompassing twelve Commonwealth countries. On Christmas Day 1953 in New Zealand she delivered the first Christmas Day broadcast ever by a sovereign from outside the United Kingdom. In her message she summed up an official attitude towards the Commonwealth which was also very much her own: "I want to show that the Crown is not merely an abstract symbol of our unity, but a personal and living bond between you and me." On 3 February 1954 she broadcast from Australia emphasising that she was visiting her dominions not as Queen of the United Kingdom but as their own sovereign: "I am proud indeed", she said, "to be head of a nation that has achieved so much."

Such sentiments would have fallen rather flat elsewhere: in South Africa, for example, with the Afrikaner Nationalists firmly in power, or in Kenya in the midst of the Mau Mau uprising. New Zealand and Australia were the most obviously receptive of the senior Commonwealth countries to royal blandishments – and still are.

Nonetheless, the great round-the-world Commonwealth tour of 1953–54 is worth some consideration as an early example of Prince Philip's impact on such events. In scope it was ambitious beyond the wildest dreams (or nightmares) of any previous British monarch: it lasted one hundred and seventy-three days; 18,000 miles were travelled in the air, rather more by sea, and 4000 by rail and road in seven hundred different drives and excursions.

The Duke of Edinburgh's influence had been felt at an early stage in the planning of the tour. It had been widely assumed that the Queen would resume the tour in Kenya, where it had been interrupted by the news of her father's death in February 1952. Prince Philip objected to this, believing that to start the tour in such a way would cause his wife unnecessary pain. It was arranged instead that the first leg of the tour would be a flight across the Atlantic to Gander in Newfoundland; because of the Mau Mau troubles, Kenya was finally dropped from the itinerary. The passage to Gander was by the BOAC airliner *Canopus* – no more nonsense about the hazards of monarchs, even heirs apparent, flying. Queen Elizabeth thus became the first British monarch to fly the Atlantic, a clear vindication of her husband's belief in the necessity to move with the times.

There were numerous examples during the tour of the Duke of Edinburgh's conviction that the onlookers merited every attention possible. When the *Canopus* touched down at Gander at 3.23 am there was a crowd waiting for them; woken from their sleep, Philip and the Queen got up, dressed, and greeted their audience, before going back to try and rest. This was symptomatic of an informality not hitherto associated with monarchs of the House of Windsor. In Jamaica the Duke was clearly disturbed that an over-enthusiastic onlooker who had thrown down his coat before the Queen in a Raleigh-like gesture was hustled away by police and later charged under the lunacy laws. Over the Christmas period in New Zealand he got up at 5 am to fly three hundred miles to attend the mass funeral of the victims of a train crash in which one hundred and sixty-six people had died.

While in New Zealand, the Duke had also insisted that it was possible for the Queen to make a brief visit to the meeting-house of Waikato Maoris although the official schedule had excluded it. In one town a man, stuck behind a dais, shouted, "Where's the Duke?" Philip left the official party, walked to where the man could see him, smiled and waved. In Wellington he read the lessons in the homely old wooden church of St Paul's. Later on, at Melbourne University, students presented him with a pair of crutches, which he handed back remarking, "Your need is greater than mine." He was also presented with a blotter which he accepted, murmuring, "This will remind me not to blot my copybook."

Prince Philip

It is not suggested that these examples of unexceptional humour, or the capacity to react spontaneously to unscheduled crowd incidents, had any profound political or social effect upon the countries visited. Psephologists record no great swing of public opinion among onlookers after a royal tour has swept by. It is not known for sure whether the Commonwealth ideal was strengthened or weakened by the great tour of 1953–54. What is clear is that the monarchy presented a more consistently human face to its overseas subjects than ever before, and for this the Duke of Edinburgh could take a good deal of the credit.

Subsequent royal tours have continued to build on the success of the tour of 1953–54 and the visit to Canada and the United States in 1951. The trend established by the Duke of Edinburgh and the Queen has continued: before the 1969 tour of Australia the original guest list was rejected as "reading like the social register", and there were royal instructions to replace some of the Melbourne matrons with Australia's "horny-handed men of toil". There have been royal "walkabouts", and, generally, a more positive attempt to meet the people.

Not that royal tours are, by some act of providence, trouble-free. Prince Philip's spontaneity of response also means that he offends some of the people for some of the time. During his Canadian tour of 1969, for example, he said, when presented with a cowboy hat at Calgary in Alberta, "Not another one?" He later made a public apology. Then in Vancouver he forgot the name of the new annexe to the city hall that he was opening: "I declare this thing open – whatever it is." More apologies: "It was raining and I wanted to get on with it: especially as the total audience was about fifteen passing shoppers under umbrellas." The annexe, however, has never recovered, and is known as the "East Thing". In Toronto he offended yet more people by suggesting that the traditional Christmas broadcast to the Commonwealth should be dressed up and called "The Queen Show". The shooting of a tiger in India in 1961 antagonised more people still. The list could be extended further, but the essential point has already been established. Shaking off the restrictions of royal protocol brings hazards; spontaneity can offend; first reactions are not always the most tactful. These are risks which Prince Philip has found well worth taking.

Royal tours overseas carry other risks: the risk of assassination and the risk of provoking violent personal and political reaction. Although the Queen is the more obvious target for such resentments,

Prince Philip is also vulnerable. Both refuse to be distracted by the possibility of violent assault. In 1961 the royal tour of Ghana went ahead despite scenes of internal disorder and against the advice of Conservative elder statesmen like Winston Churchill and Anthony Eden. The 1964 visit to Quebec was undertaken in the face of direct threats of assassination. The dilemma for the monarchy is an obvious one: to avoid potentially dangerous situations would show little confidence in the innate good will of the public; moreover, it would sever the vital, if transitory and ephemeral link between onlookers and the object of their attention.

The more dangerous incidents that have occurred on royal tours involving the Queen and the Duke of Edinburgh have been the result of the failure of the local authorities to control the crowds. In Panama in 1953 the police had failed to line the royal route and a frenzied crowd slowed the car carrying the Queen and the one carrying the Duke to a walking pace. Spectators tried to jump on the cars, and such was the lack of police control that ordinary cars were allowed to cut into the procession from side streets. Aided by "a sort of rugger scrum" of equerries and police, the Duke managed to scramble from his car and join the Queen in hers, and the procession reached its destination safely.

The incident was repeated in its essential details twenty-six years later in Oman. In March 1979 the royal couple were walking back to their car after visiting a seventeenth-century fort at Niswa, when the Queen "was surrounded by chanting boy scouts and wailing women". Prince Philip became lost in the crowd and was eventually directed to a chauffeurless car. After a couple of minutes he kicked the door of the car open and, according to the press report, said, "It's bloody hot in there. It's like an oven. And where is my driver?" As in Panama, he then became anxious for the Queen's safety and started pushing his way through the unruly crowd calling out, "Where's the Queen? Is she all right?" He then saw his car being driven away empty and was simultaneously assailed by the siren of a near-by police car. Turning to the police car, he put his hands over his ears and shouted, "Switch that bloody thing off you silly f....." Strong language, reflecting strong feelings. He eventually got into another car and rejoined the Queen. The incidents "came as a finale to a highly successful six-country tour of the Gulf States by the royal couple". Britain's diplomatic relationship with Oman seems to have survived this loss of temper and the plain speaking, which may say something, either way, about the value of royal tours.

Back in the United Kingdom, Prince Philip's patronage of a large number of organisations and good causes carries responsibilities apart from the obligation to undertake the official visits described earlier. The main responsibility is that of championing the organisation or cause, either by speaking or writing about it, or by answering press questions on the subject. Volumes of his selected speeches have been published – the first volume appearing in 1957, covering the years 1948–55. In his introduction to the second volume, *Prince Philip Speaks: Selected Speeches, 1956–9*, he wrote: "I try to say something which I hope might be interesting or at least constructive. To do this and at the same time avoid giving offence can sometimes be a ticklish business. I have come to the conclusion that when in doubt it is better to play safe – people would rather be bored than offended."

He has not, however, always chosen to follow his own rule. His public pronouncements have never been the bland, predictable, and singularly unstimulating speeches traditionally associated with the modern British monarchy. The licence he enjoys in this respect is due not only to his own extrovert nature and his capacity to state his opinions clearly, but also to his peculiar constitutional position. If he were King he would have to tread more carefully. Since he is not, he can range over a variety of topics with comparative freedom. Some of his more positive and challenging statements will be examined later.

Not all of Prince Philip's public pronouncements fizz with exciting ideas or threaten the staid and conventional with choleric collapse. There is much that is forseeable, though worthy: for example, the cause of wild life conservation, the advocacy of a greater national emphasis on scientific and technological development, the encouragement of sporting endeavour. Even when he is not acting as an advocate of change, his identification with certain causes can put him in difficult situations. One recent example was the controversy over whether Britain should participate in the Moscow Olympics of 1980. Led by Mrs Thatcher, the Conservative government had tried to persuade (some might say bully) British athletes into not going to Moscow in retaliation against the Soviet intervention in Afghanistan. The House of Commons backed up this policy with a healthy majority of 163. The British Olympic Association, however, decided on 25 March 1980 "to accept forthwith the invitation to send a team to Moscow this summer".

On the same day as the British Olympic Association's decision

52 Knights of the Garter leaving St George's Chapel, Windsor, after the ceremonial service of June 1972

53 Take that! The Chancellor of Edinburgh University conferring an honorary degree upon Miss Elsie Looker in 1956

52

53

54 Prince Philip flanked by Colombian stalwarts, with Michael Parker behind him, during his South American tour of 1962

55 Duke jokes with Magpies! Prince Philip meets the 1955 cup finalists Newcastle United at Wembley

56 Delegate at the controversial meeting of the Olympic International Sports Federations which eventually issued a statement criticising an Olympic boycott in April 1980

57 Aberfan, October 1966. Prince Philip makes contact with shocked villagers

56

57

58

59

60

"The Express is a bloody awful newspaper," said the Duke. "Ah, well," said Lord B., as they trotted him off to the Tower, "at least he takes it or he wouldn't know it was a bloody awful newspaper."

58 Police fending off Canadians rapturous at the sight of Prince Philip in Toronto
59 Prince Philip with Bing Crosby at Buckingham Palace in 1976
60 1962 *Express* cartoon featuring Prince Philip's somewhat antagonistic relationship with Lord Beaverbrook
61 A member of the Iounhanan tribe in the New Hebrides which worships the Duke of Edinburgh

62 as Lord Mountbatten welcomes Prince Philip arriving in Malta in 1949 to take up his naval command

63 ... to a Moroccan urchin in Rabat in 1964

64 ... at something up there while talking to Quintin Hogg (and nursing a polo-injured arm) in 1964

62

63

64

PRINCE PHILIP AND
THE FAIR SEX

65 with a bare-backed Diane Cilento at a 1965
film première
66 with Margaret Trudeau (pointing again)
aboard the Royal Yacht *Britannia*
67 Prince Philip's childhood friend, Hélène
Foufounis (later Cordet), with her children Max
and Louise to whom he is godfather
68 with Mrs Julius Nyerere during Tanganyika's independence celebrations in 1961

65

68

6

67

69   69 Three pillars of the Mountbatten-Windsor connection. Prince Charles, apparently justifying himself after a game of polo in 1978, is listened to by his "Honorary
Grandfather", Earl Mountbatten, and Prince Philip

70   70 Nephew and "Honorary Great Nephew" follow Earl Mountbatten's coffin to the
ceremonial funeral service at Westminster Abbey, 5 September 1979

Prince Philip spoke at the annual meeting of the Central Council for Physical Recreation, of which he is President. Though declining to get involved in the debate he said, of those involved in the controversy, "I know they are all acting in good faith." He went on to warn about the price sport sometimes has to pay in its involvement with governments: "Governments in all countries are concerned to acquire prestige through success in international sport, and so they commit themselves financially to sport. This involvement carries with it the inevitable consequence that governments acquire power to influence sport, and also the participation of sports bodies in international competition."

Rather a neutral response. If anything, tacit support for the decision reached by the British Olympic Association. Two weeks later, however, the problem re-emerged in a trickier guise. Despite the BOA's large majority for the decision reached at the end of March, not all the sports federations attached to the Association were prepared to accept the majority view. The British hockey federation gave early backing to the government's call for an Olympic boycott; fencing, swimming and yachting were undecided; and on 7 April the British Equestrian Federation announced it would not be participating "unless the Government advises to the contrary".

This decision meant that two members of the royal family, Princess Anne and Captain Mark Phillips, would not be going to Moscow, which they would have done if Captain Phillips had been selected for the three-day event. It also presented Prince Philip with a difficult decision. Over and above his family links with Princess Anne and her husband, he is also President of the International Equestrian Federation: in this latter capacity he would naturally have been expected to attend the Olympics. The British Equestrian Federation's decision not to go to Moscow, and the likelihood that other national equestrian teams would boycott the games, presented him with a weighty diplomatic problem – a problem, moreover, that he had not sought out but that had landed in his lap as a result of the legitimate exercise of his public duties. It is a problem that would not even have come the way of a less active and involved public figure. On 22 April he announced that he would not be attending the games, but at the same time helped to write a statement issued by the Olympic International Sports Federations which criticised the boycott movement. It seemed an unhappy compromise and, the following day, a Buckingham Palace spokesman claimed that the Duke had strongly opposed the first draft of the statement and had succeeded in modifying it. In fact, it seems that his own private view was that there should not be a boycott.

For all his public activity, there is one area in which the Duke of Edinburgh has no role to play whatsoever. This is in the constitutional functions of the monarchy. As he has pointed out himself, "Constitutionally I don't exist." The Queen's own constitutional position is clearly defined and understood. It is hardly a creative role, and if Parliament were to decide to dethrone her, even order her execution, she would have no option but to comply, since to veto her own death warrant would be tantamount to signing it.

The Duke of Edinburgh does not even have the task of signing any official documents. Indeed, the contents of the official boxes are none of his business. This must be difficult for a man with a well-developed capacity for looking hard and intelligently at a whole host of problems at both a national and international level. It would be absurd, however, to suppose that he bites back his opinions in private for the sake of constitutional propriety – the Queen has, for example, confided "lightly to one of the family" that "it was a good job that he was not at home" during the trauma of the 1956 Suez Crisis since "He would have been hell to live with." Nonetheless, he could not have affected events one way or the other. He has, however, fashioned an immensely creative role in public life as a respectable agent for change, and it is in this role, as we shall see, that he has achieved most for the monarchy and the nation.

15

Agent for Change

"I don't mean I did it. I was just involved in getting it done."
Prince Philip

A GROUP OF VILLAGERS in the New Hebrides islands in the Pacific Ocean believe that the Duke of Edinburgh is their Messiah and that he will soon return to them to cure all sickness and to make the old young once more. The two hundred followers of the cult expect the Duke to restore paradise on earth, and to resume his rightful place as a Melanesian – down to wearing the traditional "nambas" or penis gourd. The villagers also believe that Prince Philip runs the Commonwealth and has deliberately kept his true identity a secret from the Queen. They are convinced that when the royal yacht *Britannia* passed close to their island in 1974, the Duke confessed to his wife that "he was really a Melanesian Messiah and that the marriage could not last". There has even been an authenticated exchange of gifts between the worshippers and the object of their veneration: the Duke sent them an autographed portrait and a supply of English clay pipes; they sent him a carved wooden pig-sticking instrument about five feet long. On 19 November 1979 a Buckingham Palace spokesman admitted the exchange of gifts. He was also asked whether the Duke would wear the penis gourd on his return, and replied, "I am reluctant to commit His Royal Highness. If it does come off we will have to study that ... facility very carefully."

This piece of whimsy contains one interesting and fundamental perception of Prince Philip that most of his wife's more sophisticated subjects would instantly recognise – that he is, and has been, a powerful agent for change, though few would grant him the regenerative powers of a messiah. His capacity to introduce reforms has altered the traditional practices as well as the contemporary image of the British monarchy. At the same time he has thrown his influence behind a number of public causes that he considered to be worth supporting, though his efforts have not always been well received.

When she succeeded to the throne, Elizabeth II enjoyed a honeymoon period with the British public, rather similar to that generally accorded to an incoming Prime Minister. Her reign was hailed as the dawn of a new age – a new "Elizabethan Age". Newspapers went to great lengths to identify the "modern Elizabethans" who would restore Britain to a place of pre-eminence – ignoring the fact that the first Elizabethan England had hardly been a super-power bestriding the globe like a colossus. Winston Churchill, proud beyond measure to be the young Queen's first Prime Minister, unleashed his romantic eloquence for the occasion and made a somewhat fanciful connection with another sovereign: "I, whose youth was passed in the august, unchallenged and tranquil glare of the Victorian era, may well feel a thrill in invoking once more the prayer and anthem *God Save the Queen*."

In 1957, however, there was a sharp puncturing of the inflated bubble of royalist sentiment. Just as the Suez Crisis of 1956 had demonstrated that the days when Britain could carry out an independent, sub-imperial foreign policy were over, the next year saw the expression of a more realistic, and necessarily critical, attitude towards the monarchy. The critics were not revolutionaries of the far left, though the reaction to them might have suggested that they were. They were essentially loyalists, and, if not Establishment figures, not far removed from the British Establishment.

Lord Altrincham began it all with an article in the *National and English Review* of August 1957, in which he criticised the Queen's entourage for being "almost without exception of the 'tweedy' sort". This meant that, "The personality conveyed by the utterances which are put into her mouth is that of a priggish schoolgirl, captain of the hockey team, a prefect and a recent candidate for confirmation." He continued, "Like her mother she appears to be unable to string even a few sentences together without a written text. When she has lost the bloom of youth, the Queen's reputation will depend, far more than it does now, upon her personality . . . she will have to say things which people can remember and do things on her own initiative which will make people sit up and take notice."

Despite Lord Altrincham's protests that he meant to be a constructive and loyal critic, there was an outraged reaction to his
comments which culminated in a representative of the League of
Empire Loyalists (an organisation little heard of recently) slapping
his face during a television discussion programme. Altrincham,
who renounced his peerage in 1963, now believes that the hysterical
reaction to his article was due to the "Shintoistic atmosphere of the
post-Coronation period . . . There was a tendency – quite alien to
our national tradition – to regard as high treason any criticism of
the monarch however loyal and constructive its intent." Essentially,
the storm over Lord Altrincham's criticisms was got up by those
unwilling to countenance change, and it perhaps exhibited symptoms of the deepening mood of national insecurity. His strictures
were recognised as reasonable by a larger number of the public
than at first appeared likely: a *Daily Mail* opinion poll found that a
majority of its readers aged between sixteen and thirty-four agreed
with him, and that all age groups felt that the court circle around the
Queen was too narrowly representative.

It was possible, moreover, to recognise the accuracy of Altrincham's "priggish schoolgirl, captain of the hockey team" description of Elizabeth II. It was hardly her fault, and simply reflected the
sheltered and rather restrictive quality of her upbringing. George
VI's and Queen Elizabeth's social circle and intellectual capacities
had been strictly limited, and her own were similarly narrow.

Other critics of the House of Windsor leapt on to the Altrincham
bandwagon. Britain's most successful "Angry Young Man", the
playwright John Osborne, wrote in the October edition of
Encounter an article which, though apparently written six months
earlier, echoed Altrincham's criticism: "My objection to the Royal
symbol is that it is dead; it is a gold filling in a mouth full of decay.
When the mobs rush forward in the Mall they are taking part in the
last circus of a civilisation that has lost faith in itself and sold itself
for a spendid triviality." In the same month Malcolm Muggeridge,
man of letters and a "television personality", also wrote of "the
royal soap opera . . . a sort of substitute or ersatz religion". Muggeridge was not, of course, an "Angry Young Man", rather a
"Puckish and Sometimes Irritating Elderly Man". Nonetheless, his
criticisms, later expanded, were recognisably serious and telling,
even for those who chose to denounce him for making them.

Elizabeth II's good fortune lay not in this sudden proliferation of,
mostly, loyal critics, but in having a remedy close at hand. Her

husband certainly did not appear to be anything like the male equivalent of a "priggish schoolgirl", and his attitude, eight years later, to his eldest son's confirmation was anything but conventional. He could, moreover, spontaneously string whole paragraphs together, let alone sentences, and he had already developed the capacity "to say things which people can remember and do things . . . which will make people sit up and take notice". If the monarchy needed modernising, there already existed a consort determined to bring about reasonable change.

Some changes had already taken place before the Altrincham offensive of 1957. Smaller luncheon parties had been introduced to which, instead of relying upon representatives of the "tweedy" circle close to the House of Windsor to provide the guests, the Queen invited interesting people of all professions – scientists, academics, and so forth. Prince Philip also suggested that large-scale, more democratic garden parties should be held in the grounds of Buckingham Palace. It also seemed sensible to abolish the archaic débutante system, whereby hundreds of well-bred and rich young women paraded annually before the Queen and were thus presented at court in a sort of genteel initiation ceremony. In November 1957, a month after the Altrincham controversy had erupted, it was announced that the forthcoming season of royal presentations would be the last. Coincidence or a sensitive reaction to criticism? In tune with these modest reforms, Harold Macmillan's Conservative government gave a commitment in the Speech from the Throne in November 1957 to introduce a bill to enable the monarch to create life peers of both sexes.

In subsequent years there were more changes in the style and function of the monarchy. Formal courts, state balls and levees all followed the presentation parties into oblivion. All these reforms reflected the influence of Prince Philip. The Queen needed his encouragement and persuasion to end a good deal of the sterile formality of court life and ceremony. Her temperament and training were conservative and traditionalist, but she was able to see the rationale behind the proposed changes and to give them her full support. What her father would have made of it all may easily be guessed. It was, however, a new reign and a new monarchical style was gradually developing.

On the other hand, there has been no clean sweep of some of the ceremonies that are based on the practice of hundreds of years. The Queen continues to open a new Parliament amid scenes of great pomp and items of ceremonial which must, to some, if viewed rationally, seem absurdly comical. The Sovereign's Birthday Parade, Trooping the Colour, provides a vivid splash of colour at the height of summer, but the Queen is hardly likely to ride off to war at the head of her foot and horse guards as the symbol suggests.

The modernising of the monarchy has been an inevitable compromise which is hardly surprising since Prince Philip, the driving force behind the reforms, is no social revolutionary. He summed up his view of the modernising process in 1964 in answer to a question at the luncheon of the Foreign Press Association:

> One of the things about the Monarchy and its place, and one of its great weaknesses, is that it has to be all things to all people and, of course, it cannot do this when it comes to being all things to people who are traditionalists and all things to people who are iconoclasts.
>
> We therefore find ourselves in a position of compromise and we might be kicked by both sides. The only thing is that if you are very cunning you can get as far away from the extremists as you possibly can because they kick harder.

The object of a gradualist approach to any reform is to preserve the fundamental strengths of an institution while discarding irrelevant and offensive anachronisms. Monarchy, however, relies heavily on a sense of mystery, even awe, to maintain its appeal. Thus the changes in royal style that have taken place during Elizabeth II's reign have had to be nicely calculated. At a glance, little seems to have altered: amid economic and national decline, the British monarchy has managed to retain its gift for mounting moving ceremonial displays, often on a breathtaking scale, and always with admirable efficiency.

The Duke of Edinburgh is fully aware of the absurdities which manifest themselves in various acts of state ceremony. Once when discussing whether, during the State Opening of Parliament, the over-heavy Sword of State should be held in an at-ease position rather than held aloft during the Queen's Speech from the Throne, he said: "Incidentally the 'Sword' walks beside the 'Cap of Maintenance', which is carried on a stick. I'm not sure what could be done with that while standing at ease. Come to think of it, only the English would think of carrying a hat on a stick at a ceremony of State."

He is, however, a firm supporter of ceremonial that enhances the prestige and effectiveness of the monarchy. He approved of the plan to hold an elaborate investiture of Prince Charles as Prince of Wales in 1969. This decision, taken in the teeth of the rising storm of Welsh Nationalism, and planned partly to counter it, was meant "to 're-launch' the monarchy, as well as to launch Charles". By the late sixties it seemed appropriate to promote the monarchy as the focal point of British patriotism and to add some exceptional colour to the process. After the undoubted success of the investiture the Duke of Edinburgh, during an interview on Welsh television, defended the decision to hold the ceremony, saying: "The governing factor was that it was quite obvious that a large proportion of Welsh opinion favoured having the investiture." He added, with characteristic honesty, "The doubts were not so much about allowing the Prince to take part at all, but perhaps to what extent this sort of virtually mediaeval revival is relevant." The Silver Jubilee celebrations of 1977, on the other hand, were a more obviously national, and hence more powerful, expression of loyalty and Prince Philip played his part in them with a relaxed and self-confident dignity.

That the Queen's public persona, too, had become noticeably more relaxed by the late nineteen-seventies, was a tribute to the morale-boosting support of her husband as well as to improvements in the techniques by which she was able to present herself to her people. One example of this latter improvement could be seen in the annual Christmas Day message delivered to her subjects. On Christmas Day 1957, a few months after the Altrincham controversy had begun, the Queen delivered a memorised speech, looking straight at the television cameras for the first time. Harold Nicolson, the official biographer of George V, recorded his delight at the performance: "She came across quite clear, and with a vigour unknown in pre-Altrincham days." As the facilities for television speech-making improved, with tele-prompters, edited video-recordings and so forth, the Queen's Christmas messages became more spontaneous, more "human". Unlike the more recent softening of Margaret Thatcher's strident public image, however, it must be emphasised that the Queen's gradual improvement in her broadcasting technique owes nothing to the packaging efforts of a zealous public relations firm.

Prince Philip was the main begetter of the next logical step in presenting the monarchy with as human a face as possible – the production of the television film *Royal Family*. Screened in 1970, the film provided the Queen and her family with their most spectacular public relations achievement to date. It was not a painless achievement. Although the Queen, despite her earlier anxieties, proved amenable to the producer's requests that she should don this uniform or that, mount a horse or dismount a horse, and generally deport herself like a leading lady, her husband was a good deal less relaxed, even shouting on one occasion, "Don't bring your bloody cameras so close to the Queen!" Why the irritation in one so apparently at ease in public? His need to protect his more vulnerable wife? Anxiety lest the project should fail to enhance the standing of the monarchy? As it happened, the film was a triumph, and the Queen grew markedly more confident in public, finding unrehearsed contact with individuals in crowds much less difficult to manage.

If Prince Philip's contribution to his wife's improved, more tangible and more reassuring public image has been one of his greatest services to the monarchy, he has worked hard for changes behind the scenes as well. When Elizabeth II succeeded to the throne, he was able to supervise certain improvements in the way court and palace affairs were conducted. Apparently, however, "He leaned over backwards not to become the new broom. His suggestions and innovations weren't designed to establish himself as a new force to be reckoned with, but to help the Queen with some commonsense streamlining." Royal officials were not particularly accommodating at first, but he gradually got his way. Modern kitchens were introduced at Buckingham Palace, a system of electronic intercommunication was installed, and, much to the delight of press cartoonists, a team of business efficiency experts was consulted on the overall reorganisation of the Palace.

A good deal of the fact-finding was carried out by Prince Philip in person. He went into almost every one of Buckingham Palace's six hundred rooms, including the staff bedrooms; he walked the long underground corridors to the main kitchen; whenever he met someone during his investigations he tried to find out what they were doing and why. Among the problems that he soon identified was that of communication; before the intercom was installed, if he did anything unexpected, like ordering sandwiches, it took four men to pass on the message.

The same investigation of Sandringham was carried out. He quickly familiarised himself with every detail of the estate's management. Arguing that Sandringham's 17,000 acres could be used more efficiently to help to balance the royal budget, he backed reforms which kitchen gardeners and estate managers had long wanted. When the flax factory on the estate was closed by the government he had it converted into highly profitable pig-houses with enough room for two thousand pigs. He noticed petty details such as the relative inefficiency of the mudscraper at the garden door at Sandringham and designed a replacement. Some critics complained that he was running the estate like a battleship. On the other hand, reforms were badly needed. As Prince Philip explained in his introduction to Ralph Whitlock's book, *Royal Farmers*:

When I first went to Sandringham over thirty years ago, some of the tenanted farms were still being worked by horses. Gangs of female labour were contracted to lift the vegetable crops. Sugar-beet was hoed and topped and tailed by hand, and produce in general was bought and sold in local markets, a pattern not much changed in 200 years. On the other hand the picture of the highly intensive mechanised agricultural industry of today could not be more different.

At Windsor, too, the farms were overhauled. Shortly after the Queen's accession some of the old bullock yards, set up by the Prince Consort, were converted into laying sheds for a thousand chickens. The Ayrshire dairy herd, too, was soon being milked by machines into "travelling churns". At Balmoral, Highland cattle and other breeds were introduced and a forestry programme was initiated. The produce from Windsor and other estates supplied the royal residences, while the surplus was marketed and the profits either reinvested in the estate or put towards rendering the monarchy solvent. Prince Philip has fully merited his three terms of office as President of the Royal Agricultural Society of England.

The so-called modernisation of the monarchy in terms of its public image and the greater cost-effectiveness of its estates has been at best a partial reform. The Queen has not yet taken to bicycling in public at the head of a convoy of local officials like ex-Queen Juliana of the Netherlands. Nor have the "tweedy" courtiers and friends been weeded out – a day at Sandringham has been recently described as follows: "In a small sitting-room you find [the Queen] enjoying gin and tonic before lunch in an orange pullover, among a lot of other people dressed in tweeds;" there are a lot of dogs around, too.

The royal officials who are most in touch with the public, the press secretaries, have not become informal, chatty mines of information either. Admittedly the Queen's first, rather starchy press secretary, Commander Richard Colville, retired in 1968, but even the enlistment of Australians and New Zealanders to the press office has not brought much antipodean frankness with it. Indeed, the Australian John Dauth, who retired as assistant press secretary to the Queen in August 1980, won during his three years at the Palace "a reputation for not saying one word more than strictly necessary – and often considerably less". He left few friends in Fleet Street, which had in despair nicknamed him "Dauth the Mouth". Asked to comment on press criticism of his methods he replied, "There is a rule that members of the Royal Household do not give interviews. We have a long-standing tradition of anonymity." Hardly the views of a man anxious to communicate with the people.

The Duke of Edinburgh's capacity to communicate with his wife's subjects has been evident since he first entered the British royal family. Not that his apparent approachability means that he has the time or the inclination to talk to every Tom, Dick or Harry. His contact with the people is a commodity that is as carefully measured out as particles of precious metal. He manages, however, to give the impression of listening, caring and reacting appropriately to what he sees and hears. He is also prepared to proselytise, to campaign, pull strings and work for the causes he believes to be significant.

He is also happy to speculate about the functions of the monarchy, although the press has sometimes turned parts of his argument against him. A good example of this concerns his public remarks on the future of the monarchy in the Dominions. Of the old Dominions, the Queen remains Queen of Canada, Australia and New Zealand. In all essentials these countries are entirely self-governing; nonetheless they have a constitutional status that is atypical of a Commonwealth in which the republican form of government predominates, though these republics continue to recognise the Queen as Head of the Commonwealth.

Can the substantially anachronistic relationship of Canada, Australia, New Zealand (and seven other much smaller Commonwealth States) with the crown survive? In Australia and in Canada, the Duke of Edinburgh has looked squarely at the problem. In

Australia his remarks were considered relatively uncontroversial but when, two years later in 1969, he indulged in a similar speculation in Canada the reaction was different. In response to a question at a press conference in Ottawa, he said, about the future of the monarchy, "If at any stage people feel it has no further part to play, then for goodness' sake let's end the thing on amicable terms without having a row about it." A pragmatic and constructive response, and a far cry from George III's heavy-handed response to the manifestations of American independence two centuries before.

So far so good. He then went on to say, in an attempt to explain that monarchies should exist to serve the people and not to glorify the monarch, "We don't come here for our health." The shocked reaction to these careless and undiplomatic words was not confined to Canada. The British press got hold of the story, and soon the *Daily Mail* was asking plaintively, "Do We Need the Queen?"

Prince Philip's ability to look sensibly at the Commonwealth connection has been of value, especially as Britain's entry into the European Economic Community (which he supported) and the contraction of her overseas presence and influence has rendered the days of the Empire even more remote. Elizabeth II privately views the loss of Empire and the fragile quality of the Commonwealth ideal with some regret; after all, she was brought up to value and cherish the Empire and Commonwealth, and her speech from South Africa in 1947 to mark her twenty-first birthday contained a declaration of devotion to "the service of our great Imperial Commonwealth".

Certainly Prince Philip and the Queen still firmly support the idea of Commonwealth unity and co-operation, even though such unity is flawed and the extent of the co-operation entirely a matter to be decided by the individual member state. It is more difficult to dedicate a lifetime of royal service to the Common Market, and the British public would lack any great enthusiasm for such a cause. The Duke of Edinburgh, in fact, has recently criticised the EEC for the large subsidies paid out to community farmers. Speaking at the opening of the Perth Agricultural Show in 1979, he described the subsidies as "absolutely unreasonable and nonsensical". He was reacting to comments, shouted by an Australian farmer, about the way in which exports of Australian lamb were being hit by Common Market regulations. He went on to blame the subsidies for "huge over-production – butter and beef mountains and milk lakes which they sell at a loss to the Russians who ought to be growing more than anybody else". His reaction should not, however, be seen as an ideological response to Britain's membership of the EEC – a belated act of support for the system of Commonwealth preferential tariffs that was dealt its death blow by Britain's successful application to join the Common Market. Rather, Prince Philip was showing his natural antipathy to waste and inefficiency; the EEC was not being run in a tidy and shipshape fashion, and he spoke out accordingly.

His capacity to press for changes in the way in which British society handles its problems is well known, but his concern and his remedies can only be expressed within strict limits. He cannot campaign for any political party, or act as their spokesman – although it is clear which of the two major parties he favours. He cannot take any part in the protracted hurly-burly of public debate without pulling his punches far more than any politician would consider necessary. He is by definition a leading custodian of the dignity of the monarchy, and his public criticisms and statements must take account of that fact.

Above all, he is hamstrung not merely by his proximity to the throne but by his own social position. His passport number is 1, which, since the Queen has no passport, is an indication of his ranking in British society. By definition, therefore, there is much in that society that he cannot contemplate changing without seeming to threaten the social pyramid of which he and his wife form the apex. To consider abolishing the House of Lords, for example, would have implications for an aristocratic order of which the head is the Queen herself. To campaign for a massive redistribution of personal wealth would call into question the private fortunes and the private income of the royal family. Not that the Duke of Edinburgh sees himself as anything like a levelling force, and his views on militant trade unionists or activists of the far left are kept for sympathetic ears only.

Within these limits, he has thrown his weight behind a number of causes which could be described as progressive in a non-political sense. He is particularly good at using his presidencies and patronages to stir things up, to ask some awkward questions. His early role in promoting the work of the National Playing Fields Association, for example, has been examined in an earlier chapter.

He became President of the Automobile Association in 1951 and wrote on accepting the office that he looked forward to "taking an active part in the affairs of the Association". So active was he as President, and as a committee member when he resigned the office ten years later, that the AA must sometimes have wondered if they had made the right choice – the right choice, at any rate, for an easy life. He deluged the Association with bright ideas on insurance provision, motorway landscaping, signposting, maps, road classification, accident prevention, and so on. He was particularly anxious to cut down the amount of diesel exhaust fumes that were daily poured into the atmosphere, and fought a wily campaign to improve matters. Telling the British Medical Association that it was no good merely passing "pious resolutions" on the subject, he also wanted to know why exhaust pipes could not be vertical as on Brazilian buses. In the end, bureaucratic and political stalling blunted the initiative. It left him irritated. He was once asked why nothing came of his efforts and replied, "They're insane, that's why."

Another early example of his campaigning style was his struggle to get more public funds for the National Maritime Museum, of which he had been made a trustee in 1957. He badgered the Chancellor of the Exchequer, Peter (later Lord) Thorneycroft until the latter wrote, almost in desperation, "I pray that, with my clear conviction in the matter, Your Royal Highness will not press me further." His Royal Highness wrote a reply by return of post; it contained an unashamed threat: "I see it as my duty to pursue this matter until a satisfactory solution is reached. . . . If this is in the least embarrassing to you or to the Treasury, I am quite prepared to discuss with the Prime Minister [Harold Macmillan] my giving up the position of Trustee." In the end he got his way, though not for three years, and not without a good deal of intensive lobbying.

His capacity to threaten and browbeat is somewhat at odds with the personable and benign public style that he has developed. But his rough tactics are almost always employed behind the scenes, and mostly with those who are big enough and tough enough to look after themselves. He has a nice line in sarcasm. Once, when trying to prise money from the government for the newly founded Maritime Trust which was dedicated to the preservation of vessels of historical interest, he approached the Chief Scientific Adviser to the Cabinet, Sir Solly Zuckerman. Zuckerman suggested that models of the historically interesting ships would be a lot cheaper. Knowing that Zuckerman was Honorary Secretary of the Zoological Society, Prince Philip replied, "Dear Solly, I take your point about models. How would you react to the suggestion that the Zoo could be run more cheaply if the exhibits were all stuffed animals?"

From the beginning, Prince Philip has been an indefatigable fund-raiser for charity. His association with organisations from the National Playing Fields Association to the Variety Club of Great Britain, the Lord's Taverners, and so forth, has shown this. He writes letters to likely benefactors which, without mentioning money in so many words, usually produce some. In the United States he once dived into the Miami swimming pool of a man who promised him 100,000 dollars for charity if he would take a dip. It must have felt like combining business with pleasure.

His promotion of the Duke of Edinburgh's Award Scheme is an attempt to blow a little of the bracing fresh air of the Gordonstoun spirit through the minds and limbs of youngsters educated in very different school environments. He has consistently raised money for the Scheme, and the quarterly presentation of diplomas to those who have excelled at their projects and gained gold awards takes place at Buckingham Palace under the chandeliers, with music floating in the background. In this way the prestige of the monarchy is associated even more closely with a cause that is of particular importance to Prince Philip.

Of course, not even receptions at Buckingham Palace will melt the hearts of some of those whom the Duke of Edinburgh wishes to influence or convert to his point of view. Nor are the powerful over-awed by receiving letters on notepaper headed Windsor Castle, Sandringham, *Britannia* and the rest. A firmly entrenched bureaucrat or a minister of unshakeable resolve stands a good chance of resisting royal harassment; the harassment is, after all, only a form of lobbying, and lobbyists have to have substantial clout even to be taken seriously, let alone to get their own way. No one who has opposed him can doubt Prince Philip's clout. On the other hand, he is not elected to office, and he has no formal constituency of support at his back. Conversely, this frees him from the accusation of self-interested pleading and is a great source of strength. He can range at liberty over the whole spectrum of public activities, picking out those causes he thinks it most worthwhile to support. His arguments therefore stand a good chance of commanding more respect than those of party hacks or industry's public relations men. He can, moreover, appeal to the people over the heads of bureaucrats and politicians in his speeches and interviews. In this sense, the whole nation is his constituency. Since virtually everything that he says is considered newsworthy, this is a strong card to play.

It is a card Prince Philip plays as effectively now as when he first began to propose and press for change in certain spheres of British life. An examination of some of his most recent public pronouncements shows the scope of his interests. On 3 July 1979 he delivered a presidential address to the Scottish Association for the Care and Resettlement of Offenders. He pointed out that in 1978 the government had spent nearly £1,000,000 on academic research into crime, but that there had been little evidence that the research had produced any useful answers. He said: "With this avalanche of lawlessness threatening to engulf our civilisation, the more discussion there is about social control of crime the better." The courts and prisons faced "appalling difficulties" because the view that offenders were more in need of help and rehabilitation than of punishment meant that prisons had come to be used both for the purpose of deprivation of liberty and for the rehabilitation of offenders.

Having diagnosed a problem, he proposed a solution. Courts should divide a sentence into two parts:

The first part would be a relatively short period of punishment under humane but strict conditions, followed by a longer period of rehabilitation and training in a different establishment and under completely different conditions . . . the punishment part of the sentence might be limited to a maximum of 90 days, or whatever period is considered to be effective purely as a punishment. . . .

He went on to suggest that the second part of the sentence could be extended to enable offenders to complete education or training courses.

His intervention in the debate over the reform of the penal system won a mixed response from the Howard League for Penal Reform, which commented: "All credit to Prince Philip for beginning to give some thought to Her Majesty's prisons. But he has not said why, for ordinary offenders, the punishment or rehabilitation needs to take place in prison at all. He has not said why he gives priority to punishing offenders rather than requiring them to make reparation." Not overwhelming approval, but, more importantly, the public discussion had been carried a stage further, which is what the speech-maker had in mind.

Sport is another area in which Prince Philip has a brief to speak,

240

as President of the Central Council for Physical Recreation. He also feels strongly on the subject as a passionate sportsman himself – not to speak of the muscular traditions of the Gordonstoun ethic. He stirred up a considerable controversy about the administrative framework for British sport on 2 May 1979, the day before polling in the General Election. In an article published in the *Guardian*, Prince Philip argued that since the establishment of the Sports Council in 1972, there had been a confusing and wasteful duplication of effort between that body and the CCPR. He suggested a Royal Commission to sort out the problems.

Peter Lawson, the General Secretary of the CCPR, naturally enough agreed with his remarks and said, "British sport needs a shock wave of investment, not only to achieve international success but, equally important, to create a stronger, more self-sufficient administration for the governing bodies." Ex-rugby international, Dickie Jeeps, chairman of the Sports Council, reacted strongly to Prince Philip, saying, "It is sad the Prince appears not to recognise our contribution. . . . We are no bureaucracy. We are giving sport the leadership and the support it needs . . . many of the facts and figures he gave were distorted, inaccurate or misleading." Jeeps also deplored the fact that the Duke of Edinburgh had called for a Royal Commission on the eve of a General Election.

Denis Howell, the Minister for Sport, refused to comment just before polling day. Neil McFarlane, secretary of the Conservative Sports Committee said, ". . . I couldn't disagree more when he said he wanted a Royal Commission." Dickie Jeeps, who had been "so angry that he cancelled a meeting in the north of England to stay in London and reply to some of the charges", admitted, however, "that Prince Philip's remarks spotlight the guerrilla warfare that has been going on in British sport since the Sports Council was set up in 1972." Obviously a hornets' nest had been disturbed, although presumably for the good of the hornets. The *Daily Mirror* column dealing with the controversy was headed "Right Royal Rumpus".

Prince Philip would have viewed the rumpus as a necessary prelude to getting things right. He has commented in public on a very large number of problems, including safety standards in British airlines, the amount of unsightly rubbish in London's streets, the capacity of big business to exploit the environment, the development of remote areas, the liberating as well as the enslaving capacities of science, plant diseases and sewage disposal.

The clear-cut way in which he presents his arguments, and the range of his official and private interests, makes him one of the most quotable of Britain's public figures. The press are, therefore, always looking for juicy tit-bits. It is not that Prince Philip always sets out to make the headlines – far from it. He has said that his speeches are strictly tailored to the occasion and the company. However, "If anyone else wants to listen, that's their problem." He was once asked whether he put items into his speeches knowing that the press would lift them. He replied, "No." (A laugh) "I often take them out for that reason."

If he means what he says, his wastepaper basket must soon get filled with discarded snippets of a controversial nature when he is composing a speech. In fact, tailoring his speeches to the audience, even doctoring them to avoid giving the press too much to seize upon, has little to do with the ultimate effectiveness of the delivery. Although roughly half of his speeches never get reported, there is meat enough in the remainder to provide first-rate copy for the nation's newspapers.

The Duke of Edinburgh's relationship with the press has been referred to in earlier chapters, and has been the subject of much scrutiny elsewhere. That there should have been periods of acrimony and mutual recrimination is not surprising, given his capacity for both frankness and impatience, and stories of reporters vying with each other to see who could mention him the least are not entirely apocryphal.

Only some of the stories of Philip's retaliation against "press snooping" are true. He did ask in Gibraltar, when confronted by newsmen, "Which are the monkeys?" But he did not subsequently pelt them with nuts. He did say of a Pakistani photographer who toppled from his perch up a pole, "I hope to God he breaks his bloody neck!" He did not, however, press the button that soaked the photographer at the Chelsea Flower Show. Who did? One version is that it was David Bowes-Lyon, another that it was the man escorting him. At any rate, the photographers got wet, and the episode is etched in the public's memory.

He is quick to tell any aspiring biographer that they must not believe all that they read about him in the press, and he has certainly suffered some ugly and malicious attacks during his public life. The tradition that royalty does not answer back makes formal counter-attack extremely difficult (though it has occasionally happened), and may well explain the temptation to salve his wounds with a few spontaneous insults. There has been the occasional face-to-face confrontation as in 1969, when he led an informal discussion at a luncheon given by the Small Businesses Association. Prince Philip did not realise that among the audience were two reporters from the Press Association – or rather that one of them, Leonard Moxon, was sitting at the luncheon table taking notes, and was replaced by a colleague, John Shaw, when he went off to the telephone booth in the vestibule to catch the evening newspapers. As soon as he discovered what was going on, Prince Philip followed Moxon into the telephone booth and said angrily, "I hope you're not reporting what I've been saying. It was a completely informal discussion, and I didn't know the press were there. It's chaps like you that get me into trouble." Moxon and Shaw were, however, well within their rights and possessed Palace press cards. They later received an apology.

Eleven years later, while waiting for Prince Philip to open the British Sports Exhibition at the Stock Exchange, a reporter from the Press Association and two photographers recounted the story. They laughed good-naturedly over it. Was the press's relationship with Prince Philip still a difficult one? They thought not; time had healed the wounds. They went off to photograph and report him, and were gracefully acknowledged.

If British photographers seem acceptable to Prince Philip nowadays, foreign photographers enjoy no such privilege. In November 1979 Swedish photographers irritated him during a day's tour of Stockholm where he had been studying sporting institutions. As the cameras' bulbs kept on flashing, he turned on them and said, "Do you have to do that? If you haven't got a picture by now, you must be a bloody lousy lot of photographers."

Even if the feud between the Duke of Edinburgh and the British press is now apparently dormant, there is no guarantee that it will permanently remain so – though the signs are that it may. As long as he continues to speak and press for change, to provoke, to drop clangers and to challenge, the press will want to report him; indeed, it is essential for the causes he takes up that they should do so.

Press reaction to him is one way of assessing his worth to the nation. But is he paid the right rate for the job? The matter of royal finances is one of the aspects of the British monarchy that he has tried to bring out into the open. In 1969 he was interviewed on American television and asked how the monarchy was coping with inflation. He replied, candidly, that it would be "in the red" by 1970. The remark initiated a public debate over the financing of the royal family and whether the nation was getting value for money. During the bouts of hyper-inflation in the mid 1970s and that beginning in 1979–80, the funds paid to maintain the monarchy have been adjusted to keep abreast of rapidly rising prices and costs.

On 26 March 1980 the government, under the smokescreen raised by the budget, also announced the latest increases in the always controversial Civil List payments to the royal family. Broadly speaking, the settlement was at the level of nineteen per cent, in line with the average national wage settlements. These increases brought the royal family's total Civil List income to £3,317,300 net, all paid for by the tax-payer. Prince Philip's allowance rose by 31.4 per cent from £102,700 to £135,000, though a Palace spokesman said that in real terms the rise was 20.7 per cent. At the same time, the Queen Mother's allowance totalled £244,000, second only to that of the Queen at £2,716,300.

The finances of the royal family are labyrinthine. If it was only a matter of scrutinising the Civil List it would be easy to see what was going on. The Treasury, in fact, admits that the cost of the monarchy is impossible to compute. Government departments bear a large part of the cost of financing various royal activities: *Britannia*, which costs about £2,000,000 a year in upkeep, is paid for by the Ministry of Defence, as are the aeroplanes of the Queen's Flight; royal palaces are kept up by the Department of the Environment. These are some of the perks of the job. Then there is the income derived from the royal estates; revenue from the Duchy of Cornwall ensures that Prince Charles need not receive a Civil List allowance. The Queen's private fortune is believed to be vast, but it is impossible to know how large it really is. Prince Philip, like the Queen Mother and Princess Margaret, is liable for income tax and surtax at the standard rates on any income left after they have paid their official expenses. The Queen is exempt from the need to pay personal taxes.

Compared with other members of the royal family, Prince Philip's Civil List income arouses no specific public objection. This is some indication that he is thought to be doing his job reasonably well. Princess Anne has no such immunity from criticism, and Labour MP Willie Hamilton, commenting in the House of Commons on the 1980 allowance for Princess Margaret, deplored that £82,000 should go to such a "wayward woman". (Princess Margaret, incidentally, only received a 14.7 per cent increase.) The Duke of Edinburgh is not extravagant by nature and is prepared to weigh the cost of various purchases – a legacy, surely, from a childhood where financial security could not be taken for granted. Nor can he snap his fingers and get what he wants. He sometimes has to fight battles with government departments, for example, over who pays for items of office equipment. Presents he gives on official tours are paid for by the Foreign Office; private present-giving is, of course, his own responsibility.

His public demeanour is encouraging for those who are quick to denounce dissipation and prodigality at the top. He does not smoke, drinks moderately, dresses like any "City gent", and, now that he no longer plays polo, has no obviously extravagant pastimes. In his public activities he seems to hit exactly the right note, combining managerial alertness and efficiency with the capacity for getting along with people. This is partly an illusion. Despite his presidencies and patronages he is not accountable to a managing body in the same way as a company executive would be, and he is unlikely to be sacked as husband and consort – which is his main professional role. Nor does his smiling, generally affable public persona tell the whole story; he has bouts of "Germanic" depression, even bitterness. There are notable blind-spots and prejudices, and the temptation to indulge in private cajoling and public plain speaking sometimes reveals a less benign personality – one whose style has been described as verging "on thuggery". On the other hand, in happy contrast to royalty elsewhere, he cannot be accused of corruption or similar skulduggery. His compulsive and sometimes embarrassing honesty is both evident and, in the last resort, reassuring.

Although his prestige derives from his position as husband of the monarch, it has been sustained and arguably increased by his capacity to work for change and by his ability to display a considerable range of emotions in public. Even his occasional fits of irascibility make it easier for his wife's subjects to identify with him, showing him to be something more than a smiling ceremonial mask. Above all, he appears to work hard which is a virtue, particularly in others, that the British public holds dear. There are, of course, his long vacations at Christmas and Easter and particularly during the summer, though they work out at rather less than those taken for granted by university dons and their students. Nonetheless, in the words of Michael Parker:

I don't think he's let up. I've watched it over the years, and he keeps up this incredible pace, and I've actually said to him from time to time, "Hey – what about it? It's time you eased up somewhat." And, you know, he grins a bit, and he says, "Well, what would I do? Sit around and knit?" There's never been a word of complaint, about his work, or his life. And I only hope that . . . the United Kingdom shows its gratitude for what he's done . . . for the constant flogging up hill and down dale and around the world, and in and out of film premières ad nauseam, and making hundreds and hundreds of speeches, and never really stopping. Because they're the most extraordinarily lucky country to have him.

If the Queen were to abdicate to make way for Prince Charles, though this appears unlikely to happen in the foreseeable future, it is difficult to see Prince Philip sinking back into a serene and contemplative retirement. His vigour and enthusiasm seem unaffected by his proximity to his sixtieth birthday, and, even if one day he becomes confined to a wheelchair, one can imagine him taking the same lively interest in his environment and in the course of world events.

Vigour and an enquiring mind, however, are not necessarily laudable in themselves; tyrants and gangsters may be similarly endowed. The Duke of Edinburgh's claims on posterity are more worthy than the capacity to drive himself hard and to ask pertinent questions. Quite simply, he has transformed both the external image and the internal realities of the House of Windsor. The monarchy now appears less staid and more relevant than when he married the heiress to the throne more than three decades ago. Time, admittedly, has been on his side, and a more open society has encouraged the development of a more open monarchy. Nonetheless, his role as an agent for change has been a most significant one – something which even his critics would find difficulty in denying. Even if his various achievements were to die with him, he would have one tangible memorial – that his future descendants will bear the surname Mountbatten-Windsor. The man who, as an infant Greek prince, was carried into exile in a cot made from an orange box, has made his mark.

PRINCE PHILIP'S GREEK & DANISH ANCESTRY

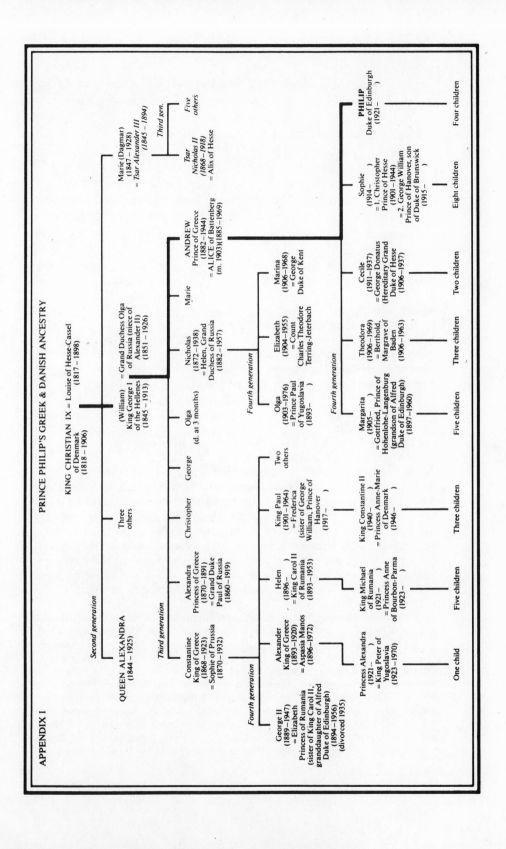

KING CHRISTIAN IX = Louise of Hesse-Cassel
(1818 – 1906)   (1817 – 1898)

Second generation

QUEEN ALEXANDRA
(1844 – 1925)

Three
others

(William) = Grand Duchess Olga
King George I   of Russia (niece of
of the Hellenes   Alexander II)
(1845 – 1913)   (1851 – 1926)

Marie (Dagmar)
(1847 – 1928)
= Tsar Alexander III
(1845 – 1894)

Third gen.

Tsar
Nicholas II
(1868 – 1918)
= Alix of Hesse

Five
others

Third generation

Constantine
King of Greece
(1868 – 1923)
= Sophie of Prussia
(1870 – 1932)

Alexandra
Princess of Greece
(1870 – 1891)
= Grand Duke
Paul of Russia
(1860 – 1919)

Christopher

George

Olga
(d. at 3 months)

Nicholas
(1872 – 1938)
= Helen, Grand
Duchess of Russia
(1882 – 1957)

Marie

ANDREW
Prince of Greece
(1882 – 1944)
= ALICE of Battenberg
(m. 1903)(1885 – 1969)

Fourth generation

George II
(1889 – 1947)
= Elizabeth
Princess of Rumania
(sister of King Carol II,
granddaughter of Alfred
Duke of Edinburgh)
(1894 – 1956)
(divorced 1935)

Alexander
King of Greece
(1893 – 1920)
= Aspasia Manos
(1896 – 1972)

Helen
(1896 –   )
= King Carol II
of Rumania
(1893 – 1953)

King Paul
(1901 – 1964)
= Frederica
(sister of George
William, Prince of
Hanover)
(1917 –   )

Two
others

Olga
(1903 – 1976)
= Prince Paul
of Yugoslavia
(1893 –   )

Fourth generation

Elizabeth
(1904 – 1955)
= Count
Charles Theodore
Terring-Jeterbach

Marina
(1906 – 1968)
= George
Duke of Kent

Fourth generation

Margarita
(1905 –   )
= Gottfried, Prince of
Hohenlohe-Langenburg
(grandson of Alfred
Duke of Edinburgh)
(1897 – 1960)

Theodora
(1906 – 1969)
= Berthold,
Margrave of
Baden
(1906 – 1963)

Cecile
(1911 – 1937)
= George Donatus
(Hereditary Grand
Duke of Hesse)
(1906 – 1937)

Sophie
(1914 –   )
= 1. Christopher
Prince of Hesse
(1901 – 1944)
= 2. George William
Prince of Hanover, son
of Duke of Brunswick
(1915 –   )

PHILIP
Duke of Edinburgh
(1921 –   )

Princess Alexandra
(1921 –   )
= King Peter of
Yugoslavia
(1923 – 1970)

King Michael
of Rumania
(1921 –   )
= Princess Anne
of Bourbon-Parma
(1923 –   )

King Constantine II
(1940 –   )
= Princess Anne-Marie
of Denmark
(1946 –   )

One child

Five children

Three children

Five children

Three children

Two children

Eight children

Four children

APPENDIX II

The Man and his Offices

THE SUMMARY BELOW has been compiled from the master copy of *The Patronage Book of HRH the Duke of Edinburgh* which is kept in Buckingham Palace. The book is a ring folder, one and a half inches thick, which contains a very brief biography of Prince Philip, as well as an up-to-date list of his various presidencies, decorations, patronages, foreign honours, membership of a host of clubs and associations, university honours, and so on. It is a staggering, even awesome, testimony to his involvement in hundreds of organisations, and a reminder of the persistent demands made upon his time and good will.

To present the whole list would amount to reprinting the *Patronage Book* itself. Instead, only Prince Philip's present and more significant presidencies and patronages are listed; most of his Memberships, Honorary Life Memberships, Trusteeships, and Chairmanships have been omitted. Thus a few columns of print are all that is left of sixty-six closely set pages. To show how full the complete list would have been, the patronages listed under the letter "A" have been reproduced in full. Under subsequent letters, a mere sample of offices have been chosen. Some pieces of information do not appear at all. For example, Prince Philip is patron or honorary member of seventeen golf clubs (mostly royal clubs), and enjoys a similar relationship with over one hundred Service Clubs and Associations, and seventy-two Yacht Clubs. Again, he has nearly one hundred and sixty cups, schools, locomotives, prizes, boats, awards, trophies and so forth named after him. Even with the omissions, the final list seems impossibly full.

EDINBURGH, Duke of, *cr* 1947; His Royal Highness, The Prince Philip (Mountbatten), KG 1947; KT 1952; OM 1968; GBE 1953 (Grand Master of the Order); PC 1951; *b* Corfu, 10 June 1921; only *s* of HRH Prince Andrew of Greece and Denmark, GCVO, and of HRH Princess Victoria Alice Elizabeth Julia Marie, elder *d* of the 1st Marquess of Milford Haven, PC, GCB, GCVO, KCMG: *m* 20 November 1947, Her Royal Highness The Princess Elizabeth, now Her Majesty Queen Elizabeth II, of England, elder *d* of the late King George VI; three *s* one *d*. *Educ:* "The Elms", Paris; Cheam School, Berkshire; Salem, Baden; Gordonstoun School, Morayshire; and Royal Naval College, Dartmouth. Served in Royal Navy, since 1939; Midshipman, 1940; Sub-Lieutenant, 1942, Lieutenant, 1942; Lieut. Commander, 1950; Commander, 1952; Admiral of the Fleet since January 1953.

Appendix II

Served in World War II, 1939–45, with the Mediterranean Fleet, in Home Waters, and with the British Pacific Fleet in South-East Asia and Pacific; mentioned in despatches, Battle of Cape Matapan, March 1941; Admiral, Sea Cadet Corps since 1952; Captain General, Royal Marines, since 1953; Extra Master of the Merchant Navy, since 1954. Naturalised as a British subject on 28 February 1947, adopting the surname of Mountbatten. Granted the title, style and attribute of Royal Highness, 19 November 1947. Cr Baron Greenwich of Greenwich in the County of London, Earl of Merioneth and Duke of Edinburgh (in the Peerage of the United Kingdom) 20 November 1947. Personal ADC to His Majesty King George VI, 1948–52; introduced and took his seat in the House of Lords, 1948; Privy Councillor of Canada since 1957. Decorations: Africa Star; Atlantic Star; Burma Star (with Pacific Rosette); Croix de Guerre (France) with Palm, 1948; Greek War Cross, 1950; Italy Star; 1939–45 Star; War Medal 1939–45, with Oak Leaf. Granted Precedence next to Her Majesty, 1952. Granted the style and titular dignity of a Prince of the United Kingdom of Great Britain and Northern Ireland, 22 February 1957. Member of the Council of the Duchy of Cornwall since 1952; Ranger of Windsor Great Park, since 1952; Lord High Steward of Plymouth, since 1960. Field-Marshal, since 1953. Colonel-in-Chief, Army Cadet Force, since 1952; Colonel of the Welsh Guards, since 1953; Hon. Colonel, University of Edinburgh Training Corps, since 1953; Hon. Colonel, Leicestershire and Derbyshire Yeomanry, 1957–69. Colonel-in-Chief, The Queen's Royal Irish Hussars, since 1958; Colonel-in-Chief, The Duke of Edinburgh's Royal Regiment (Berkshire and Wiltshire), since 1959; Colonel-in-Chief, The Queen's Own Highlanders (Seaforth and Camerons), since 1961; Colonel-in-Chief, Royal Electrical and Mechanical Engineers, since 1969; Colonel-in-Chief, the Intelligence Corps, since 1977. Marshal of the Royal Air Force since 1953; Air Commodore-in-Chief, Air Training Corps, since 1952; Hon. Air Commodore, RAF Kinloss, since 1977. Admiral of the Fleet, Royal Australian Navy, since 1954; Field-Marshal, Australian Military Forces, since 1954; Marshal, Royal Australian Air Force, since 1954; Colonel-in-Chief, Royal Corps of Australian Electrical and Mechanical Engineers, since 1959; Colonel-in-Chief, Australian Cadet Corps, since 1963. Admiral, Royal Canadian-Sea Cadets, since 1953; Colonel-in-Chief, Royal Canadian Army Cadets, since 1953; Air Commander-in-Chief, Royal Canadian Air Cadets, since 1953; Colonel-in-Chief, Royal Canadian Regiment, since 1953; Colonel-in-Chief, Cameron Highlanders of Ottawa (Militia), since 1967; Colonel-in-Chief, Royal Hamilton Light Infantry, since 1978; Colonel-in-Chief, Queen's Own Cameron Highlanders of Canada (Militia), since 1967; Colonel-in-Chief, Seaforth Highlanders of Canada (Militia), since 1967. Admiral of the Fleet, Royal New Zealand Navy, since 1958; Colonel-in-Chief, Royal New Zealand Infantry Regiment, since 1958. Field Marshal, New Zealand Army, since 1977; Marshal, Royal New Zealand Air Force, since 1977; Hon. Colonel, Trinidad and Tobago Regiment, since 1964; Hon. Colonel, Confederate Air Force of Harlingden, Texas, since 1976.

Patron: Alfred Hospital, Prahan, Victoria, Australia, since 1951; Amateur Boxing Association, since 1952; American Club in London, since 1952; Anglers' Co-operative Association, since 1965; Anglo-Finnish Society, since 1955; Anglo-German Foundation for the Study of Industrial Society (British Patron), since 1972; Anglo-Swedish Society, since 1954; Anguilla Recreation Fund, since 1964; Army Boxing Association, since 1952; Army Officers' Boxing Club, since 1952; Association of British Aero Clubs and Centres Ltd, since 1954; Association of

Cricket Umpires, since 1973; Association for Science Education, since 1961; Association of Societies of Art and Design, since 1967; Australian Marketing Institute, since 1963; Australian Outward Bound Trust, since 1966 (Australian Outward Bound Memorial, 1960–66); Australian Rugby Football League Board of Control, since 1955; Auto Cycle Union, since 1961; Braemar Mountain Rescue Association, Patron & Life Member, since 1968; Britain-Nigeria Association, since 1961; British Association for Commercial and Industrial Education, since 1952; British American Alumni, since 1976; British Crafts Centre, since 1979; British Driving Society, since 1973; British Heart Foundation, since 1961; British Productivity Council, since 1964; British School of Archaeology at Athens, since 1952; British Trust for Conservation Volunteers, since 1970; Canadian Power Squadrons, since 1963; Charities Aid Foundation, since 1974; Cheam School Association, since 1973; City of London Club, since 1974; Coal Trade Benevolent Association, since 1977; Council for Nature, since 1958; Council of St George's House, Windsor, since 1965; "Cutty Sark" Society, since 1952; Dawson City Museum, since 1960; Eltham, Greenwich and Woolwich Chambers of Commerce, since 1967; English Schools' Football Association, since 1952; Finmere Show, since 1960; Fleet Air Arm Museum, 1973–83; Forty Club, since 1960; Friends of the Royal Academy, since 1977; Game Conservancy, since 1973; Gamekeepers' Association of the United Kingdom, since 1959; Greenwich Festival, since 1975; Highland Fund, since 1963; Hurlingham Polo Association, since 1952; Industrial Society, since 1952; Institute of Chemical Engineers, since 1968; Institute of Marketing, since 1952; International Association of Cape Horness (British Section), since 1977; Jesters Club, since 1954; Leicestershire and Derbyshire Yeomanry Old Comrades, since 1975; London Federation of Boys' Clubs, since 1947; Lords Taverners, Patron & 12th Man, since 1950; Middlesex County Cricket Club, since 1966; Modern Pentathlon Association of Great Britain, since 1958; Mount Everest Foundation, since 1977; Muscular Dystrophy Group, since 1966; National Savings Committee, since 1952; National Voluntary Civil Aid Services, 1977–82; Naval Officers' Association of Southern Africa, since 1955; Norfolk Island Flora and Fauna Society, since 1968; Outward Bound Trust, since 1953; Outward Bound Trust in Canada, since 1969; Pakistan Society, since 1953; "The Queen's Trees" Campaign, since 1977; Research and Development Society, since 1970; Royal Air Force Museum, since 1968; Royal Canadian Regiment Association, since 1971; Royal Fowey Yacht Club, since 1952; Royal Marines Museum, Portsmouth, since 1974; Royal National Institute for the Deaf, since 1958; Royal Tournament, since 1952; Royal West Norfolk Golf Club, since 1952; Sail Training Association, since 1955; St Andrew's Jubilee Trust, since 1977; Scottish Baroque Ensemble, Hon. Patron, since 1974; Society for Nautical Research, since 1980; Society of Industrial Artists and Designers, since 1969; Society of Model Aeronautical Engineers, since 1955; Thames Sailing Club, since 1959; Travellers Club, since 1952; University of Cambridge Engineers' Association, since 1953; Vancouver Rowing Club, since 1975; Voluntary Services Overseas, since 1961; Wedge Entomological Research Foundation, since 1974; Wildfowlers' Association of Great Britain and Ireland, since 1967; Windsor Home Park Cricket Club, since 1954.

President: Aidis Trust, 1979–83; Amateur Yacht Research Society, 1976–80; Australian Conservation Foundation, 1971–76; British Amateur Athletic Board, since 1952; British Commonwealth Ex-Services League, (Grand President), since 1974; British Commonwealth Games Federation, since 1955; Central Council of

Physical Recreation, since 1951; City and Guilds of London Institute, since 1951; Council for National Academic Awards, since 1964; David Davies Memorial Institute of International Studies, 1979–83; English Speaking Union of the Commonwealth, since 1952; Fédération Equestre Internationale, 1964–80; Uffa Fox Memorial Community Centre and Nautical Museum (President of the Trustees), since 1974; Guinea Pig Club, since 1960; Historic Churches Preservation Trust, since 1952; King George's Fund for Sailors, 1978–83; National Federation of Housing Associations, 1975–80; Naval and Military Club, since 1979; Royal Agricultural Society of the Commonwealth, since 1958; Royal Bath & West Southern Counties Society, 1981; Royal Commission for the Exhibition of 1951, since 1965; Royal Household Cricket Club, since 1953; Royal Merchant Navy School, since 1952; Royal Mint Advisory Committee, since 1952; Royal Society of Arts, since 1952; Royal Yachting Association, 1975–80 (Hon. Member since 1948); Schools Science and Technology Committee (Standing Conference), since 1971; Scottish Association for the Care and Resettlement of Offenders, 1978–80; Scottish-Icelandic Association, since 1965; Technical Education Council, 1975–80; World Wildlife Fund – British National Appeal, since 1961.

Chancellor, University of Wales, since 1948; University of Edinburgh, since 1952; University of Salford, 1967–71; University of Cambridge, since 1976. Master of the Corporation of Trinity House (an Elder Brother since 1952). Chairman of Council of the British Red Cross Society, 1970–73. Royal Governor of Charterhouse, since 1953. Patron and Trustee of the Duke of Edinburgh's Award, since 1961. Grand Master of the Guild of Air Pilots and Air Navigators, since 1952. Admiral of the Honourable Company of Master Mariners, since 1957. Master of the Bench of Inner Temple, since 1954 (Treasurer for 1961). Visitor of the Institute of Technology, Manchester, since 1957. Membre Permanent of the Jockey Club of France, since 1962. Life Governor of King's College, London. Trustee of the King William IV Naval Foundation, since 1969. Liveryman of the Worshipful Company of Mercers, since 1959 (Freeman since 1953). Member of the Court of Governors of the National Library of Wales, since 1949. Trustee of the National Maritime Museum, Greenwich, 1948–76. Chairman of the Duke of Edinburgh's Committee, Queen's Award to Industry, for 1965 only. Member of Committee of Management of the Royal National Lifeboat Institution, since 1957. Honorary Academician of the Royal Scottish Academy, since 1963. Commodore of the Royal Sydney Yacht Squadron, 1961–68 (Patron since 1953). Commodore of the Royal Yacht Squadron, 1961–68 (Admiral since 1952). Visitor of St Catherine's College, Oxford, since 1962. Permanent Master of the Worshipful Company of Shipwrights, since 1955. Trustee of the Tower Hill Trust, since 1969. Hon. Member, Honourable Artillery Company, since 1954. Visitor of Upper Canada College, since 1955. An International Trustee of the World Wildlife Fund, since 1961 (President of the British National Appeal). Liveryman of the Worshipful Company of Fishmongers (Freeman since 1947). Also Patron, President, Hon. Member, etc., of some 540 other organisations, public bodies and clubs, including: *Hon. Member* of the Anchorites Club, the Castaways Club, the Savage Club, the Goat Club, the Mudhook Yacht Club, St Edmund's Hall Teddy Bears' Club, the Grand Order of Water Rats, the "Punch" Table, the Concrete Society, Sydney University Tiddlywinks Society, the Danish Dragon Club, the Welsh Beekeepers Association; *Member* of the Bar Yacht Club (and Admiral), the Four Hundred Club, the British Dragon Association, the International Order of Characters (US); *Life Member*, "Le Bon Viveur", the Porcupine Rod and Gun Club (Timmins, Ontario); *Patron*, the Royal Naval Lay Readers Society, the

Lucifer Golfing Society, the Society of Registered Male Nurses, the Cardiff Medical Students Club, the Egham and Thorpe Royal Agricultural Association, the Canadian Cutting Horse Association, the Windsor Forest Bowmen; *Hon. Colonel* of the Honourable Order of Kentucky Colonels; *Deputy Sheriff* of Harris County, Texas; *Hon. Fellow* of the Institute of Public Cleansing.

Freeman or Hon. Citizen: Acapulco; Belfast; Bridgetown; Barbados; Cardiff; Chicago; Dar-es-Salaam; Edinburgh; Glasgow; Greenwich; London; Los Angeles; Melbourne; Montevideo; Nairobi.

Foreign Honours: Order of the Superior Sun, Afghanistan; Grand Cross of the Order of San Martin, Argentina; Grand Cross of Honour, Austria; Grand Cordon of the Order of Leopold, Belgium; Hon. Member of the Most Esteemed Family Order, Brunei; Medal of the Order of Dogwood, Canada; Knight of the Order of the Elephant, Denmark; Chain of the Most Exalted Order of the Queen of Sheba, Ethiopia; Grand Cross of the Order of the White Rose, Finland; Grand Cross of the Order of George I, Greece; Grand Cordon of the Supreme Order of the Chrysanthemum, Japan; Chevalier-Grand-Croix, Order of the Golden Lion, Luxembourg; Commander of the Order of the Golden Ark, Netherlands; Grand Cross of the Order of St Olaf, Norway; Grand Collar of the Order of Prince Henry the Navigator, Portugal; Member of the Distinguished Order of Izzuddin, Republic of Maldives; Hon. Member, Darjah Utama Temasek, Singapore; Member of the Order of the Seraphim, Sweden; Grand Cross, Yugoslav Star; Grand Cordon, National Order of the Leopard, Zaire; 1st Class Order of the Brilliant Star, Zanzibar.

Honorary Degrees held: Hon. D.Sc. from Council for National Academic Awards; Universities of Adelaide, Delhi, Reading, Salford, Southampton, Victoria in Canada; Hon. Ll. D. from Universities of Malta, Cambridge, Edinburgh, Karachi, London, Wales. Other honorary degrees from Engineering University, Lima, Peru; Royal College of Art; University of California, Los Angeles; Oxford.

Publications: Selected Speeches, 1948–55, OUP, 1957; *Prince Philip Speaks: Selected Speeches, 1956–59,* Collins, 1960; *Birds from "Britannia",* Longman, 1962; (with James Fisher) *Wildlife Crisis,* Hamish Hamilton, 1970; *Dilemmas in Conservation* (Fourth Jane Hodge memorial lecture), 1973; *The Queen's Award to Industry; report of the 1975 Review Committee under the chairmanship of HRH the Duke of Edinburgh,* 1975; *The Environmental Revolution: Speeches on Conservation, 1962–77,* Deutsch, 1978; *Philosophy, Politics, Administration* (Rede lectures at Cambridge University, 1979), 1979; various articles, forewords, etc.

Heard of Him, Never Met Him

by NICHOLAS MONSARRAT

Gentlemen, the toast is Prince Philip,
Duke of Edinburgh,
Which makes a nice switch,
Because usually Prince Philip, Duke of Edinburgh,
Is the toast;
And the things they do to that 50-year-old battered slice of bread –
Everything from buttering it up,
Or smothering it in ham,
Or smearing it with the rancid oil of envy,
To carving it into bite-sized pieces
For the spiteful to chew on –
Would make any self-respecting club sandwich
Resign from the club.
Yet it is an honour and a privilege to propose this toast
Because I am a King's man
And a Queen's man
And the Duke's man,
Believing that people behave better under a monarchy
Than under any presidential yoke
Or some hard-boiled egg of a dictator,
And that those who believe so
Should say so; and that,
Borrowing from another duke, another forthright battler,
The Duke of Wellington,
They should publish and be damned,
In a good cause.

I have never met him,
And I sure won't meet him now –
This contribution
Will earn me no royalty.
But I have *nearly* met him seven times altogether,
And they are all worth recording
For a variety of reasons

253

Which have nothing to do with history
And everything to do with loyalty,
And respect, and admiration, and allegiance –
All the old-fashioned words
Good for a giggle on TV,
Bad for a modish reputation,
True for all time.

*   *   *

THE FIRST TIME was long ago and far away
In the hoary old year of 1947,
When he was not yet in the public domain,
And Princess Elizabeth, the predestined bride
(I shall be coming to her later)
Was then at the marvellous age of twenty-one
And (for public consumption anyway)
Still foot-loose and fancy-free.
But there were rumours among the knowing and the pseudo-knowing
Of a young man waiting somewhere in the wings;
And when she,
And her father the King,
And her mother the Queen,
And her sister, who still had the sweetly-pretty label
Of Princess Margaret Rose,
Arrived at Cape Town on the Royal Tour of South Africa,
There was just a chance that this sailor-suitor would come out of the wings
And into this rare and splendid sunshine.
I *might* have met him then,
Being, for my sins (what sins? In those days I had hardly begun!)
Head of the British Information Service in South Africa
And co-opted also as a Royal Tour commentator.
But he wasn't there on that day,
And it was my loss, and his loss too
Because he missed a truly glittering occasion
When the battleship *Vanguard*
(The biggest afloat, and, for a change, *ours*)
Came out of the morning mist of Table Bay
Like a great grey friendly ghost
And nudged alongside the quay –
All the towering 43,000 tons of her –
As gently as a pram into a crèche
Without cracking an egg;
And the flags flew, and the guns saluted, and the crowds roared,
And against the enormous stone curtain of Table Mountain
And out from this great bristling ark of a ship,
The family came ashore.

254

Perhaps, on second thoughts, it was just as well he wasn't there.
It might have been
Rather too daunting an encounter
With one's future in-laws.

*   *   *

THE SECOND TIME I never met him was 1952,
And that's still long ago and far away,
But that time turned into a time of immortality,
Or rather, of mortality taking its toll, and
Brusquely, cruelly, finally, and beyond any argument
Thrusting the torch upon new players, new mortals,
A new generation of the Lord's anointed
Or of sacrificial goats,
Whichever way you choose to look at it.
The Edinburghs (as total London snobs called them,
Pretending a familiarity they would never dare put to the test)
The Edinburghs were holidaying in Kenya,
Literally up a tree, if the number one suite of the Tree Tops Hotel,
Which is perched on an enormous fig-tree in the Aberdare Forest
In Kikuyu country,
May be so designated.
After that strange tree-sojourn, it was thought
That they might finish off their tour in South Africa,
Where we were ready for them,
And my little British Information machine was ready for them also.

At dusk, beneath that ancient, patriarchal fig-tree,
The animals came down to drink at the water-hole:
Elephant and hippopotamus, gentle gazelle and ungentle lion,
Striped zebra, armoured rhinoceros, odious hyena,
All taking time off from strife
To slake their evening thirst,
While round them the expectant forest
Waited to give them cover again,
And the hotel flood-lights (which they took to be another moon)
Pin-pointed this royal gathering.
It must have been a marvellous setting
And the prince and princess must have been very happy there,
Very excited, very moved,
Watching the beasts come down to drink
Within the truce-lines in the heart of the Old Chief's country.
But in far-away London, on that same night,
Death himself came down to drink.
He drank the tired King,
And the news broke into their watching, or their sleeping,

Prince Philip

In what must have been the strangest place in the world to receive
News of a King's death, and especially a father's death.
That was the end of that.
All we saw of them in South Africa
Was on the news-reels a week later
(No television in South Africa then, nor now either):
A sad, moving, tremendous moment when the new Queen of England
(It was difficult to get used to that word
After fifty-two years of kingship)
Appeared in the open doorway of the plane
Which had brought her from Kikuyu country
To a country now her own.
Behind her was a supporting star, in all the senses,
This same man I never met;
And he, like all the world, attended this lonely moment of majesty
As she came down the draped steps
Towards the clustered black hats and funeral penguin suits of her Cabinet
And into history.

                    *   *   *

THE THIRD TIME was the nearest miss of all
And the most exciting of all,
Because it was almost my own occasion
And this time I *would* meet the Prince, by explicit royal command.
I had written a book,
And out of it they had made a film
Which was to have its première at the Leicester Square Theatre
On March the twenty-sixth, 1953,
In aid of a good solid sailors' charity,
And attended by the entire Board of Admiralty,
And a shining cluster of Sea Lords,
And Earl Mountbatten, and King Hussein,
And me,
And the supporting star again, the Duke of Edinburgh,
Whom we would meet afterwards.
In fact, a memorable night, for memorable reasons,
Was in immediate prospect.
But on the very eve, when all was poised,
And I couldn't have been more excited
If I had been starring in the film myself,
Death drank again:
Old Queen Mary died, full of years, full of that family love
Which a nation also knows, and feels.
Promptly the lights went out, as they had to,
And court mourning descended. Said *The Times*:
"The Duke of Edinburgh has cancelled all his engagements",

And among all his engagements was us.
Collapse of author,
Robbed of the handshake and all that went with it;
And sad also for a special reason –
I was damned sure he would have enjoyed the film
Because he knew all about the cruel sea himself,
At first hand.

*   *   *

THE FOURTH NEAR-MISS was another Royal Tour:
Canada, this time, a country of magical variety and attraction,
A country I liked so much
That I had just resigned from my British Information job
To stay on there and enjoy it the more.
If I had still been in the service
I would at least have been on deck
When the customary duke-baiting started,
And the reporters flocked round,
Hoping he would say something wrong
(He did: He criticized Canada's fatuous drinking laws)
Hoping he would do something wrong
(He did: He sprinkled them with a little water from a hose,
By happy accident, and enjoyed it)
While the photographers called out:
"Hey, dook! This way!"
And looked round for laughs,
And the good old Canadian general public
Which does not give a continental four-letter frolic for the monarchy
Except on the ignoble three-tier system
Of the snobbery, or the show, or the chance of juicy fiasco,
Waited for the ignoble fun.
But as it turned out, he did very well without me.
They had picked on the wrong man.
Eventually the crude French wilted
And the rude press gave up,
And the man in the street
Turned to his neighbour, and said:
"You know, this guy's *all right*!"

*   *   *

THE FIFTH TIME was Canada again,
Canada under a gorgeous summer sun,
Canada at the lake-side,
Canada, and the promise of some blissful sailing
In the Duke of Edinburgh's Cup for Dragon Yachts, 1958.
I had one of these elegant toys,

And the Duke himself had another, called *Bluebottle*,
And *Bluebottle* was shipped out to have a crack at the trophy
On our own home water of Lake St Louis, at Montreal,
With HRH at the helm,
And a whole flock of dragons from all over
Fiercely seizing their chance to breathe fire down each other's necks.
I was all set to race;
I even had a joke ready, in case we won
And I had to make a speech:
"The presence of His Royal Highness
"Has certainly given these proceedings
"An extra fillip."
(Well, it's not too bad
For after dinner.)
But perhaps it was just as well that suddenly I had to sprint down to New
     York
For one of those absurd television turmoils
Which hold out prospects of dollars by the literal million
And then whip them away again.
One moment they just *love* your idea,
And they're going to make a pilot film immediately –
"You *gotta* be here!
"We're all juiced up!
"This thing is sensational!"
But when you arrive, it's "Sorry, the front office
"Has gone sour on it."
One minute the man says:
"They're jumping up and down at CBS!"
And the next, he can't even remember your name.
But still I went down, at an hour's notice, on this fruitless, futile effort,
And so missed the race,
And the Duke,
And the splendid trophy,
And that terrific joke to crown it,
And all for less than nothing.
My crew, to say the least, did not win either;
So all I have to show for that one
Is a silver bottle-opener inscribed:
"Duke of Edinburgh's Cup, Royal St Lawrence Yacht Club, 1958."
When I came back, my crew said:
"You missed a good man."
I knew that already, damn it.

                    *   *   *

CHAPTER SIX was set on this same Lake St Louis,
When the Queen and Prince Philip

Were due to sail up river in the royal yacht *Britannia*,
To open the St Lawrence Seaway –
That 2,000-mile masterpiece of maritime engineering
Which could now carry salt-water sailors, for the first time,
Into the very heart of a continent.
The whole yacht club fleet of two hundred boats, big and small,
Dressed over all with every stitch of bunting we could buy,
Was turned out to greet them;
And I, now possessed of the fastest Chris-Craft cruiser on the lake
(And also the desperate shame of being a chauffeur,
Instead of a true sailor)
Was designated as "POLICE LAUNCH",
With unlimited powers to order all my friends out of the fairway,
And a splendidly accoutred RCMP corporal
To back me up.
Britannia came out of the Montreal mist
Like *Vanguard* before her,
But this time the ship was a true yacht,
Blue and shapely as a magpie in flight,
Slicing her way up-stream like *Bluebottle* herself
On a noble scale.
We circled, and dipped our ensign, and then took station
A few yards off her starboard bow
(There was a cruiser and lots of destroyers hanging about,
But we were the *Police*, the civil power, the guardians.)
And when we looked up,
There, thirty feet above us on the upper bridge,
Was Prince Philip himself,
With his personal escort, who happened to be an old friend,
Minister of Transport George Hees,
The man in charge of the whole Seaway project.
We looked at the Prince
And the Prince looked at us;
We looked at George Hees
And George Hees looked away quickly
(I suppose there *were* a few bottles lying about,
And the smart Mountie corporal
Must have been lost among the half-dozen of my rackety friends
Who had been allowed to join the party.)
I shouted "Good morning, George!"
And George continued talking to the Prince
(No doubt about the pollution of the St Lawrence River),
And when he was not doing that,
Staring straight to the front,
A very figure-head of aloof if borrowed majesty.
Well, we weren't going to have that sort of thing

Prince Philip

From old George Hees,
Who was a drinking pal before he became a Cabinet Minister,
So I said: "All together now! – One, two, three! –
"GOOD MORNING, GEORGE!"
In a shout which rang across the lake
And made even the police corporal jump;
Whereupon Prince Philip smiled,
And walked to the other wing of the bridge,
While George Hees looked down, and gave us a wave –
The smallest wave I ever saw, a sort of half-mast flicker,
Like a woman drying her nail varnish –
And then joined his august charge
Well out of sight of this unseemly rabble.

That was in 1959
Still long ago, and far away,
But at least I got into earshot.

        *   *   *

NOW COMES THE SEVENTH and last time
Of me and the man I never met;
Though this time I came closest to it
And, privately, I count it as my one and only score,
And it was only just the other day.
We have a friend
Who is a one-subject bore,
And the one subject is herself;
Over the years she has become
Sole Minister of her own Interior
And Life-Time President (unopposed)
Of the British Boring Board of Control.
She is a sculptress
(I am changing the role a little
To protect the guilty)
And, by one of those strange turns of fortune
Which make one feel the world is grotesquely, permanently unfair,
She was invited to a party at Buckingham Palace.
"Oh, it was so *dull*!" she told us,
Her eyes swivelling up to heaven
Like a pietistic Virgin Mary doll.
(How can it possibly be "dull", to go to Buckingham Palace
For the first time?)
"But I did talk to Philip –" (the bloody impudence
Of that form of address!)
"And of course I asked him if he knew the work of Ariosto Vascovec;
"You know – the Pole who did that marvellous inert abstract thing

"We have out on the patio.
"Can you imagine? – he looked absolutely blank!
· "Obviously he'd never heard of Vascovec,
"And I had to explain everything,
"And especially the attitude Vascovec took
"In that article he wrote for *Nuances*
"About my own Spatial Inruption experiment –
"Well, it's more of a *movement*, isn't it? –
"That everyone is talking about these days.
"Do you know, Philip wasn't in the least interested!
"In fact he didn't even pretend!
"All he did was nod now and again
"And then he suddenly started talking about boats!"

At that heartening, even joyful moment,
I felt that I had met the man at last,
And that long-ago-and-far-away
Was here and now.

(from *The Twelfth Man*, ed. Boddey, M., Cassell, 1971)

BIBLIOGRAPHY

Airlie, Mabel, Countess of, *Thatched with Gold*, Hutchinson, 1962

Alexandra of Yugoslavia, Ex-Queen, *Prince Philip: A Family Portrait*, Hodder & Stoughton, 1959

Andrew of Greece, HRH Prince, *Towards Disaster*, John Murray, 1930

Arnold-Brown, Adam, *Unfolding Character: the Impact of Gordonstoun*, Routledge, 1962

Asquith, Lady Cynthia, *The King's Daughters*, Hutchinson, 1937

Baker, George, *HRH Prince Philip, Duke of Edinburgh*, Cassell, 1961

Boddey, Martin (Ed.), *The Twelfth Man: the Lord's Taverners in honour of their patron*, Cassell, 1971

Boothroyd, Basil, *Philip: an informal biography*, Longman, 1971

Butler, Peter (Ed.), *The Wit of Prince Philip* (with cartoons by Giles), Frewin, 1965

Campbell, Judith, *Elizabeth and Philip*, Arthur Barker, 1972

Cathcart, Helen, *HRH Prince Philip, Sportsman*, Stanley Paul, 1961

Channon, Henry, *Chips: the Diaries of Sir Henry Channon* (Ed. Robert Rhodes James), Weidenfeld & Nicolson, 1967

Christopher of Greece, HRH Prince, *Memoirs*, Hurst & Blackett, 1939

Connell, Brian, *Manifest Destiny*, Cassell, 1953

Cookridge, E. H., *From Battenberg to Mountbatten*, Arthur Barker, 1966

Cordet, Hélène, *Born Bewildered*, Peter Davies, 1961

Crawford, Marion, *The Little Princesses*, Cassell, 1950

Dean, John, *HRH Prince Philip, the Duke of Edinburgh*, Robert Hale, 1954

Dimbleby, Richard, *Elizabeth our Queen*, Hodder & Stoughton, 1953

Duff, David, *Mother of the Queen*, Frederick Muller, 1965

Duncan, Andrew, *The Reality of Monarchy*, Heinemann, 1970

Edgar, Donald, *The Queen's Children*, Arthur Barker, 1978

Frewin, Leslie R. (Ed.), *More Wit of Prince Philip*, Frewin, 1973

Frewin, Leslie R., *The Royal Silver: Anniversary Book*, Frewin, 1972

Frischauer, Willi, *Margaret, Princess without a Cause*, Michael Joseph, 1977

Gordon, Caryl R., *Wings*, private publication, 1969

Hamilton, Gerald, *Blood Royal*, Anthony Gibbs & Phillips, 1964

Hamilton, W. W., *My Queen and I*, Quartet, 1975

Hatch, Alden, *The Mountbattens*, W. H. Allen, 1966

Hibbert, Christopher, *The Court at Windsor*, Longman, 1964

Heckstall-Smith, Hugh, *Doubtful Schoolmaster*, Peter Davies, 1962

Hilton, James, *The Duke of Edinburgh*, Frederick Muller, 1956

Holden, Anthony, *Charles, Prince of Wales*, Weidenfeld & Nicolson, 1979

Hollis, Sir Leslie, *The Captain General: a life of HRH Prince Philip*, Herbert Jenkins, 1961

Bibliography

Hough, Richard, *Louis and Victoria, the first Mountbattens*, Hutchinson, 1974

Hough, Richard (Ed.), *Advice to a Grand-daughter: Letters from Queen Victoria to Princess Victoria of Hesse*, Heinemann, 1975

Judd, Denis, *The House of Windsor*, Macdonald & Jane's, 1973

Judd, Denis, *George V*, Weidenfeld & Nicolson, 1973

King, Stella, *Princess Marina*, Cassell, 1969

Lacey, Robert, *Majesty: Elizabeth II and the House of Windsor*, Hutchinson, 1977

Laird, Dorothy, *How the Queen Reigns*, Hodder & Stoughton, 1959

Lee, Arthur S. Gould, *The Royal House of Greece*, Ward Lock, 1948

Liversidge, Douglas, *Prince Philip, First Gentleman of the Realm*, Arthur Barker, 1976

Longford, Elizabeth, Countess of, *The Royal House of Windsor*, Weidenfeld & Nicolson, 1974

Look Magazine, *England's Most Misunderstood Man*, July 1964

Marie Louise, Princess, *My Memories of Six Reigns*, Evans, 1956

Masson, Madeleine, *Edwina*, Robert Hale, 1958

Martin, Kingsley, *The Crown and the Establishment*, Hutchinson, 1962

Mountbatten of Burma, Earl, *The Mountbatten Lineage*, private publication, 1958

Mountbatten of Burma, Earl, *Eighty Years in Pictures*, Macmillan, 1979

Morrah, Dermot, *Princess Elizabeth, Duchess of Edinburgh*, Odhams, 1950

Morrah, Dermot, *The Work of the Queen*, William Kimber, 1958

Nicholas of Greece, HRH Prince, *My Fifty Years*, Hutchinson, 1927

Nicolson, Sir Harold, *George V*, Constable, 1952

Noel, Gerard, *Princess Alice*, Constable, 1974

Peacock, Lady Irene, *HRH Princess Elizabeth, Duchess of Edinburgh*, Hutchinson, 1949

Peacocke, Marguerite, *HRH The Duke of Edinburgh*, Phoenix House, 1961

Petrie, Sir Charles, *The Modern British Monarchy*, Eyre and Spottiswoode, 1961

Philip, HRH Prince, *Selected Speeches 1948–55*, OUP, 1957

Philip, HRH Prince, *Prince Philip Speaks: Selected Speeches 1956–59*, Collins, 1960

Philip, HRH Prince, *Birds from 'Britannia'*, Longman, 1962

Philip, HRH Prince, and Fisher, James, *Wildlife Crisis*, Hamish Hamilton, 1970

Philip, HRH Prince, *The Environmental Revolution: Speeches on Conservation, 1962–77*, Deutsch, 1978

Philip, HRH Prince, *Philosophy, Politics, Administration*, (Rede lectures at Cambridge University, 1979), 1979

Pope-Hennessy, James, *Queen Mary, 1867–1953*, Allen & Unwin, 1959

The Queen, a Penguin Special, 1977

Röhrs, H. & Tunstall Behrens, H., *Kurt Hahn*, Routledge, 1970

Shew, Betty Spencer, *Royal Wedding*, Macdonald, 1947

Skidelsky, Robert, *English Progressive Schools*, Penguin, 1969

Taylor, A. J. P., *Beaverbrook*, Hamish Hamilton, 1972

Terraine, John, *The Life and Times of Lord Mountbatten*, Hutchinson, 1968

Thomas, James & Parker, Michael, *The Duke of Edinburgh's World Tour, 1956–7*, Pitkin Pictorials, 1957

Thomson, Malcolm, *The Duke of Edinburgh*, Odhams, 1953

Tisdall, E. E. P., *Royal Destiny*, Stanley Paul, 1955

Townsend, Peter, *The Last Emperor, Decline and Fall of the British Empire*, Weidenfeld & Nicolson, 1957

Townsend, Peter, *Time and Chance: an autobiography*, Collins, 1978

Wainwright, David, H. E., *Youth in Action: the Duke of Edinburgh's Award Scheme 1956–66*, Hutchinson, 1966

Wheeler-Bennett, Sir John W., *King George VI, His Life and Reign*, Macmillan, 1958

Whitlock, Ralph, *Royal Farmers* (with a foreword by Prince Philip), Michael Joseph, 1980

Wulff, Louis, *Elizabeth and Philip*, Sampson Low, 1947

INDEX

Admiralty, 90, 140
Airlie, Lady, 113, 115, 128, 134
Aitken, Max, 198
Albert, Prince Consort, 18, 19, 116, 138, 143, 151–2, 154–8, 169, 195, 234
Alexander, Prince of Hesse, 26–7, 30
Alexander I, King of Greece, 33, 46, 47, 81
Alexander II, Tsar, 26
Alexander III, Tsar, 27, 37
Alexandra, Princess of Greece (daughter of King Alexander), 47
Alexandra, Princess of Greece (daughter of George I), 38
Alexandra, Queen, 24, 35, 37, 40, 41, 46, 56
Alexandra, Queen of Yugoslavia, 23, 95, 97; on Princess Alice, 31, 32–4; on Prince Andrew of Greece, 36; on Philip, 59–60, 79, 81, 82, 87, 88, 104, 113–14, 133, 142, 146–7, 151, 192–3, 203–4; on Earl Mountbatten, 99; in Second World War, 100–2; marriage, 105, 106; on Balmoral, 118; at Philip's wedding, 134, 135; on Princess Margaret and Peter Townsend, 181
Alexandra, Tsarina (Alix), 27, 41
Alexandria, 100–1
Alfonso XIII, King of Spain, 28, 55
Alice, Princess, Grand Duchess of Hesse, 26, 27, 28–9
Alice, Princess of Greece (Prince Philip's mother), 24, 30, 58; marriage, 30, 35–6, 40–3; character, 31–4; religious beliefs, 31, 33, 63; financial position, 40, 59, 61–2; children, 43, 48, 49–51; exile in Switzerland, 46–7; seeks Prince Andrew's release, 55; marriage ends, 63–4; returns to Athens, 78–9; in Second World War, 95–6, 101, 109; and Philip's marriage, 125; death, 31, 32
Aloro, Julie, 128–9
Altrincham, Lord, 228–9, 230, 232
Amalgamated Society of Woodworkers, 129
Anatolia, 53–4, 57
Andrew, Prince, 161–2, 172, 173, 174
Andrew, Prince of Greece (Prince Philip's father), 125, 194, 202; in exile, 16, 46–7; marriage, 30, 35, 40–3; character, 36; family background, 36–8; relationship with Philip, 36, 78, 79, 82–3, 169; education, 38–40; resigns from Greek army, 43–4; in Balkan Wars, 44–5; in First

World War, 45–7; returns to Greece, 47–8, 49–52; and Turkish attack on Anatolia, 52–4; accused of treason, 54–6; escapes from Greece, 56–9; marriage ends, 63–4; in Second World War, 101; death, 109, 110–11; Philip's resemblance to, 189–90
Anne, Princess, 186, 201, 225; birth, 140, 144, 146; education, 173; character, 174; marriage, 196; financial position, 244
Annigoni, Pietro, 36
Aosta, Duchess of, 41, 134
Aosta, Duke of, 41
Argentine Polo Association, 213
Armstrong-Jones, Lady Sarah, 187
Arnold, Dr Thomas, 69
Aspasia, Queen of Greece, 81–2
Asquith, H. H., 137
Athens, 33, 34, 43, 78–9, 95, 147
Athlone, Earl of, 139
Attlee, Clement, 109, 116, 130, 131, 149, 151–2
Australia, 108, 211, 220, 222, 235–6
Automobile Association, 237–8

Baden, Berthold, Margrave of, 66, 67, 69, 71–3
Baden, Prince Max von, 67, 68–9
Balfour, Arthur, 137
Balkan Wars, 44, 52
Balmoral Castle, 117–21, 234
Baltimore Sun, 167
Barcelona, Count and Countess of, 134
Baron, 184–5, 186
Bateman, 139
BBC, 21, 166, 233
Beatrice, Princess, 28
Beaverbrook, Lord, 99–100, 194, 197–200
Beaverbrook newspapers, 193, 197–200
Berck-Plage, 60
Bernhard, Prince of the Netherlands, 134, 158, 204
Bevan, Aneurin, 129
Birds from Britannia, 207, 208
Birkhall, 136
Birley, Sir Robert, 70
Blanc family, 59
Blower, Agnes, 49, 50–1
Blumenfeld, Eric, 72
Bonaparte, Lucien, 59
Bonaparte, Princess Marie, 38, 59

265

Index

DENIS JUDD is an historian who has written many books including biographies, royal and military histories and historical novels. He is a Fellow of the Royal Historical Society.

At present, Dr. Judd is Head of History at the Polytechnic of North London. He lives in London with his wife and four children.

THE MOUNTBATTEN LINEAGE FROM GRAND DUKE LOUIS II OF HESSE
(Showing Daughter's Children)

Grand Duke Loui
of Hesse and the R
1777–1848

Grand Duke Louis III
of Hesse and the Rhine
1800–1877
m.
Princess Mathilda of Bavaria
1813–1862

Prince Charles of Hesse
1809–1877
m.
Princess Elisabeth of Prussia
1815–1855

Princess Alexander of Hesse
1823–1888
m.
Countess Julie of Hauke
Created Princess of Battenberg
1825–1895

Three
others

Grand Duke Louis IV
of Hesse and the Rhine
1837–1892
m.
Princess Alice
of Great Britain and Ireland
D. of Queen Victoria
1843–1878

Prince Louis
of Battenberg
1917 1st Marquess
of Milford Haven
1854–1921

Princess Marie
of Battenberg
1852–1923
m.
Gustaf
the Prince of
Erbach-Schönberg
1840–1908
4 children

Prince Alexander
of Battenberg
1874 Sovereign Prince
Alexander I of Bulgar
1857–1893
m.
Johanna Loisinger
1865–1951
2 children

Grand Duke Ernest Louis
of Hesse and the Rhine
1868–1938
m. 1894
Princess Victoria Melita of Edinburgh
1876–1936
1 daughter
m. 1905
Princess Eleonore of Lich
1871–1937
2 sons

Princess Elisabeth
of Hesse
1864–1918
m.
Grand Duke
Serge
of Russia
1857–1905

Princess Irene
of Hesse
1866–1935
m.
Prince Henry
of Prussia
*Grandson of
Queen Victoria*
1862–1926
3 children

Princess Victoria
of Hesse
1863–1950

m.

Same Person
Prince Louis

Hereditary
Grand Duke
George Donatus
of Hesse and
the Rhine
1906–1937

Louis
The Prince of
Hesse and the Rhine
1908–
m.
Margaret
*Daughter of
Lord Geddes*
1913–

Princess
Elizabeth
of Hesse
1895–1903

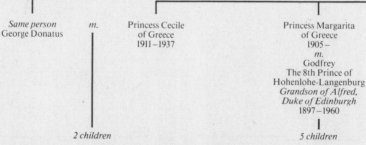

Same person
George Donatus

m.

Princess Cecile
of Greece
1911–1937

Princess Margarita
of Greece
1905–
m.
Godfrey
The 8th Prince of
Hohenlohe-Langenburg
*Grandson of Alfred,
Duke of Edinburgh*
1897–1960

2 children

5 children